Praise for *Seven Letters from Paris*

"A charming story, and a delightful tribute to the power of a good old-fashioned love letter."
—*Peter Mayle, bestselling author of* A Year in Provence

"*Seven Letters from Paris* is a real-life fairy tale. You'll be rooting for this bubbly American heroine and her *prince charmant*."
—*Elizabeth Bard, author of* Lunch in Paris: A Love Story

"*Seven Letters from Paris* is the story of a sexy, passionate, whirlwind romance twenty years in the making...and worth the wait. Sam shows us all the power of second chances and following your heart."
—*Teresa Rhyne, number one* New York Times *bestselling author of* The Dog Lived (And So Will I)

"Enchanting. A captivating real-life fairy-tale romance that will have you reading slowly so you can savor every delicious word. Castles included!"
—*Janice MacLeod, author of* Paris Letters

"*Seven Letters from Paris* is a celebration of *l'amour* across cultures and across decades. Samantha Vérant's voice is winningly funny, curious, and warm. She embraces France, and her French love, with an all-American enthusiasm that is nothing if not infectious."
—*Hilary Reyl, author of* Lessons in French

"Samantha Vérant's *Seven Letters from Paris* renewed my belief in the power of true love and made me believe that miracles can happen!"
—*Jamie Cat Callan, bestselling author of* French Women Don't Sleep Alone

"Wonderfully engaging and endearingly honest. This serendipitous romance between Samantha and Jean-Luc has to be one of my favorite memoirs set in France. I adore it."

—*Samantha Brick, author of* Head Over Heels in France: Falling in Love in the Lot

"Two star-crossed lovers must go up against the passage of time, the difficulty of distance, and many hilarious dinner-party faux pas to make their forty-something cross-cultural romance survive. Reading this book is like eating a bowl of strawberries in the sunshine. It's a delicious and joyful story from beginning to end, one that makes you hold your breath and clutch your heart with vicarious excitement as you're carried along what must be one of the sweetest love stories that's ever been told."

—*Torre DeRoche, author of* Love with a Chance of Drowning

"A true story of long-lost passion found, but also a cautionary tale on the importance of small gestures and romance in everyday life."

—*Jennifer L. Scott, author of* Lessons from Madame Chic

"A sweet and comical modern love story of one woman's happily-ever-after."

—*Wendy Lawless, author of* Chanel Bonfire

"Imagine a chronically insecure Cinderella spurning Prince Charming. Twenty years later, she finds her life at a dead end—and the Molotov cocktail of regret, curiosity, and the Internet explodes to break her out of the eternal jail of personal demons. *Seven Letters from Paris* is a glorious life-affirming testament to the power of love to change everything—and the enduring intoxication of France and a sexy Frenchman. (I was Googling my first love by page 15.)"

—*Jo Maeder, author of* Opposites Attack *and* When I Married My Mother

"Samantha is the friend anyone with a French rail pass would love to travel with: she's carefree and fun—yet she's seriously determined to stick to the itinerary. Too bad the stop in Paris wasn't scheduled for longer—to include more time with the gorgeous Frenchman she met in the bistro!

You'll tear up reading this inspiring love story set in Paris and the South of France. And you'll giggle and cheer as the Franco-American lovers reunite in time to conquer French bureaucracy—and even bankruptcy—in order to tie the knot. *Seven Letters from Paris* is sweet, touching, and real—as well as chock-full of information on how one American navigated international regulations in order to sail off into the horizon with her Frenchman."

—*Kristin Espinasse, author of* Words in a French Life: Lessons in Love *and* Language from the South of France

"In a world where love letters and romantic overtures have all but disappeared, it's reassuring to know that feelings committed to a page still have the power to bring two people together. Samantha and Jean-Luc were clearly destined to be reunited and their story is an inspiration for anyone still searching for a soul mate."

—*Patricia Gucci, author of* In the Name of Gucci

"Not since *Dangerous Liaisons* has French letter writing been this exciting."

—*Helena Frith Powell, author of* Two Lipsticks and a Lover

"Inspirational and heartfelt, this book illustrates that it's never too late to change directions in life. Vérant's story reveals how having the courage to follow your heart and take a big leap when you're feeling stuck can put you on the path that you're truly meant to follow."

—*Holly C. Corbett, national magazine editor and coauthor of* The Lost Girls: Three Friends. Four Continents. One Unconventional Detour Around the World.

"Watch out, Walt Disney. Samantha Vérant has lived—and vividly shared—a happily ever after story complete with castles and a dark and handsome hero. But unlike the Disney princesses, Samantha's own honesty, soul-searching, brave leaps into the unknown, and willingness to laugh at her own foibles make her a role model for today's woman."

—*Candace Walsh, author of* Licking the Spoon:
A Memoir of Food, Family, and Identity

"Fairy tales come true in Samantha Vérant's utterly winning debut memoir. Effervescent, enchanting, and wise, *Seven Letters from Paris* is a paean to second chances, the power of hope, and the risks real love requires. A romantic page-turner."

—*Christina Haag*, New York Times *bestselling author of* Come to the Edge: A Love Story

Seven Letters from Paris

A MEMOIR

Samantha Vérant

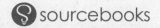

This book is a memoir. It reflects the author's present recollections of her experiences over a period of years. Some names and characteristics have been changed, some events have been compressed, and some dialogue has been re-created.

Published by Sourcebooks, Inc.
P.O. Box 4410, Naperville, Illinois 60567-4410
(630) 961-3900
Fax: (630) 961-2168
www.sourcebooks.com

Vérant, Samantha.
  Seven letters from Paris : a memoir / Samantha Vérant.
    pages cm
(trade : alkaline paper) 1. Vérant, Samantha—Relations with men. 2. Vérant, Samantha—Marriage. 3. Vérant, Samantha—Correspondence. 4. Paris (France)—Biography. 5. Women—France—Paris—Biography. 6. Americans—France—Paris—Biography. 7. Love-letters—France—Paris. 8. Reunions—France—Paris. I. Title.
  DC705.V47A3 2014
  944'.36108411092—dc23
  [B]

                                2014016020

          Printed and bound in the United States of America.
              VP 10 9 8 7 6 5 4 3 2 1

For Jean-Luc,
mon Prince Charmant, who opened up my heart
and taught me that love isn't rocket science.

Author's Note

This is a true story. There are no composite characters or scenes; however, I did change the names of select individuals to protect their identities, as well as to thwart the potential threat of having an onslaught of Molotov cocktails lobbed through my bedroom window. Conversations are not verbatim, but reconstructed from my elephant-like memory to the best of my abilities—thankfully, there are no quizzes on French conjugations in this book. Some sequences of events were compressed or omitted completely, because they slowed down the pacing, didn't drive the story at hand forward, or bordered on being TMI. (Yes, even in memoir there is such a thing as *too much information*.) So instead of going down into the *Guinness Book of World Records* for the longest memoir ever written, I stick to the pertinent details and facts that led me on a yearlong—and still continuing—love adventure. And I invite you, dear reader, to join me.

Think of it as a whole long day and a whole long night, shining and sweet, and you will be all but awed by your fortune. For how many people are there who have the memory of a whole long day and a whole long night, shining and sweet, to carry with them in their hearts until they die?

—Dorothy Parker, "The Lovely Leave"

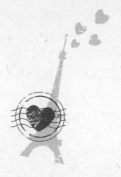

Preface

Tonight I'm cooking from the heart, choosing self-belief over fear.

Although I've always been a culinary adventuress, experimenting with recipes ripped from the pages of *Bon Appétit* and *Gourmet* since the age of twelve, Jean-Luc and I usually prepare this particular meal together—him manning the stove, me the eager sous-chef, slicing and dicing the parsley, shallots, and garlic. Now, thanks to his gentle coaching, I'm a little more confident when it comes to the art of preparing flammable French cuisine. And I can't let a little heat scare me out of my own kitchen.

The time has finally come to conquer my anxiety of flambéing—on my own.

On the first strike, the match hisses to life, trailing a wisp of smoke. I take a step back, reach out my arm, and touch the lit tip into the pastis with a steady hand. Flames flare up and the aroma of the anise-flavored liqueur permeates the kitchen. The blaze settles into a simmer, and I let out the breath I've been holding in. My technique is still not flawless though; to the cat's delight, one plump shrimp tumbles onto the floor. Bella lifts her haunches and pounces on her prey. I may not have the pan flip down, but I have one very happy, pint-sized panther.

After setting the timer, I twist the knob on the burner to low, which will allow the flavors of the pastis to infuse the shrimp just a bit more. Jean-Luc has already set the table outside, and I step out into the garden to join him. "Wine?" he asks.

I nod and take my seat within earshot of the kitchen, noting my husband's handsome profile, his manicured sideburns, and his chiseled jaw with the five o'clock shadow as he uncorks the bottle of Cabernet d'Anjou.

I am just as attracted to him as I'd been when we first met over twenty years ago.

Right as we're about to clink glasses, the timer in the kitchen buzzes. Before I can move a muscle, Jean-Luc says, "Stay. Stay." He flies out of his chair and into the house. A few seconds later, he rushes back to the deck and places a glossy black paper bag on my dinner plate. I can make out the name of a jeweler: *18k, Montres et Bijoux.*

I point, my mouth dropping open. "But you weren't supposed to get me anything—"

"I wanted to." He shrugs and blows air between his lips like only a Frenchman can do without looking silly.

"But the shrimp—"

"Can wait a minute. I turned the burner off." He motions to the bag. "*Ouvre-le.*"

He doesn't need to translate his words into English. With a shake of my head, I reach through layers of hot pink tissue paper to discover a bracelet resting in a satin-lined box. The clasp is delicate, but Jean-Luc manages to hitch it in seconds. The strand twists on my wrist and a small amethyst heart rests on my pulse, its facets glittering in the candlelight. Something about the way the light flickers on the jewel, almost beating, brings on a moment of complete clarity. I look to the starlit sky before meeting Jean-Luc's gaze, trying to find my breath. I can only whisper, "Thank you."

Jean-Luc's hands clasp onto mine. "Sam, you never, ever have to thank me."

Oh, but I do.

Three years ago, when I left a loveless marriage, filed for bankruptcy, became a dog walker, and moved back in with my parents in Southern California, I thought things couldn't get any worse. But then, in a moment of longing and memory, I used the Internet to track down Jean-Luc and rekindle an unfinished romance from decades before. Tonight is our second wedding anniversary.

This is the story of how I rebooted my life and restarted my heart.

Seven Letters

I didn't know how I'd survive the wreckage.

As the latest casualty of a company-wide layoff, I was an out-of-work art director in Chicago, and new employment opportunities—freelance or otherwise—were hard to come by. The big bad wolf of credit card debt had huffed and puffed and blown any kind of financial freedom away. Anger and resentment had taken its toll on what started out as a happy marriage. For eight years, I'd been sharing the guest bedroom with my dog, Ike. It was no wonder my husband Chris and I didn't have kids, save for one furry "replacement child."

My fortieth birthday loomed around the corner, and I didn't know in which direction to head when all roads seemed to lead straight to rock bottom. So on the evening of May 6, 2009, I met up with the one person I'd hoped could shove me onto the right path or, at the very least, lift me out of my funk.

Tracey listened to me bitch and moan and groan for a good half hour. Then her lips curved into a catlike grin. She grabbed the bottle of Pinot Noir off the bar and filled our glasses to the top. Before red wine spilled everywhere, I grabbed my glass, eyeing her with suspicion. No yellow feathers stuck to her lips but, having been her best friend for over twenty-five years, I knew she was up to something—always scheming, that Tracey. "Spit it out already, Sylvester."

"Nineteen eighty-nine. Twenty years ago. Paris."

And just like that, the tune of our depressing conversation switched from a song titled "Stormy Nights" to "Happy Days," and we reveled in our past, reliving each moment by glorious moment in a wild romp down memory lane. We sounded a lot like the two middle-aged women in that legendary commercial from the eighties—the one where they reminisce about their trip to Paris over a cup of coffee. One woman said, "I loved that waiter," and they both giggled and sighed. "Jean-Luc."

Then again, our 1989 Parisian adventure couldn't be compared to a mere coffee commercial; it was the dreamiest escapade we'd experienced in our lives, our biggest adventure. *La vie en rose*, Paris seduced our souls. Not only did we become bewitched with Paris's breathtaking architecture, culture, and art, Tracey and I both found romance on her historical streets. But *my* Jean-Luc wasn't a waiter; he was a sexy rocket scientist, who spoke near-perfect English, thanks to his job within the aerospace industry and international collaborations. And we would have been totally remiss if Patrick (his equally handsome friend) didn't play a major role in this lively conversation.

I am still thankful that Tracey and I hadn't fallen for the same guy.

A spark lit Tracey's dark brown eyes, a brow lifted high. She leaned forward and whispered, "Do you still have Jean-Luc's letters?"

She knew full well I had them. "They're packed up somewhere at home. Why?"

"Because we're going to create a blog called *The World's Most Beautiful Love Letters*. People will submit their letters to us, and we'll reject or accept them by comparing them to Jean-Luc's. His letters will set the bar."

As a distraction from my disaster of a life, her idea piqued my interest.

We finished off our bottle of wine and discussed possibilities for the blog. I agreed to give it some serious thought, but I wasn't totally convinced by Tracey's enthusiasm. Posting Jean-Luc's love letters on a public forum and comparing them to others would cheapen them. I hadn't communicated with the guy in twenty years. And what if he somehow stumbled onto this "love blog" and recognized his words? Wouldn't that be just a tad humiliating? I definitely didn't want to humiliate *myself*. What I needed to do was track down those letters, give them a good read, and then make a decision. It was after midnight and I was all talked out. Perhaps it was from the way I'd tapped my fingernails on my wine glass that Tracey finally picked up the hint.

"Do you need a ride home?" she asked.

"No, the walk will do me good."

"Up to you—"

"Really, I'm fine."

"Think about the blog, Sam." Tracey set her glass down, gave me a big hug, and then shimmied her shoulders out of the restaurant, singing, "The love blog is a little old place where we can blog together. Love blog, baby. Love blog, bay-beeeeeeeee."

Leave it to my best friend to bastardize the B-52s for the sole purpose of making me laugh. With a bounce in my step, I booked it out of the restaurant and raced the two blocks home, unearthing Jean-Luc's letters priority *numero uno*.

I was a woman on a mission. I nearly killed myself pulling the first plastic container out of the storage closet. It fell to the floor with a resounding thud, narrowly missing my head. Thankfully, my husband was out of town on business so the noise wouldn't bother anybody save for the downstairs neighbors and my dog. Ike, curious about the commotion, plodded into the hallway, his breath a green cloud hanging over my shoulder. No matter. Stroking Ike's velvet ears with one hand, I flipped the top of the container open with the other. Photo albums. Childhood modeling photos. Random memories from my past.

Six containers later, I was still coming up empty handed, and I was about to give up when I counted the boxes scattered on the floor.

Seven. The exact number of letters I'd received from Jean-Luc. It had to be some kind of sign.

But surely, I was setting myself up for disappointment.

At first glance, the last container didn't look promising—it was filled with files, tax returns, and old employment stubs. But then I held my breath, removed a few binders, and hallelujah, my quest for momentary happiness was fulfilled in the form of an aqua blue plastic folder filled with old letters. With careful fingers, I pulled Jean-Luc's letters out and inspected them closely. In pristine condition, they appeared to have been written only yesterday, even though thousands of yesterdays had since passed. All the pages were beautiful cream parchment embellished with black ink. Compared to my chicken scratch printing, Jean-Luc's handwriting was poetic, artful. I stacked the letters in order, curled up on my couch, and I read:

Letter One
Paris, July 28, 1989

My Sweet Samantha,

I really don't know how to begin this first letter, not because of nothing to say, but rather, I've got so many things to lay on this paper I can't find my thoughts. I have no dictionary here to write perfect Shakespearean English, so excuse the mistakes I have made and the ones I will certainly make.

Please don't think it's easy for me to express my feelings in a letter, but when your heart beats for somebody, I believe it's best not to hide it. Perhaps you believe it is too quick to declare my feelings. Perhaps most people would think that it is, but I don't care about the way others live, because I'm doing what I need to do to express myself to you. None before you opened my heart in so little time, but with you, all my barriers exploded into a thousand pieces.

Sam, I know it will be difficult for us to keep a strong relationship, but in my life I've learned "where there is a will, there is a way," and I believe in it. I found in you a girl with kindness, so many qualities which can make a man happy. I liked your way to be funny, your kind of foolishness, your passion for art, but mostly I loved your presence by my side. I miss your voice. It still sings in my head like a sweet bird filled with plenty of happiness. You put thousands of suns in my mind...like a fairy. So thank you for the time we shared together—filled with both tenderness and joy.

It would be a disaster if we stop this passion between us. And I am a man who cannot live without passion. It's the nerve of my being, the best we can do. I felt it that evening at the restaurant—an unspoken connection. I had to communicate with you, or I'd be disappointed in myself if I didn't know the outcome. So for this passion, I'm going to try my best to save it. I really want to live something exceptional with you.

When your train departed the station, I didn't ask where you would be staying in Nice. You made me crazy—crazy for you, of course. I would have been able to join you over the weekend. My head was in the clouds and today, all day long, I was very angry with myself for being so stupid. You told me to come with you, but I didn't think about the weekend. Sure, Sam, I would have done that for you.

I really desire for this story to be great—both romantic (yeah!) and erotic (hmmm!) at the same time. I wanted to give you so many pleasures in order for you to keep me deep in your mind, and I'm a little frustrated not to have done it. Still, you remain my pretty girl, the girl I care a lot for. We have so many things in common—both intellectually and physically—and it's hard to find both attractions in the same person. So when you find her, you don't want to let her go. I really want to be with you, even if it's complicated. We have to move forward together—hand in hand, heart with heart, skin on skin.

I can't finish this letter. It's crazy. I'm crazy too!

Jean-Luc's words were an aphrodisiac, food for the love-starved. Reading them was better than bingeing on chocolate, and I consumed his letters with a voracious appetite, each page more beautiful and poetic and romantic than the next. His words were exquisite, full of passion and promise. Much as he'd written, I felt my heart beating on every word. It had definitely needed the jump start.

I admired his courage. I'd never been one to express my emotions. Not like him. And God, at that point, what I would have done to have just one measly ounce of passion in my life. But there I sat on the couch, wondering what had happened, trying to figure out the point in time when everything I'd once dreamed for had just gone wrong. I had nothing—just debt and a dead marriage, guilt and fear. Where was my everything? I held onto Jean-Luc's letters.

Tracey's idea to use these letters as some kind of love barometer, well, her concept had sprouted wings and flown right out the window, and I found myself gripped by the strong hands of guilt and regret. In 1989, Jean-Luc had written me seven beautiful letters in an attempt to keep the spark between us lit.

And I never wrote him back.

Not one word.

Pas un mot.

Ghosts from the Past

My God, what an idiot I'd been. Punctuated with passion, Jean-Luc's letters still heated my soul twenty years later. So why hadn't I written him back in 1989? I needed to find the answer. By searching my past, I figured, maybe I could figure out my future—because I didn't want to live the rest of my life in a passionless marriage or become a meanspirited, coldhearted spinster. If there was ever a time to change everything in my life, it was now.

Setting Jean-Luc's letters aside, I jumped up from my seat and turned on every light in the apartment. Ike lifted his big head, a look of irritation crossing his face. My furry old kid, complete with a graying muzzle, slowly stretched his way off the ottoman. He shot me another "look" before dragging his paws down the hallway, the effect sounding as if he wore fuzzy slippers. And there it came—the creak. He'd jumped onto the bed in the guest room—our bed, since I had moved out of the room I used to share with Chris.

I sat on the couch, questions gnawing at my brain: Why would a married woman keep so many letters that supposedly meant nothing to her? Did I really care that much about what the other sex thought of me? Had I needed to keep mementos to prove I was loved? As if to answer me, a card fell to the floor. I picked it up.

My hands shook with disgust and disappointment. It was from my biological father, Chuck.

A crazed man with blue eyes and dark, curly hair stood in front of a comically oversized cake under a Happy Birthday banner, holding a gun to his head. Guests surrounded a table, all in exaggerated death poses, tongues hanging out, eyes rolled back. Chuck had written a banal message on the inside of the card, closing the note out with "Well, here's the birthday card I modeled for. Love you."

Granted, it was better than the other birthday card he'd sent a few years later, the one with a woman dressed in a trench coat and lacy lingerie—the printed text reading, "Play with it again, Sam."

I pushed both cards face down into the folder, questioning whether to throw them out. Truth be told, I was questioning everything.

My husband had always accused me of having "abandonment issues" because of Chuck—or as I called him, the Mother Chucker. Suffice it to say, I'd always harbored a deep resentment for my biological father. Anybody of sane mind would. After a year and a half of marriage, he left my mother and me for another woman. Stole the car. Drove off into the California sunset. Left the door to our apartment open so the cats escaped. Didn't even leave a note. I was six months old, jaundiced and colicky. My mother was twenty-one years young, fearful of her future. Even worse, the Mother Chucker's family wrote us off too, cutting off all correspondence.

Still, life went on for my mother and me—and it was a much better life. When I was six, she married the man I proudly call my dad, Tony. As a precocious five-year-old, I probably played a tiny role in his decision to marry us when I looked up at him with wide blue eyes and asked, "Will you be my daddy?" And no, my mother did not prompt this question. It was all me—a little girl who wanted to complete the family circle.

Tony accepted my proposal and Mom married him one year later. I wore my hair in Shirley Temple ringlets to their wedding. Our life was great, no, fantastic, all rainbows and marshmallows and unicorn-perfect, or at least, it was to me. Chuck wasn't around to veto the judge's ruling, and my dad formally adopted me when I was ten.

Two months after my adoption had gone through, my mother gave birth to my baby sister, Jessica. Thanks to Peter Mayle's book *Where Did I Come From?*, I knew enough about the facts of life when I stated matter-of-factly, "Dad is going to love her more than he loves me. She's his *real* baby. And I'm not."

Then I burst into tears.

Mom and Dad sat me down and explained that just because my dad didn't make me during one of his happy sneezes (as depicted in the book) it didn't mean I wasn't his real daughter. Love didn't come from just DNA. I was still jealous of the attention my sister received but, for the time being, the issue had been resolved. I forgot about my adoption, my old last name. I was a Platt and proud of it.

Until the day I was reminded I wasn't born a Platt at all.

Which brings me back to Chuck.

Deadbeat daddy-o first made contact when I was twelve years old—right when I was in the throes of puberty, right at the time I didn't fit in. As if life wasn't confusing enough. Naturally, his wish to get to know me upset my mother, but she gave me the choice to speak with him or not. Curious about my origins, I'd hoped to get some answers. Like, why? Why did he leave my beautiful mother? Leave me? Yet I was too nervous to ask these questions.

Soon after this first phone call, the gifts arrived—a red suede coat from Saks and a pair of diamond earrings. Like that could make up for *never* paying child support. In eighth grade, I lost one of the earrings. A jealous classmate destroyed the jacket; the blue pen marks scribbled on the back of it couldn't be removed.

After he made this initial connection, I sent Chuck some photos of me. In return, he sent a picture of himself roller-skating down the Santa Monica pier wearing a leopard-print banana hammock. And then as quickly as he skated into my life, out he skated again, proof that leopards—especially the kind that wear Speedos—never change their spots.

Many years would pass before Chuck would contact me again. Somehow he managed to track me down at Syracuse University the summer before my family moved to London for my dad's job, and he got in touch with me, asking if there was anything I needed. Why yes, came my reply. I told him of my plans to travel Europe, how I'd be working all summer waitressing to pay for the trip, and asked him if he wouldn't mind donating two hundred dollars to my travel funds.

"No problem," he'd said. "The check is in the mail."

For weeks, I stalked the postman. And every day was the same. He would watch my face turn from expectant to a look of pained disappointment. He'd do a little dance, shifting his weight from one foot to the other. My eyes would search his face for an answer. His voice was always apologetic—as if it was his fault he'd brought me bad news. The check never showed up and once again, Chuck disappeared from my life.

I swore to write him off.

But I didn't.

Always the optimist, or maybe the type who always goes back for some more pain and punishment, I gave Chuck one more chance to prove himself when my family moved from London to Newport Beach. Regardless of my feelings toward him, I couldn't ignore my curiosity that summer. Chuck lived an hour away. The timing felt right. I was twenty-one, a bona fide adult, and the urge to meet this man face-to-face was strong. So I did what any red-blooded American girl would do. I called him.

Amazingly, he answered. I asked him to meet me for lunch. He accepted my invitation and we agreed to meet at some trendy café. I swore my mother to secrecy, not wanting to upset my father, the man who raised me. It would be a clandestine meeting. The next day, I drove two hours on the hell that will always be the 405, to the 10, to Pacific Coast Highway, nervous to confront the man who was half-responsible for my creation. Surprise, surprise, there he stood outside the restaurant. He hadn't blown me off.

Over lunch, as he talked and talked—mostly about himself—I

inspected Chuck like he was some kind of bizarre attraction at a freak show, trying to see if we shared any similar characteristics. Like mine, his eyes were blue, but they were darker, didn't have the hints of green or the golden sunburst surrounding the pupils. His hair was also dark, curly, almost black, and his complexion was darker too. But the worst thing about him was his smile. Oh, the joy in his face made me nauseous. Who was this person seated across from me?

Then Chuck did the unthinkable. He dragged me all over the restaurant, introducing me to people as his *daughter*. Sourness filled my mouth, my meal threatening to come back up. The man was a complete stranger. After I left the restaurant, I never spoke to him again.

I had my answer. Little did I know, Chuck would influence the many bad decisions I'd made concerning the opposite sex. I'd developed a pattern—going after guys who didn't want me, dumping the guys who did. If somebody liked me, there must have been something wrong with them. After all, my biological father, my own blood, had left me high and dry.

Out of sight, out of mind. Before the Parisian fling with Jean-Luc could crush my heart into tiny little pieces, I returned to my studies at Syracuse University, never to be heard from again. I didn't write Jean-Luc back because I *liked* him. Which, to me, made all the sense in the world—no risk, no broken heart. Instead of setting myself up for the fall of all falls, I avoided any kind of real intimacy.

Now, twenty years later, I hoped it wasn't too late to put a stop to the cycle. I'd been so afraid of falling in love I'd never truly done it.

With nothing to lose, I made a decision.

I was going to apologize to Jean-Luc.

Letter Two
Paris, July 30, 1989

My Lady and Sweet Samantha,

Your souvenir from France is missing you very much. Everything in me misses you. I want so much to share my time with you that this letter links us together. I am in front of the paper as I could be in front of you—talking with you, but unfortunately not able to exchange touches and kisses. Every time I leave my apartment, I wonder if you are calling me from Nice without me being able to get to the phone. It's quite an unpleasant feeling.

If you had stayed, in a couple of days, I would have been able to show you the fabulous French castles and Normandy—a souvenir to your patriots who came forty-five years ago to be killed on the beaches. I would have liked to have shown you Paris and France through French eyes, for you to understand our way of life, different from the bread and wine bottle under the arms. Through the knowledge of France, it's me I want you to know. Every Frenchman's life is tightly linked with his nation's history.

Sam, I want you to know I feel like a kid writing a letter to his first girlfriend. In my life, I've known lots of girls, but few I've really liked or even loved. Don't think that I've got (as we say in French) a "sugar heart," that I fall in love with every girl I meet. It is really not my way of life. But it's so marvelous to care for someone, to share thoughts, to live for someone else. Life is great.

Sometimes funny things change your life with the strength of a hurricane. You don't know how or why, but it does. I like to write when I feel my heart beating on every word.

I am a boy from the sea, heated by the sun of Provence, but your heat is greater and makes my blood boil in every part of my body. My brain, usually cool, is burning in such a matter that I don't recognize it. You are a witch on the run from Salem, aren't you?

Samantha, believe me when I said I felt so well with you, so well loved in your arms. Your tenderness toward me showed me we were in harmony.

Our adventure is not of a tourist meeting a stranger in a foreign capital. It wasn't my purpose since the beginning. You are the Sam I cherish. I hope you share my feelings. In your blue eyes, I want to be lost for a long, long time.

Avec amour et désir,
Jean-Luc

The Love Blog

Now, it wasn't like I thought Jean-Luc had been pining away for me all these years, sitting around in some Paris flat, crying out, "Oh, Samantha, you broke my heart! I'll never fall in love with another woman. Why didn't you write me back? Why? Why? Why?"

First of all, if he'd said those words, they would have been in French. Second, he probably wouldn't even remember me. Third, I was fairly certain that he was a player—after all, he was an attractive, smooth-talking Frenchman. Honestly, he could have written dozens upon dozens of letters to other girls.

This did not change my mission.

By apologizing to Jean-Luc, I was facing myself one regret at a time, making amends with my past—a kind of twelve-step program for the emotionally disabled. First on the agenda: find him.

I sat at the dining room table with my laptop, opened up a browser window, and plugged his name and occupation into the search bar. Of course, I didn't know if professionals in his field actually *called* themselves rocket scientists, but it was a start.

I held my breath and…

Forty-two thousand results showed up—the first listing being Jean-Luc Picard. Now I'm no Trekkie, but I knew my Jean-Luc wasn't captain of the USS *Enterprise*. Had he been wearing the adult-sized, tight-fitting maroon and black onesie when I met him in Paris, our relationship would have turned out a lot differently …meaning it never would have happened. This minor glitch, however, did not leave me discouraged. How many French rocket scientists could possibly have shared his exact name?

Well, his last name, anyway.

Using a little trick I'd learned to pare things down, I Googled Jean-Luc's full name in quotes. Once again, I clicked on search. This was much more promising at thirty-nine results. I clicked through each and every one, which included reading a PDF dissertation relating to the aerospace industry. What was a high-enthalpy hypersonic project? Entry and reentry to and from the Martian atmosphere? I may not have understood one word I'd read, but *beam me up, Scotty*. A modern-day Mata Hari, I'd tracked down my rocket scientist.

My limited comprehension of what he did for a living put aside, I now found myself in even more of a conundrum. I couldn't just shoot off some arbitrary message. What would I say? "Dear Jean-Luc, you may not remember me, but I'm the somewhat neurotic woman you met twenty years ago in Paris. You wrote me seven beautiful love letters. I never wrote you back. Well, I just want to apologize. Sorry, it wasn't you; it was me. Hope all is well, Samantha."

No. Definitely not.

Considering how overdue my response was, I needed to do something more, something special, maybe even a little poetic. Tracey's idea about the love blog began to look good, with some major— and I mean major—tweaks. Forceful as the running of the bulls in Pamplona, the idea charged into my brain. I called Tracey to put the kibosh on her million-dollar idea. '

"I thought about Jean-Luc's letters today," I began. "And there's no way I'm posting his letters online so we can compare them to others." I wasn't exactly breaking the news gently, but at least I got to the point quickly. "Trace, I came up with something a little bit different." Excitement made my voice quiver. "Your idea about the love blog wasn't so bad. In fact, it inspired me." I caught my breath.

"I'm going to write a seven-post blog, the same number as the letters he wrote me, recounting our time in Paris. Then I'm going to send the link off to Jean-Luc along with my delayed apology."

I'd half-expected her to belt out Timbaland and One Republic's song "It's Too Late to Apologize" to add some shock value. She didn't. "I'm so glad you're taking some initiative. After all, I only came up with this whole 'Love Blog' thing to kick your mind into a better place." She paused. "You needed a good kicking."

Regardless of Tracey's true intentions, her plan worked. Suddenly, Jean-Luc and his letters were all I could think about. The memory was pure happiness, and I needed more. "Please, find the photos from our trip," I begged. "I'm dying to see them."

"Not seeing those pictures won't harm you one bit, but by staying in your marriage, you're killing yourself. So when are you going to leave Chris?"

And I'd always thought I was a "till death do you part" gal. "When the timing is right."

"The timing will never be right."

"It's just so hard to leave. Staying is easier. My confidence is shot."

"Don't be such a drama queen," she said. "Stop making excuses."

When my best friend had turned into a relationship guru, I'd never know.

That evening, before I went to bed, my husband called. We talked for a few minutes. Nothing out of the ordinary. He told me about his trip. My voice was chipper enough, but my thoughts were elsewhere. He told me he missed me. He'd see me in a few days. Out of habit, I told him I missed him too, couldn't wait to see him. Guilt weighed me down like an iron suit I couldn't shake off. I didn't miss him.

Not at all.

In the beginning, I'd been attracted to my husband's entrepreneurial spirit, his drive and dedication, his quirky sense of humor. He had a nice house on Chicago's north side with a spectacular garden and a beautiful magnolia tree. I was a twenty-seven-year-old optimist and thought we could build our future together. For the first couple of years, we'd been the clichéd happy couple, hosting dinner parties and going out on the town, taking amazing trips. But after a couple of failed businesses, things changed. He began comparing us to other couples, friends of his or mine who had bigger houses, made more money, had kids. I opted for sleeping in the guest room with my dog, blaming my husband's buzz saw snoring for the room change. Behind closed doors, the facade of the happy couple was stripped down until only anger (him) and resentment (me) were left.

We hung up. I pulled up my blog and I wrote the first post. I didn't have any passion in my current life, but at least I could relive the glory days of my past. Swept away in my Parisian adventure, the first post was followed by the second, my fingers taking on a life of their own. I called my sister and gave her the URL. I alerted a few other friends via email.

"Why didn't you ever tell me about Jean-Luc?" my sister Jessica screamed into the phone the next morning.

"Jessie, it's not as if we shared things back then. Eight-year-olds don't give out the most stellar relationship advice."

She snorted. "So that's why you never confided in me?"

"Pretty much," I said. "But the times have changed."

Really, when it all came down to it, there wasn't much dissimilarity between a thirty-nine-year-old and a twenty-eight-year-old—especially when the former is a bit crazier than the latter. Whereas I was definitely my mother's daughter, Jessica had our dad's more pragmatic mind. Still, our age difference wasn't as important as it had been in the past, especially since she'd experienced a bit of life herself by now.

"I want to read those letters," said Jessica. It wasn't a request but a demand. "Scan them in and email them to me."

"No."

"Why?"

"Because they're better in person."

She sighed. "Fine. I want to come visit soon anyway."

Jessica wouldn't let me off the phone until I promised to carry on with my story. I checked the comments on my blog a few minutes later, and the consensus from the few followers I had was the same. This story was incredibly delicious, a lip-smacking, chocolate-covered bonbon, complete with a creamy center. I found myself craving Jean-Luc's words, a sweet addiction masking the sourness of my will to divorce Chris.

I recounted our first meeting at the Parisian café, where our eyes had locked across the room, hoping this blast from the past would awaken Jean-Luc's memories, praying he'd remember our time together. The email to him was a bit harder to compose. It took four days, countless drafts, and a few dozen calls to Tracey to come up with an apology that didn't border on sounding insane. Day five came. According to the plan in my head, it was time to invite Jean-Luc to visit the blog. Before sending my letter off into cyberspace, I called Tracey.

"This is nuts," I said. "It's been twenty years. I should just take those posts down."

"Don't you dare," said Tracey. "Finish what you've started. I know you, Sam. You want to do this."

Did I? Unlike a paper letter, I couldn't run to the mailbox and rip up the email before the postman retrieved it. I tapped my mouse on my desk, deliberating, staring at my computer screen. Then again, what was I so scared of? It was only an apology—one he might not even receive. In a "now or never" moment, I held my breath and clicked that send button before I could change my mind. I watched as the load bar sent the email off. These were modern times, and what was done was done.

From: Samantha
To: Jean-Luc

Subject: My Letter Is Long Overdue

Dear Jean-Luc,

In case you are wondering, yes, this letter is twenty years overdue.

Last week, I came across your letters (I've always kept them), and I felt a strong need to apologize to you. Profusely. You wrote me seven of the most beautiful letters I've ever read and I never found the courage to write you back. I tried tracking you down a few years later, but you'd moved on. Unfortunately, the Internet wasn't as powerful as it is now.

Back then, the way you expressed your feelings for me, the way you wrote, so passionate, so romantic, was very intimidating. No matter how hard I tried, my words came out wrong. Needless to say, the bin in my dorm room overflowed with crumpled pieces of paper.

But this reason only scratches the surface. It's time to fess up and get to the real one.

Right before I left for Paris, my biological father entered into my life. As quickly as he appeared, he once again disappeared. Which really messed up my head. To be brief, because of him, I always pushed people— men—away, especially when they got close. And you got too close.

So there you have it. And I'm truly sorry.

With all this said, I'm recounting our story on a blog. My intention is not to embarrass you, but because your words were so beautiful, I have posted snippets of your letters. And because of the way I am, I am bring- ing a little humor to our story. I'm on the fifth blog post now, but the story will last seven posts, the exact number of letters you sent me. A little poetry on my part? If you don't write back, naturally, I'll understand.

Take care,

Samantha
www.sevenloveletters.blogspot.com

I didn't think about the time difference or the fact that I'd just sent off an email to Jean-Luc's work address on a Friday night. No, I refreshed my in-box every two minutes, hoping for an instant response, fantasies toying with my head.

"I forgive you," he'd write.

To which I'd answer: "Thanks. I knew you'd understand. And didn't I mention it? I want to leave my husband. I don't know how to do it. Have any advice?"

I Want a Divorce—and I'm Taking the Dog

It was time to pick Chris up at the train station, both of us having agreed that sitting in Chicago airport traffic in rush hour would prove futile. On my way over, two police cars blocked my route. From the looks of it, a drug bust or car theft had gone bad—there were cops standing with their weapons drawn and a pissed-off criminal in baggy jeans ducking into the back of a cruiser. I sat in my car, nervous—and not because of the scene being played out in front of my passenger window. Ten minutes passed. My cell phone rang.

"Where the hell are you?"

"I'm on my way. There's been some kind of—"

"Jesus Christ, Sam. Just get here quick," he said, and then the phone went dead.

The cops finally let me by. The trendy neighborhood was packed with cars. About a half a block from the train station, I took a right just after Wicker Park and called my husband. He was confused about where I'd told him I'd parked and wouldn't give me a second to explain. I blared the horn when I finally saw him, although something in me wanted to just drive away. He stormed toward the car. My quivering smile faded into a frown. Chris threw his suitcase into the back and crawled into the passenger seat, slamming the door. "Gee, don't look so happy to see me."

"I was, but then—"

"Nice welcome."

On the drive home, I could barely see through tears of anger and frustration. We fought the entire way. About what? It didn't matter; it never did. I pulled the Jeep into our parking spot and slammed my hand on the steering wheel, sobbing. When did he get so angry? When did I get so sad? Our marriage didn't start out this way. For a while, it was great.

He apologized. He'd lost his temper. He was tired. He didn't feel well.

I was tired of the excuses.

I was tired of the explosions.

I was just plain tired.

We made it upstairs to the apartment. From his bag, he handed me two bottles of Jo Malone perfume. Apparently, he'd spent an hour picking them out with the saleswoman in London. I was supposed to mix the dark amber with ginger lily and nectarine blossom with honey to customize the scent. He asked if I liked them. I sprayed my wrists and assured him I did.

I wiped my tears away and thanked him. Maybe I was overreacting. Maybe there was something in this marriage that could be saved. Yet, if there was, why did my heart cloud up the moment I saw him? Why did I feel more like myself when he wasn't around? How was it that somebody could press all the wrong buttons, making you feel like half a person? How was it that I found myself pushing all the wrong buttons too?

I'd reached my tipping point.

Chris snored away, napping on his green overstuffed chair. I just stared at him, a bit numb, wondering who this man I was married to was. I didn't recognize him. How did I let things get like this? Snoring aside, it was almost as if I couldn't stand the way he breathed. I found myself having a "Black Widow" daydream, killing him off in a plane crash.

Not good.

Before Chris could meet his premature death, he woke up and

grabbed his keys off the kitchen counter. "I'll be back later. I'm working out and then I have a lunch meeting."

Depressed, I lay on the couch, watching a plane soar by in the pale blue Chicago sky, listening to the birds chirping away. Freedom was hard to come by when this life weighed me down. I called up my recruiter to ask if any job opportunities had popped up.

"Sorry, Samantha," she said. "The pulse in the advertising world of Chicago is dead. There's nothing right now, but I'm hoping things will pick up soon though. I'll call you the second I hear of anything."

There I was, hoping to find work as an art director, a creative director, a designer—a job I no longer enjoyed, maybe never had. I'd fallen into this vocation because it was the game in which my dad had successfully played. He was a sought-out executive, and my father's stamp on the advertising world was the reason we moved around so much.

Tracey and I often joked that we'd been able to see a lot of the world because of my parents' moves—from Chicago to Boston, Boston to London, London to California, California to Virginia to Tucson then back to Virginia and back to California again. To think, I wasn't even a military brat like my mom had been. Nope, my dad was a Mad Man, an ad man.

Our family's relocation to the East Coast affected me more than most, taking place at the end of my junior year of high school while I was attending the Chicago Academy for Performing and Visual Arts for theater and voice. Although I stayed involved with the drama club after the move, it was in a suburb south of Boston at Cohasset High School where art became a part of my life. By senior year, my dreams had metamorphosed, and I'd decided to trade in arias and monologues for a sketch pad, paints, and pastels. Instead of singing "One" on Broadway, I would end up at Syracuse University, majoring in advertising design in a last-ditch effort to make my dad proud. Upon graduation, it didn't take long for me to understand this dream simply wasn't mine. Seventeen years later, I was an out-of-work designer who wanted to redesign her life.

I needed to get my head together, to focus and figure out exactly what it was I was looking for, so I decided to take Ike for a long walk. It was a beautiful, warm spring day, the sun was shining, and the birds chirped out sweet songs. The sidewalk was busy, filled with families—and babies.

They were everywhere.

Mothers walked by pushing strollers or holding toddlers' hands. A preppy dad wore a chic BabyBjörn carrier with a bouncing, blue-eyed baby boy in it, all smiles. It was almost a cosmic joke, the world reminding me I would be turning forty in a few months.

And I was childless.

Then, just to hammer this unfortunate fact into my head, a woman strolled past, accompanied by her toddler who sported an "I just learned to walk" grin on her drool-covered face and bumped into my knees. The little girl smiled a gummy smile, big blue eyes twinkling. My heart lurched.

My friends always asked when I planned to get pregnant, right after they'd scared me to death about the horrors of childbirth. Forgive me, but I didn't like being told that my nipples would turn large and brown and possibly dangle like little toes, my nose would widen, and I'd pass gas a lot, and not at the most opportune times. Sure, I understood "mommy weight" and morning sickness, but green discharge and incontinence?

In my heart, I know I could have gotten over all my fears. I loved children. But with constant easy excuses, my fear always took the lead. The world was in shambles. Kids were expensive; we couldn't afford them. We needed to spend more time together. We wouldn't have a life anymore, wouldn't be able to travel, go out. What if the kid had birth defects? Things weren't stable enough. We were too old.

The fact of the matter was that if I had really wanted to have children with Chris, we would have had them already. I needed somebody to tell me what a wonderful mother I'd be, what a wonderful a woman I was—and Chris wasn't doing that for me. Shuffling my feet, I headed up to the apartment and straight to my lifeline: my computer. When Jean-Luc's name popped up in my in-box, I nearly fainted. Stupefied, shaking my head, quivering in my white Keds, I stared at his name for what seemed like hours, and when I finally garnered the courage to click the email open, I had to reread his message five times to make sure it was really him.

From: Jean-Luc
To: Samantha

Subject: Re: My Letter is Long Overdue

Dear Samantha,

As I wrote in my first letter, I don't know how to start this letter. Twenty years of memories are crashing into my head like waves. Twenty years exactly from now. How do I lay down words that have been sleeping, preserved somewhere, but a bit covered by the dust of the time?

Honestly, when I first saw your email, I didn't believe it was you, the pretty and joyful Samantha I let go away forever. I thought if I clicked on your blog link, I'd be sent to some porno site and get trapped. But like you did with me, I did a little research, and I Googled your name—a different last name than before.

I remember the platform at the Paris Station—Gare d'Austerlitz or Gare de Lyon? My brain is still a little foggy. We said our good-byes, but an adieu quickly replaced it. Of course, at this time, everything in my head was pushing me to climb onto this train, to carry on our love adventure in the South of France. I should have retained my ardor. A lack of courage? During the next nights and days, I blamed myself. I've blamed myself so many times.

Your message and the blog are like a stormy wind sweeping away the dust off my memory. Billions of words are coming through my thoughts, one pushing another. I too tried a few times to seek you out, to find a way to contact you, but life decided another way for us.

Don't blame yourself. In my head you were a princess (my American princess), and the accuracy of your narration is fantastic. I feel ashamed to not have back all these thousands of details of our story. Ashamed. I hope I'm not embarrassing you. I'm just putting words on this "white sheet" without discrimination even after twenty years.

I did not know how to start this message, and I'm still troubled to finish it. I am stopping now. Too many words to write. Too few fingers to tell them.

Hoping this first message will not be the last.

Take care,

Jean-Luc

Over the next week, a flurry of new letters began—one after the other, email after email. For the first time in my life, I didn't hold back and I completely opened myself up to him. It was easy to do behind a computer screen. My fingers flew across my keyboard, tapping away, revealing bits and pieces of my situation to Jean-Luc—what had gone right and mostly what had gone wrong. A bit reminiscent of an era gone by when war-torn lovers could only communicate through letters, we shared every hope, dream, and fear, every mistake. We accepted each other's faults, no fingers pointed, no judgments passed. Write. Point. Click. Send. I've got mail!

Our communication went into overdrive, and we exchanged three to four emails a day, some of them in French. Since I hadn't spoken a word of the beautiful language in over twenty years, I relied on Google Translate to help me out. Language barrier aside, I was communicating with somebody like I never had before. Like my husband and I never had.

I soon learned that Jean-Luc had never married the mother of his children, a ten-year-old boy named Maxence and a twelve-year-old girl, Elvire. Jean-Luc and Frédérique had split up in 2002, and in the midst of a midlife crisis, he took up with a younger woman he'd met while traveling for work—a relationship that was short-lived. He shared custody of the kids and visited them on the weekends until cancer took Frédérique's life in October 2006, one week before Max's seventh birthday. As a single dad, Jean-Luc's world spun around his kids. But he had recently married a very young Russian physicist, Natasha, who, instead of love, showed only tolerance for his children. He and Natasha had been in an on-again-off-again relationship for three years before he'd succumbed to the pressures of marriage. He'd thought the stability would change the strained relationship she'd had with the kids. Apparently, it didn't. She turned more manic, he fell out of love, and now he was in the process of filing for divorce.

In a way, it sounded like he needed me as much as I was beginning to need him. I wondered if there could be something more between us than this budding virtual friendship, especially after he'd described the exact color of my eyes without seeing me for twenty years, but I pushed the thought into the back of my mind.

While Jean-Luc had provided an anonymous support system of sorts and had given me a much-needed confidence boost, I wasn't leaving my marriage because of him. But what he represented—that something else, something wonderful, existed for me—was another story altogether.

He was hope.

It took me ten days to find my courage. First came a big fight with Chris, then two vodka martinis numbed all my fear. With my blood alcohol level hovering somewhere between bravery and foolishness, I finally told my husband what I should have told him many years earlier: "I want a divorce. And I'm taking the dog."

Instead of fighting for me, Chris left for his father's house, and the cavalry came a-runnin', hoofs a-poundin' and horns a-blazin'.

"Tracey, please tell me I'm not a bitch."

"Sam, you're *not* a bitch."

"Am I doing the right thing?"

"You know you are. Now don't ask me again."

Click.

"Jess, I'm leaving him."

"Tell me when and I'll be there."

"Next weekend?"

"Done."

Click.

"Mom, can I come home?"

"I'm driving with you. When do you want to leave?"

"Jess is coming to help me pack. So not this weekend, but the next."

"I'm booking my ticket."

Click.

"Tracey, tell me I'm not a bitch."

"You are *not* a bitch."

"I'm doing the right thing, right?"

"You don't want my answer."

"What do you mean?"

"I don't like the way he—" She cut herself off midsentence. "I'm keeping my opinions to myself until you leave and the divorce is final."

Point taken.

Click.

The Hangover

While I waited for my sister to arrive, the correspondence between Jean-Luc and I intensified—three to five emails a day, mostly him giving me words of support. Since Tracey still hadn't unearthed the photo album from our European adventure, the only picture I had of him was a hazy imprint in my memory—a photo of us standing on the white steps of Sacré-Coeur. In any case, I was dying to see what my rocket scientist looked like now, how he'd fared throughout the years. I sent him a few goofy pictures of me, taken with the camera on my computer, and asked him to send me one in return. He complied.

I opened up the attachment, which he'd sent as a Word doc, and…and…and…it must have been his idea of a joke. The first picture was of Jean-Luc, but he'd cropped his head completely out of the shot, so all I could see was a body (which looked rather good, slim and fit) wearing a nice tailored suit. The caption under the photo read: "A beheaded guy twenty years later, head in the sky. Just your average, run-of-the-mill rocket scientist."

I scrolled to the next photo, which was of his daughter and son smiling on a tram in the Pyrénées Mountains. Elvire had beautiful auburn hair and blue eyes, and she would be an absolute knock-out when she was older. His son, Maxence, was not only adorable, but with a confident attitude to boot, he would definitely be a real heartbreaker. So Jean-Luc had made some nice-looking kids, but I wondered: What did *he* look like?

There was one more photo.

It was a flower in his garden?

He was killing me.

Either he was a pro at torturing people without inflicting actual pain, or there was something dreadfully wrong with him. Maybe some horrible accident, an aerospace experiment gone bad, had left him horrifically disfigured. I grabbed the phone and dialed the number to the one person I'd been sharing every last juicy detail with, every word, every sentence, every letter since his first response.

"Jean-Luc sent me a photo, but he cropped his head out of it."

Tracey spit out a laugh. "He's probably bald."

"Maybe," I said.

You could drive a four-mile-long train through the pause that followed. I wondered: Did I really care if he was losing his hair? We were only exchanging emails. My computer dinged. There was a new message from Jean-Luc.

"There's something else," I said, my voice drifting off.

"What? What is it?"

"He just sent a message. He wants to call me."

"Well, don't let me stand in your way. Ciao."

Click.

I stared at the computer screen for a minute. This phone call could change everything. Was I ready to open up my life to Jean-Luc in real time? Moreover, could I do it? It was time to find out.

It took several minutes to type three simple words: "Call me now." Thirty seconds after I sent the email, the phone vibrated on the dining room table. Before the phone shimmied onto the floor, with my nerves sparking like live wires, I made my move and answered.

"Hello?" I questioned, even though I knew exactly who was on the other end of the line. My voice shook. My heart hammered against my ribs. Back and forth, I paced the length of the hallway.

"Samantha." Even with one word, deep, strong, and sultry, Jean-Luc's voice carried the confidence I lacked. "For this first conversation, could you speak slowly?" he continued. "English isn't my first language. Sometimes it's hard to understand on the phone, and I don't want to miss one word that comes out of your mouth."

"This is weird," I said.

"Weird? How?"

"I'm sorry. It's just that I haven't spoken to you in twenty years. And the way we've connected in our letters, well, I'm finding this all pretty strange." I went quiet for a moment. "I was only trying to apologize to you, but things…I don't know. I just find this all a little bit crazy—"

"Sam?"

Oh God, this was so awkward. "I'm sorry."

"Never, ever apologize. You have nothing to be sorry for."

It was time to change the subject before I apologized again. Plus, my curiosity was killing me. "Your children are absolute angels. I love their photos, but when are you going to send me a picture of you? With your head in it?"

"I'm a little bit afraid that I am no longer this handsome guy you once knew. Right now, I'm in between Richard Gere for the gray hair, but closer to Bruce Willis for the lack of it. I'm not photogenic. Really, I'm not. As for you, Sam, and your pictures, you are so very pretty. I could never miss you on the street, no, never."

I smiled to myself. He was nervous too. "Just send me one photo, please, just one."

With a sigh, he agreed.

Once the initial shock wore off, Jean-Luc led the conversation, which I was thankful for. His sentences glided easily off his tongue. We discussed his looming divorce, how he'd had an initial meeting with an attorney, and how Natasha wasn't completely aware of his intentions yet. Meanwhile, call waiting was clicking in, along with dozens of emails and text messages coming in from Chris, heart-breaking and pleading, asking me to think about the good times. My responses to Jean-Luc came out in one-word answers, sounds—uh huh, yep, yes. It seemed he had everything figured out. I, on the other hand, was flipping out.

"Are you okay?" asked Jean-Luc. "You've barely said a word."

"I'm fine," I lied. My eyes leapt to the clock in the kitchen. "Jean-Luc, I'm really sorry, but I have to leave now to pick my sister up."

"I understand," said Jean-Luc. "And remember, you never have to apologize to me. For anything."

We hung up and I sat at the dining room table, elbows on the table, supporting my head with my hands. The scent of the dark amber with ginger lily and nectarine blossom with honey still lingered on my wrists, conjuring the memory of the argument that happened minutes before Chris had given the two bottles to me. Nausea crept into my stomach. The perfume only masked my unhappiness—it was a temporary fix.

My cell phone buzzed with a text message from Jessica, alerting me to the fact that her plane had landed early, and she was now taxiing to the gate. I texted her back with an "I'm on my way. Meet me outside of baggage claim." I figured by the time she disembarked and retrieved her bags, I had about forty-five minutes to navigate the twenty-minute drive. It was early enough in the afternoon to evade rush hour, there were no Cubs or Bears games, and so I had a couple of minutes. Before I left for the airport, I wrote Jean-Luc a quick email, thanking him for his support and explaining why I was so despondent during our phone call.

We weren't even up the stairs when Jessica made her demand. "I want to read those letters."

"Me too," piped Meg, a friend of ours whom we had picked up on the way back from O'Hare.

"Which ones?" I asked. "The old ones or the new ones?"

Jessica threw her suitcase onto the floor in the guest room. "How many new ones are there?"

"I don't know. Fifty? A hundred?"

"Shut the front door," said Jessica. "Does he write you in French?" I nodded. Her baby blue eyes went wide. "And you remember it? From high school?"

"Not at all," I laughed. "Thank the powers that be for Google Translate."

Or maybe not. According to Jean-Luc, the letters I'd been writing him in French were completely nonsensical, and I'd have to write him back in English to clarify my thoughts.

Meg shrugged her shoulders. "I visited your blog. I want to read the seven letters."

We strolled into the living room, zigzagging through the boxes and containers. The two girls took a seat on the couch, both with expectant expressions, hands in their laps, pursed lips. Teasing them with an overly dramatic sigh, I retrieved the letters from the nightstand and handed them over. While they busied themselves reading, oohing and aahing, I made myself useful by pouring the wine. Then I checked my computer to find Jean-Luc's response to my earlier email.

To: Samantha
From: Jean-Luc

Subject: Re: Thank You

Sam,

I talked too much and did not let you sufficiently explain your situation. Sorry for my behavior, but I was so nervous the words just flooded like a river from my mouth. Don't feel guilty. You are courageous, not a coward. You have to do what is right for you and you only. I am besides you whatever the stormy weather brings.

Thank you for being here and for your nice soul.

Jean-Luc

My nice soul? Even with all my deepest and darkest secrets revealed, Jean-Luc still saw me as a saint. I sucked in my breath.

Meg looked up at me with tears in her eyes. She held out the letters. "Oh my god. I want this."

So did I. Until that moment, I just hadn't realized how much. I averted my gaze and nervously fingered the rings I still wore on my left hand. Naturally, this act did not go unnoticed. Jessica grabbed my hand and released it immediately as if I had a deadly and contagious disease. "Why the hell are you still wearing those?"

"Give me a break. After nearly twelve years of marriage, you get used to some things. And I did try taking them off, but I felt so strange, so naked without them."

"Oh, please." Jessica's expression changed her face from Kewpie doll into Chucky. She brushed her long blond hair off her shoulder in defiance. "You're getting divorced. That's why I'm here, right? To help you pack?"

There it was, the dreaded "d" word. I didn't know what scared me more: the finality of it all or the fear of the unknown. "Jessie, I'm not divorced yet. I need some time to get used to the thought. Please, no judgments." I grabbed my coat. "Let's just go to dinner."

A twentysomething woman popped through the open sunroof of a stretch limo, a glass of champagne in hand. Her T-shirt depicted a bride dragging a groom by the hair. I had to squint to make out the words above the caricatures: "I got one." Oh yes, it was the quintessential bachelorette party.

Since I was seated at one of Chicago's crowded outdoor cafés, the reasonable thing for me to do would have been to raise my glass of wine in offer of congratulations like the other patrons, but a single, bitter thought held me back. I wanted to scream, "Don't do it!" and it took sheer willpower not to. I just stared at the girl and bit down on my bottom lip. Unfortunately, the bride-to-be caught my gaze before the limo drove off.

She yelled: "I'm getting married..."

To which I instantly replied at the top of my lungs: "I'm getting divorced!"

The chatter of nearby conversations ceased.

Forks and jaws dropped.

What can I say, besides I had a knee-jerk reaction?

Jessica and Meg spit red wine all over the table—a waste of a perfectly good Pinot Noir if you ask me—and everybody in the restaurant, and I mean everybody, stared in my direction with what I can only describe as shocked bemusement. I sank into my seat and shrugged my shoulders in mock apology. Within seconds, laughter rocked the patio, glasses were raised higher, and shouts of encouragement came from every corner.

"Smart move, girlfriend!"

"Men suck."

And I think I made out the words, "Can I have your number?"

Jessica jabbed me in the ribs, her blue eyes watering with tears of laughter. She could barely get her words out. "I can't believe you just did that."

Neither could I.

"It's good to have the old Samantha back."

Jessica's statement threw me. "What's that supposed to mean?"

"Well, you've got a spark, a light in your eyes."

"Chris wasn't a bad guy," I muttered. "He just wasn't the right guy for me."

"Gee, I've never heard that one before." Jessica snorted and continued. "What you're doing is so brave."

Me? Brave? If I were brave, it wouldn't have taken me six years to garner up the courage to end things. If I were brave, I wouldn't have asked for a divorce in a Hiroshima-like explosion after drinking two martinis with a lemon twist. "It's the way I ended things. It wasn't right."

"What way would have been better?" asked Jessica. "Look, you finally said what was on your mind. So it was fueled by alcohol. Big deal. Get over it. Seriously, how many marriages end in a good way?"

I nodded, thankful that at least we didn't have children to complicate the matter. "Still, I should probably have 'Beware: I'm an evil, soon-to-be-forty-year-old divorcée' tattooed on my forehead."

"No, you're definitely not evil," said Meg. "And that thing with the bachelorette was damned funny. People are still laughing."

I gulped back my last sip of wine. "I guess timing is everything."

Meg lifted her glass. "Here's to timing."

Tired beyond all belief, I went home early and crawled into bed, only to wake up the next morning with a serious hangover. It wasn't from the wine we'd had at dinner, but from fear. Jessica and I spent all day packing up the rest of my things. I flipped through old photos. Even the pictures were alien, the life I'd shared with the soon-to-be-ex galaxies away. When we were finished, it saddened me to see everything from the past thirteen years taped into ten medium-sized moving boxes. Jess and I dropped them off at the local mail station, sending them to my parents' house via UPS. This added another nine hundred dollars to my already dangerously high credit card debt.

I would take all my valuables and breakables in six plastic containers in the rental Jessica had helped to arrange. In California, Ike could swim and go to the beach; he wouldn't have to struggle up three flights of stairs, huffing and wheezing. Chris and I had both agreed the lifestyle change would be good for our furry kid.

Jessica walked by the dining room table and picked up the Nambé salt and pepper shakers, which had been a wedding present. She dropped them into one of the open containers. "You might need these."

Like I needed a hole in my head. I pulled them out. "I'm trying to pack light."

She crinkled her brows. "But you're hardly taking anything."

I looked at the furniture, at the things we'd accumulated over the years. "It's just stuff."

Reminders of a life I was leaving behind. But I knew moving on wouldn't be easy.

Two days before I hightailed it out of town, my husband returned to our apartment, needing closure. He also wanted to say good-bye to Ike. No matter how Jean-Luc's letters affected me, no matter how hard I tried to fight it, I opened up the door and welcomed guilt back into my life. Chris told me what a wonderful woman I was, how he wanted to start a family with me, everything I'd needed to hear. We talked about everything, every sin we'd committed against one another, the good and the bad and the ugly, and we confessed and professed. For once, blame was left out the equation. He almost convinced me to stay. Almost.

"While you were gone, I started communicating with another man," I said.

"You're having an affair?"

"No," I said. "Just exchanging emails."

I was expecting an explosion. It didn't come. A vision of the man I'd married almost twelve years prior flashed in my memories—a man no longer recognizable to me.

"Well, stop," he said. "Do it now. End it. For us."

Maybe Chris was right. Maybe there still was an *us*. But if there was, why did I feel like it was too late? I kept those reservations to myself.

"Okay," I agreed, wondering if there was something, a lifeline, in this marriage I could hang on to.

We talked and we cried and we talked.

After twelve years of misunderstandings and hurt feelings, we were finally communicating, but the damage had been done, the flames smoldering for far too many years. Guilt set in. I was drowning. The demise of our marriage could only be blamed on one person: me. I never expressed my feelings to Chris, and over the years, everything I'd once felt for him had just shut down. I was so detached, so emotionless; I didn't recognize this cold side of myself. When communication broke down, even bigger problems emerged.

It was too late. Love didn't come with a switch I could turn on and off when I wanted to.

I finally met his eyes. "I'm still going to California,"

"I know." Chris wrung his hands. "Maybe this separation will be good for us."

Ike followed me into the guest bedroom. Feeling like utter crap, I pulled out my computer and backed up my blog, archiving it to my desktop before deleting it. Then I sent Jean-Luc an email, ending our affair of letters. I didn't deserve his friendship. I was a spineless coward who had agreed to a temporary split with Chris just to avoid a war.

In the morning, before Krakatoa could erupt, spouting off in molten anger, Chris left the apartment, heading off on another business trip. From the balcony, I watched him get into the taxi. He looked up at me. I looked down on him. When he drove off, a dark cloud lifted off my heart. I could breathe again.

Letter Three
Paris, August 3, 1989

My so sweet Samantha,

I really don't know where you are at this time, but my spirit walks with you during your whole trip. Your blue eyes remind me of the sky of my country, a deep blue and sparkling light. Your body smells like the perfumes found all over Provence, but even Provence can be jealous of your freshness. Your skin is so sweet, so beautiful and soft, smooth as the petals of a rose. I want to smell and taste every inch of your body, to awaken all of my Latin senses. You bombarded my head with rockets of tenderness. My head may explode like the fireworks shot off on Independence Day.

Samantha, I miss you very much. I think all of my letters can be proof of this. Sure, I may sound crazy, but banality is not a way to live life; passion is. We were all made in a moment of passion because love is a bond between two people, two hearts, and two bodies. Everything should be about passion. When I love, I do it with passion or it's dead right from the beginning.

I felt something so different with you, so powerful. I was attracted to you the first second we met. I really want to be something different for you, to bring you what you look for in everything. Sam, perhaps you won't believe me, but you are the first person to cause such a reaction in all my senses. I'm not a mystic. I'm just Jean-Luc, burning in a way I've never known before you. And you are Samantha, a kind of well-loved witch!

Paris misses you in order to tell you its entire story. I would like to present you my country, which I am sure you will love. I had so many things to tell you, to show you, to give you. When your train left the station, I felt so sad and alone. I just want you, through these letters, to know me a little better. Answer me quickly. I miss you. This night I will jump into the memory of your eyes to find you again.

Love,
Jean-Luc

Hello, Thelma, or Is It Louise?

I eyed the bottle of vodka on the kitchen counter, then the clock, and then the bottle. How about a martini, Sam? It's five o'clock somewhere, right? And then I felt like a freak. My God, it wasn't even ten in the morning. Instead of bending to the temptation of drowning out my emotions, I headed for the master bath. I didn't need a shrink to tell me alcohol veils reality for a moment, oftentimes making it worse. And I certainly didn't need to be told I looked like total crap. All I needed to do was face the mirror. Who was that person? She'd really let herself go.

I was covered in black dog hair and I'd been wearing the same sweats for three days. My hair was greasy, my stomach was bloated, and my eyes were bloodshot. Not only that, there was a planet-sized zit on my chin. It used to be a source of pride for me to look nice—heels and makeup, lip gloss over lip balm. Grimacing, I pulled out the tweezers and plucked away, certain the old me lurked around somewhere.

Fifteen minutes later, I stepped into the shower…

Good lord, the hair on my legs was long, and my bikini line was reminiscent of the jungles of the Amazon. Break out the weed whacker. It was time for this woman to get some of her pride back. One hour and fifteen minutes later, it was time to go pick my mother

up at the airport. I didn't know if I was ready for her. Not that she'd
be checking out my bikini line.

I made it to the airport just in time, pulling up to baggage claim
as planned. I stared at my mom for a moment or two. In high school,
rumor had it the boys at school didn't show up at the basketball
games for the games, or to see me cheerlead, but rather to check her
out. While you could tell we were definitely mother and daughter, I
was a more sinister version of the apple to her tree—my nose a little
bigger, my blue eyes smaller, and my lips thinner. I'd tried to rectify
that last physical insecurity with an injection of collagen when I
was twenty-seven, only to end up with a bruised mouth I'd paid two
hundred dollars for. I've since decided thin lips are sexy.

As usual, my mom looked fantastic, all tan and blond and bubbly
and perky, a wide super-white smile spanning her face. She got into
the car. "What's that on your chin?"

"It's a stress zit." I lowered my voice. "Please don't talk about it. It
will hear you, causing another one to appear."

"Toothpaste will get rid of it. Or tea tree oil. Do you have any tea
tree oil?"

"Ugh. Can we please not talk about it?"

"Sam, don't be rude. I'm only trying to help."

"I know, Mom, thanks. For everything." I bit down on my bottom
lip. "Can we change the subject?"

"Of course. What do you want to talk about?"

Anything but my stress zit. "Tell me that story again."

"Which one?"

"The one where you picked me up after not seeing me for a while,
when I lived with Nanny and Poppy."

"Oh, those three months without you were the worst in my life,"
she said. "You were my little girl, my angel. I couldn't take another
second without you. When I was settled in Chicago, Nanny
and I decided to meet at the midway point, at a Holiday Inn in
Kentucky. You guys were late. I was pacing the lobby of the hotel,
waiting. Finally, I saw Nanny's red Dodge Duster pull into the

parking lot, saw your little strawberry blond head in the backseat. I screamed, 'My daughter, my daughter!' People must have thought I was crazy."

"And then—"

"I ran out into the parking lot, opened the door, pulled you out of your car seat, and twirled you around and around, me crying like a fool, you giggling away. Once they figured out what was going on, everybody in the lobby applauded. They were pressed up against the window of the hotel, I swear."

I shot my mom a sideways glance. She was getting all teary eyed. I was too. "Do you ever regret it?"

"What?"

"You had to put your dreams aside." I choked back my words. "For me."

My mom had had big aspirations when she was younger. She was going to be a famous ballerina, dancing in *Swan Lake*, fluttering around in tutus and pink satin toe shoes with the New York City Ballet. At the age of eighteen, she'd moved to Manhattan to pursue this lofty ambition. She moved into one of those group apartments for girls, living with hopeful actresses, models, and dancers. As she waited for her dancing career to take off, she cocktail-waitressed at one of New York's most illustrious clubs, Salvation, on West Fourth and Seventh. Rock stars hung out there—legends like the Beatles and the Rolling Stones, along with wannabes like the guitar-playing Chuck, whose claim to fame was jamming with Jimi Hendrix.

A small-town Southern girl who moved around from military base to military base in her youth, my mother had never met a guy like Chuck before: he was a bad boy, dark and dangerous. He swept her off her feet and they married then moved to California, where he pursued his dreams of becoming a musician and she put her dreams on hold, working as a sales clerk in a clothing boutique. When she became pregnant with me, her toe shoes were hung up on a hook of unfulfilled dreams.

"Sam, dreams change." Mom squeezed my hand. "And I've been living vicariously through you. I've tried to give you all the opportunities I didn't have. Like performing arts school. Like college."

I gulped. "Well, at least you were a top model in Chicago."

"A top junior model," she corrected. "That's how I supported us. It was just you and me—"

"Until Dad came along."

Before she'd met Tony, we lived in a basement apartment and she sometimes worked two jobs to pay the bills when bookings were slow. She made sure I had everything I needed—food on the table, clothes on my back, or a new Barbie doll. Funnily, I had never realized how very poor we were. She'd always provided for me, surrounding me with love.

My mom may not have achieved her dream of becoming a prima ballerina, but her love of dance turned into a career in the fitness industry. Now she was a volunteer, teaching yoga at the Greater Los Angeles Veterans Administration, helping veterans overcome post-traumatic stress disorder, brain injuries, and drug and alcohol addictions—a program she was instrumental in creating that was now going nationwide. I was so proud of her.

I was about to find myself in the same position she'd found herself in so long ago—broke, heavyhearted from a breakup, and about to move back home to her parents. The only difference was that I wasn't twenty-one with a small infant; I was almost forty and childless. It dawned on me that our lives may have taken different paths, but my mother was exactly like me. I could talk to her—really talk to her—and not just about the latest beauty treatments. With a thirty-five-hour road trip ahead of us, we had plenty of time.

"I know we talked about leaving on Sunday, but can we leave tomorrow?" I asked.

"I think that's an excellent idea."

In the morning, we loaded up the rental minivan. Soon, the Chicago skyline disappeared from the rearview mirror. Fear had me shaking in my gym shoes. I clenched my teeth. My mother sat in the passenger seat, so excited she was practically bouncing up and down, a wide smile plastered on her face. Twenty miles into the drive, she blurted out, "I spoke to the woman who walks our dogs, and she's looking for some help. I suggested you."

"Why? Does she need a website designed?"

"No, actually, she needs more dog walkers."

"Wait. What?"

"It will be good for you until you land on your feet."

"Great. Just great," I said.

I had nothing but a mountain of debt. I was about to turn forty and I was moving back in with my parents. I'd just left the man I'd spent thirteen years with. I'd sabotaged my love affair of letters with Jean-Luc. And my mother had just asked me if I wanted to become a dog walker. This was not the way I'd mapped out my life.

My knuckles turned white as I gripped the steering wheel. "They have bridges in Los Angeles, right?"

"Yes. Why?"

"So I can throw myself off one when we get there."

"Sam, that's not funny." She huffed. "So when we get home, we have some work to do. Obviously, you need to have your hair highlighted. And look at those nails. They're a mess—"

"Yeah, I'm sure the dogs will judge me. They *are* from Malibu."

My mother shot me her patented look, a half-disgusted sneer, half pout. The kind of look that made me feel bad in one flash second. "Don't be so rude. You don't have to walk dogs if you don't want to. I'm only trying to help."

"I'm sorry, Mom. I'm dealing with a lot on my plate right now. I'm feeling overwhelmed." I felt terrible for snapping at her, but I wasn't in the mood to plan anything. I was all talked out. "I have an idea. Why don't we listen to one of those books on tape you brought?"

"I know exactly which one," said my mom.

She'd come prepared.

As Elizabeth Gilbert, a woman also leaving a long-term marriage, narrated her book *Eat, Pray, Love* along the not-scenic route to Omaha, Nebraska, we passed blurred cornfields and cows, cheese shops and strip clubs. We drove through a town named Marseilles, right when Liz said, "I wanted out of a marriage I didn't want to be in." Although it was in Illinois, I couldn't stop thinking of France and a certain someone who lived there.

My mom was at the wheel when my cell phone buzzed. It was a text from Chris, calling me a freak, along with a few other choice words, for taking the salt and pepper shakers. I was about to call Jessica who, unbeknownst to me, had clearly decided I needed to spice up my life, when another text came in. Apparently Chris was in the process of hiring a divorce attorney who would work on both of our behalves, and since our marriage had essentially been over for more than six years, it was going to be quick.

Stunned, I read the messages out loud. I realized Chris was lashing out, but if there was ever a proverbial nail in the coffin, those two texts had hammered my decision in. I deleted the messages and I didn't respond. Forget about a separation. I knew I was never going back.

"You need to hire your own attorney," Mom said. "You have to protect your best interests."

"I am. I left him."

"What about money?" she asked.

"Mom," I said. "Everything is gone. There's nothing to split."

"I'm surprised you didn't leave him years ago," she said.

I knew how she felt about my husband. I'd been put in the middle of them, defending one against the other, which was tiring to say the least. In Chris's mind, I was married to him and therefore he was the only person who mattered in my life. I was the wife. Period. The fights about my mom started two years into our marriage, creating more than a wedge; it had driven us apart. As much as my mom had protected me over the years, I also protected her. To me, it wasn't a big deal that she occasionally interrupted our meals with phone calls. Look what she'd given up for me. But Chris didn't see it that way.

"I wanted to."

My mom pinched her lips together, her eyes narrowed into a glare. By the way she was breathing, I could tell she wanted to say something else on the subject. For once, she held back. "Sam, I've said this to you time and time again. The most important thing for me is to see you happy. You've been punishing yourself for far too long and you're not the martyr type. Now that you're leaving him, I'm noticing positive changes."

"Like what?"

"For one thing, you're actually talking to me again, not brushing me off." She squeezed my hand tightly. "It's good to have the old Sam back. I've missed you."

Jessica had said the exact same thing. I wondered how much marriage had changed me.

We arrived at our hotel at a little past eight in the evening and ordered room service. My mom and I got comfortable on the bed, both of us wearing yoga pants and T-shirts. I pulled out my computer and handed her Jean-Luc's letters from 1989 while I checked my email. Stunned, I stared at Jean-Luc's latest message, which described his scientific view of faith, how nature hates empty spaces and unbalanced systems, and how the world needs to be filled with wondrous things. Since he'd been on a business trip to Germany, I was pretty sure he hadn't read my last message. The more I thought about what I'd written to him, the more like an idiot I felt. "I wish I hadn't ruined things with Jean-Luc with the last email I sent," I muttered. "He's going to hate me."

Mom peered over her reading glasses. "Well, what you wrote couldn't have been that bad."

"No, it was pretty bad." I pulled up the email, cleared my throat, and I read. "Everything in a relationship is passionate in the beginning. But like a star, this kind of intensity fades in brightness over time. After time, things get comfortable—like an old pair of socks, holes included. I'm still leaving Chris, but I need some time to figure out what exactly it is that I'm looking for. Really, you are a truly incredible man, a gift. Our whirlwind of letters caught me off guard. And I wouldn't trade them in for anything in the world. I will be here for you. But right now, this love affair of letters has to stop, and I can only be your friend."

From his spot on the bed, I swore, even my dog groaned.

"You wrote Jean-Luc a 'Dear John letter'? Why on earth would you do a thing like that?" asked my mom.

"I was confused."

"And now?"

"I'm not." I shook my guilt-ridden head. "I've been discussing all these pent-up feelings with Jean-Luc. I look forward to his emails. I look forward to writing him back. He knows everything about me."

"Everything?"

Technology had connected Jean-Luc and I in a way I'd never thought possible. I'd opened up my soul to the man. "Everything."

"It sounds like Jean-Luc is very supportive of you. You're just writing letters. It's not like you're getting married to him and moving to France—"

I raised my brows.

"Oh, come on, Sam. I know you're a dreamer, but be realistic. You haven't even seen him in twenty years—"

I pulled up the photo he'd finally sent. "In the first picture Jean-Luc had sent me, he'd cropped his head out of it. I emailed him back, begging for a picture with his head in it. So he sent me a picture of him in his twenties, dressed in drag at a party. He finally sent this picture last week, explaining he's no longer the handsome guy I once knew." I turned the screen toward my mom. In this picture, Jean-Luc wore a black suit, the jacket of which had a dark teal lining, and a crisp white shirt. Although he'd cropped the very top of his head out of the picture, most likely hiding the fact that he was, indeed, losing his hair, it didn't matter. He looked so sexy standing there with his rugged manly-man looks, his hands in his pockets, drawing attention to his broad shoulders and trim waist.

"It's funny, the image I have of him in his youth is faded, but this man has gotten better with age."

My mom's eyes went wide. "You write him back now. Apologize."

So with my mother breathing over my shoulder, clucking on and on about how good-looking Jean-Luc was, and what a nice suit he wore, and how his soul patch was so sexy (just like Bruce Springteen's!), and what a wonderful writer he was, and how sweet he was to me, I did, all the while hoping it wasn't too late. Not that I dreamed of moving to France or anything like that.

No, not me; it never crossed my mind.

From: Samantha
To: Jean-Luc

Subject: Greetings from the road!

Dear Jean-Luc (still my Prince Charming, I hope),

Please forgive my indecisiveness (a typical Libra trait). I now have clarity. Please ignore the last email I sent. I can't let "guilt" lead my heart, but I do need to spend time for myself. My trip back to California and the time I will spend there with my family will allow me to do just that.

I used to keep my emotions all bottled up inside, internalizing everything. With you it is very different. I feel like I can talk to you or write to you about anything. So thank you. You have to promise me you won't let me avoid subjects that make me uncomfortable. Communication is the backbone of everything. On this, I speak from firsthand experience. Really, you know more about me than anyone. For you, I want to be an open book. Can we please, please, turn the page?

Sam

"There," I said. Once again, I pressed the send button while holding my breath. "It's done."

"Do you think he'll respond?" Mom asked.

"I don't know. But I won't blame him if he doesn't." I shrugged and then said matter-of-factly, "Mom, I really need to talk about Chuck."

Her face paled. "What about *him*?"

"He kind of gave me a complex, showing up in my life when he did and then disappearing." I squeezed my eyes shut. "It's hard, because I know I'll never know the answer why."

"Why what?"

"Why, if I'm his daughter, didn't he try to get to know me better?"

"I'm sure he loved you. In his own way."

"No, no, he didn't. How could he? He doesn't even know me. Never did. I met him once. I know this now, but it's impossible to love somebody you don't communicate with. That's what killed my marriage."

I went on to explain how, during the times I was in correspondence with Chuck, I felt that my adopted dad, even though he had always treated me as his flesh and blood, loved my sister more because she was his. I explained how Chuck was an unhealthy ghost in my life, an evil poltergeist floating over all my relationships, one that I needed to get rid of once and for all. I told her how his leaving her, leaving us, had affected the way I carried out my relationships with men.

My mother's eyes filled with tears, threatening to explode. "I hate him. I hate what he did to us."

"Mom, Mom, I'm sorry, I don't want you to cry," I pleaded. I didn't want her to cry because if she started up, I'd start up too.

"Oh, Sam," she said with a sniffle. "I hope you know, we were only trying to protect you. I guess we should have talked about it—about him—more."

"Well, we have plenty of time," I said. "Who knows how long I'll be staying with you—"

"I know." She nodded her head enthusiastically. "I'm so excited."

"Me too, Mom. Me too. I'm starting a new life."

The thought both thrilled and scared the pants off me at the same time.

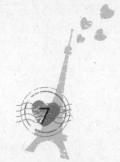

When Life Goes to the Dogs

Three days later, Mom, Ike, and I pulled the minivan up to my parents' house—my new home. I should have been happy that my mom and I survived a thirty-hour road trip in a loaded-down minivan. I should have been happy that my supportive parents were taking me in. I should have been happy that I had a private room with its own bathroom, complete with a balcony overlooking their sparkling pool. But I wasn't happy. I was ashamed.

My mom was exhausted from the long trip. She excused herself to take a nap, suggesting I do the same. Instead, I unloaded the car, my former life slapping me in the face. The container filled with my old design projects reminded me I used to be self-sufficient, a go-getter. Now, almost forty, jobless, and debt ridden, I had to rely on my parents to put a roof over my head. The more I unpacked, the more ridiculous I felt.

Why did I bring so much crap? What was I going to do with the wedding china? Host a dinner party and say, "Oh this? It was from my first marriage. Pretty, isn't it?" Soon, I had six containers and ten boxes sorted into piles: things my parents might want—like the china, since they'd gifted most of the set anyway; things I would keep, namely a few pieces of art, photo albums and yearbooks, jewelry my parents and grandparents had given me, and my blue plastic folder of letters; things I would throw away, like old pay stubs and papers; things I would donate—all my DVDs, books, and a pile of clothes I hadn't worn in years.

When I was finished, I was left with just three containers and two suitcases.

It was the rudest of awakenings.

This was it? This was my life? This was all I had left? I clenched the Nambé salt and pepper shakers in my hand, deliberating, finally placing them in the "to keep" pile. For me, they were symbolic, a reminder of all the bad choices I'd made.

Looking more like a zombie who'd just crawled out from the earth than his vibrant daughter, I must have been unrecognizable to my dad when he came home from work. He walked into the kitchen, unable to hide the concern in his watery green eyes. Even worse, I hated asking him for help when he'd done so much for me over the years, but certain things couldn't be ignored. Like the fact that in California you need a car, especially when your family lives three miles up a long, steep canyon road with no public transportation. To get a car, I needed money, which I didn't have. My mom, dad, and I sat at the kitchen table trying to put a logical game plan together. Dad scratched his stubbled chin. "Sam, honey, I'm taking off work tomorrow so we can go to some car dealers."

He'd always been there for me when I needed him, but my dad was a workaholic who never took a day off. Family vacations were rare, and so our time to bond together was spent on the weekends. When I was little, he'd take me to the IHOP on Sundays, where I'd order piles of blueberry and chocolate-chip pancakes smothered in strawberry syrup and he'd read the paper and try to ignore the waitresses' flirtations. I'd make it a point to let those ladies know I had a mom, she just wasn't with us—a little girl's way of saying "back off, lady, he's taken."

In high school, these daddy-daughter dates turned into dinner and a movie, the latter of which usually involved seeing something my mom, a romantic comedy kind of gal, didn't want to see. It was on one of these outings, at the age of seventeen, that I discovered a lump, just shy of my left breast, under my armpit. The whole evening I was like one of those old paintings of Napoleon Bonaparte, but instead of one hand tucked into my shirt, my hand was sneaking a feel under my armpit in the darkness of the theater. On the ride home, I burst into tears. "Something is wrong with me."

My dad took me to the doctor the following day and to the hospital a week later, when I'd had the fibroadenoma, a benign tumor, removed. Although it wasn't breast cancer, the worry crinkling his eyes stayed until I'd woken up from the operation. Just like the worry written on his face now. "Dad, you don't have to take off work. I'll be all right."

"I've already arranged it. It's settled. We'll help you out for a couple of months until you land back on your feet. Have you thought about how much you can afford for a car payment?"

Car payments? I felt sick. Land on my feet? I'd landed flat on my back. But I was the daughter my parents never worried about, the fearless one, the one who got up on stage, the one who never let life get her down. I kept all my reservations to myself.

Bodhi, my parents' bear-sized golden retriever, placed his big head on my lap and gazed at me with soulful eyes. Jack, the bichon, danced his funny dance, standing upright and pumping his little arms up and down. Gunnar, the Brittany spaniel, sniffed Ike, who was curled up on his dog bed and panting. The dogs reminded me that I had one temporary fix to my financial mess: dog walking. Of course, I knew I wasn't going to become an overnight millionaire walking dogs, but I figured I'd soon land some kind of job in advertising or design. I had about four months, maybe five, to make some money and get my finances in order. I hoped to keep some of the freelance clients I'd had in Chicago, as they promised to keep me busy.

"I think I'll be able to afford around two-fifty a month," I said.

My dad set his coffee down on the glass kitchen table. "How are your finances?"

Nonexistent. I have nothing, nothing but pride and hope.

"I have a couple of hundred dollars in the bank. I'm looking into cashing in my 401(k). And I want to sell some of my jewelry." I rubbed my temples, trying to push back the monstrous headache that had begun river-dancing in my head the moment the word "finances" was mentioned. "I also have my unemployment."

My mom wrung her hands. "I can't believe after nearly twelve years of marriage, you have nothing but a few pieces of art and the clothes—"

"Anne, don't start," said my dad, cutting my mom off. I shot him a sideways glance and a grateful half smile. My dad squeezed my shoulder and continued, "How much do you think you can get for your jewelry?"

"I have no idea."

"And bills?"

"There's health insurance, my cell phone, and credit cards."

"And the amount you owe on your cards?"

"Twenty grand."

Silence filled the room. Even the dogs stopped panting. I put my head in my hands. Saying everything out loud just made it all that much more real. Now, I'd love to say I was addicted to designer clothes and shoes, which would offer an explanation for this gut-twisting, made-me-want-to-vomit-in-my-mouth amount of debt, but I was no Carrie Bradshaw. Christian Louboutin, Jimmy Choo, and Manolo Blahnik had never set foot in my closet. Accumulated over the years, the cost of married life soared one dollar at a time—a few moves, two failed businesses, groceries, dentists, doctors, maybe a plane ticket or two, things of that nature. I was to suffer the consequences.

The vein in my mom's forehead throbbed. "He should pay. He left you with nothing—"

"But I left him—"

"I just hate—"

"Anne, you're not helping matters," said my dad.

"Mom, stop. Dad's right. In order for me to move on, I can't think about Chris. I have to figure things out on my own. Please." My nails created half-moon indentations in the flesh of my palms. I clenched my teeth so hard I thought I'd break a tooth or two. "God, Mom. I don't want you and Dad to feel the need to dig me out of this hole. In fact, I refuse. Unbelievably, I'm an adult now. Hopefully, my finances will clear up. Hopefully, I'll get a job. Hopefully, things will work out."

But I knew hope could only get me so far.

At the very least, I had one thing going for me. Jean-Luc finally wrote me back:

From: Jean-Luc

To: Samantha

Subject: Re: Greetings from the road

Hi Sam,

Concerning the letter I received, it is true to say that it troubled me significantly. Since you were confused, consumed with a high level of guilt, and a person in front of you was able to promise you even the moon to not lose you, everything and anything was possible.

BUT according to your words in all your letters, I was really not expecting such a change. It crossed my head, but never stayed. I understood your marriage was concrete, anchored in reality, whereas I was just a shadow behind words, known only for a few weeks and one day of passion. I thought about the arguments he probably used to confuse your mind. I was thinking that I am a man, and I know men. Whether they are American, British, or French, men know women are often driven by the guilt. They can "play" with that.

I don't know your husband except from your words, and I tried to find all levels of understanding through them to get the best knowledge about the situation. I imagined you fragile for some instants…always with your guilt. Sam, take your decisions for you and you only. Don't

take any decisions for me. You have to feel good with yourself first. I
will be waiting for you, if it is your wish and your desire.

Kisses to my pretty princess.

P.S. This night, look at the sky and you will see a bright point moving;
that's the space station. I wrote something on it for you. Watch it with
your heart. The future will be bright. Believe it.

That evening, in the dark, I stood on the balcony off my room,
searching for that damned space station for hours and hours. Maybe
I was having a severe bleached blond moment, but as I looked up
toward the sky, I'd hoped to discover "*Toujours Samantha*" blinking
in big ball Christmas lights. Certainly, it could happen in the movies,
so why not in real life? To my utter disappointment, no such message
appeared in the starlit sky, just a few satellites bouncing around as
sporadically as my thoughts.

In the state of California, unemployment had reached an all-time
high, peaking at nearly 13 percent. Lucky me, I was a number in
these statistics. While I could have delayed my job search to settle in
a bit, I'd decided to meet with a recruiter to see what opportunities,
if any, existed. Now that I had a car (and the bills that went along
with it), if I wasn't able to get a full-time gig, at the very least I
could pick up some freelance design work. The recruiter raved over
my portfolio and said she could get me working right away. Even
with the depressed state of the economy, I was optimistic. So while
I waited for all the wonderful design opportunities, it was time to
launch into my new day job.

Nothing could have prepared me for the perils of dog walking
in Malibu.

In the first house I visited, a black-and-white photo of a woman
sat on the entry table. She stood naked in the middle of a street,
waving a large feather boa over her head. Her very large breasts
couldn't be ignored.

"Um, is that our client?"

"You should see some of the other pictures," said Stacy, the owner of Whiskers and Tails and also an instant friend. Her clean-scrubbed face broke out into a wide grin. "They're, um, interesting."

Stacy originally hailed from Boston, which explained both her laid-back demeanor and her ambition. A producer by trade, dog walking was her side business to pay the bills. As two creative types, we connected immediately, surviving Malibu's neurotic pet owners one dog at a time.

My eyes darted across the hall to a photo of a much, much older man, who looked like Santa Claus, save for the fact he was naked with the woman from the other photo in a bathtub. I choked on my tongue.

"They're nudists," explained Stacy.

"To each his own. As long as it doesn't affect me."

But their lifestyle choice would affect both Stacy and I—like the day the nudist husband was home and we came face-to-face with his pecker, nothing but a screen door separating us. It was funny, in an "oh my god, did we really just see that" way, and we snorted back our laughter as we scrambled to get the leashes on the dogs and get them out of the yard, into the car, and to the beach. The man just stood there as if nothing was out of the ordinary. I realized my dog-walking training sessions weren't for just the dogs but for dealing with their human owners.

Besides making a friend in Stacy, dog walking, if one ignored the occasional weirdness, came with its perks. Day after day, I walked up and down the canyons of Malibu, quickly losing fifteen pounds and getting back into shape. This new version of the soon-to-be-divorcée diet also included daily double shots of wheat grass instead of double shots of vodka. And the pale pallor of my icy Chicagoan complexion was aglow, tanned by the California sun.

To go along with my svelte figure, the nudist client gave me boxes and boxes and boxes of clothes, each garment still with its tags on. And while the fake-fur-covered bustier or the black sequined pants were not quite my taste, I would find use for the many, many dresses. Brand-new used clothes from a nudist. Ah, but my life was filled with irony. At any rate, I'd dropped two sizes and fit into my skinny jeans.

Not that the dogs I walked cared.

June quickly turned into July, and some days were better than others. Now a self-proclaimed divorcée dog walker, I came up with my own tag line—picking up crap and my life one piece at a time. Every day I received calls or texts from my soon-to-be-ex-husband. Like he'd promised in that first round of texts, Chris had hired an attorney to file our "uncontested divorce," pushing to end our marriage very quickly, but he was also still hanging on to the concept of "us." The court date, for which I would not have to appear, was set for the end of July. My emotions were all over the place. I was happy I'd finally found the courage to move on, yet I really didn't like hurting somebody else in the process.

In addition to twice-daily emails, Jean-Luc and I talked on the phone two or three times a day, sometimes for hours. I was so comfortable with him, one time I even fell asleep. He stayed on the line, just listening to my breath rise and fall until he had to go to work. Unfortunately, my parents didn't have an international calling plan, and along with the car and all my other bills, I didn't know how I'd ever pay them back when we received a six-hundred-dollar phone bill. Job opportunities, according to my recruiter, who'd changed her tune, were few and hard to come by.

Thankfully, we were able to switch my parents' phone service to one that included three hundred minutes of international calling for an extra seven dollars. It was a little late, but there was nothing I could do about that. Jean-Luc switched his phone plan as well, getting a much better deal with unlimited calling to sixty countries for a few euro extra a month. From there on in, if I needed to call him, I would, and then he'd call me back.

Of course, at home I did my best to pitch in. I walked all of the dogs, went to the grocery store, and prepared all the meals, something my dad really appreciated—especially my signature dish of filet mignon served on a crusty crouton and artichoke bottom with béarnaise sauce. Before I came home, I think my yoga teacher of a mom had them both on some kind of weird starvation diet consisting of coffee and kitchari—an Indian cleanse comprised of mung beans and vegetables. Being creative in the kitchen kept me sane. With so much time on my hands, I could experiment more— cooking everything from chicken paprika to lobster thermidor to fresh crab cakes with a tarragon sauce.

My life could have been worse. My parents' house was beautiful, a vine-covered Spanish-style hacienda overlooking the canyon, complete with a pool and gardens full of hummingbirds, roses, and jasmine. But I couldn't just live at home in la-la-land paradise forever, the personal chef to my parents.

I was a realist. And I had my pride, damn it.

On top of all this, Ike's health was declining rapidly. A week or two after I arrived in California, I took my fur-covered replacement child to a new vet. As usual, he was the biggest baby in the waiting room, hiding between my legs, his body shaking violently from his nose to the tip of his tail. The Chihuahua next to us showed more courage. Doctor Lisa took one look at my furry kid and gave her diagnosis.

"It's obvious," she said. "Ike has laryngeal paralysis, a disease common to Labrador retrievers."

I stroked Ike's velvet ears. "Laryngeal paralysis? Is it bad?"

Dr. Lisa pinched her lips together. "I'm not going to lie to you. It can get bad. The problem is the nerves and muscles that control Ike's laryngeal cartilages are losing their function—they're paralyzed— which makes it difficult for Ike to breathe, eat, swallow—"

"What causes it?"

"It's idiopathic."

My bottom lip quivered. "Can it be fixed? Cured?"

"Medical treatments are only aimed at reducing swelling or just calming down the dog. If his condition continues to get worse, to the point where it becomes debilitating, surgery is the next step.

But with or without surgery, there is always the risk of developing aspirational pneumonia."

Pneumonia had caused the death of my very healthy grandfather, Poppy, when he was hospitalized after choking on a poorly made brownie and rupturing his esophagus. The pneumonia started in the hospital. If a brownie was the catalyst to kill off a very fit war hero, my dog was doomed. Ike inhaled his food.

"What do I do?"

"Limit his physical activity and keep him out of the heat."

I had to do something more, something to keep my dog in the best possible condition. My furry kid wasn't feeling well, and I wanted to give him the best care I could get. "You have an acupuncturist on staff, right?"

"Yes."

"Do you think it would help?"

"I'm up for anything natural. It's worth a shot."

I took Ike for a hot dog at the Mutt Hutt in Malibu's Country Mart and then for a walk on the beach. One of the greatest, and also one of the saddest, moments I'd ever shared with my dog was just sitting with him on the beach that day, my arms wrapped around his neck. Together, we watched the waves breaking onto the shore and the pelicans soaring across the sky, and Ike licked my face, which he only did on very rare occasions, as if to say, "Thanks, Mom. You gave me a great life."

I buried my face in his fur and hugged him close.

Everything hit me all at once. The floodgates opened, the tears streaming down my face far from fake. Hugging Ike tightly to my chest, I let it all out; I finally cried. I cried for the loss of my marriage. I cried for my dog's health. I cried for just about everything. I also forgave myself. For everything.

If life was the sum of the choices I'd made, I was just going to have to make better decisions. Starting now.

Play It Again, Sam

In the beginning of July, Jean-Luc had taken the kids away to Scotland for a two-week summer holiday, and our communication slowed. Instead of twice daily emails and our two-hour-long phone calls, I was lucky to hear from him every three days, and only if he was able to find an Internet café. The one time he did manage to call, he put his children on the phone. This I was unprepared for. Elvire, his daughter, was first.

"*Bonjour,*" she said, her voice soft and sweet.

"Hi, I mean, *bonjour. Ça va?*" Although they were only kids, I was a bit nervous.

"*Oui. Ça va.*" Yes. I'm fine.

A mile-long pause.

"*Et vous?*" she asked.

"*Moi? Ça va bien aussi.*" Another pause. I asked her about her trip. "Scotland, I mean, *L'Écosse? C'est bien?*"

"*Oui.*" We listened to each other breathing. She burst into laughter. "*Je vous passe mon frère.*"

I wouldn't have wanted to talk to some strange tongue-tied American woman I'd never met before either. And then Jean-Luc put his son on the phone. The moment Maxence's voice reached my ears, I was surprised that a ten-year-old boy could possibly have a voice that low. To make matters worse, I couldn't understand one word he said. He laughed and passed the phone back to his dad.

"Sorry, honey," said Jean-Luc. "They were both very curious about you, breaking my balls a bit."

Jean-Luc explained that Maxence had been looking over his shoulder at the Internet café and he'd wanted to know why I'd addressed my emails to Jean-Luc as *mon écureuil* (my squirrel), *mon loup* (wolf), *mon Yeti* (bigfoot or sasquatch), and *mon* Shrek—all animals or characters that Jean-Luc had at one time or another referred to himself as over the course of two months of correspondence. I could his imagine his son's laughter, deep and throaty, his daughter's giggles, airy and soft, as they peered over his shoulder trying to figure out what I'd written.

The French have always had funny expressions for terms of endearment. Jean-Luc, like most French parents, referred to his children as *mes puces*, or my fleas. One time Jean-Luc called me *ma biche*, which, hearing the pronunciation as "bitch," I took as highly offensive, until he explained it meant "my doe." Normally though, Jean-Luc called me his American princess, which led to me referring to him as my "frog"—which was inspired by the fairy tale *The Princess and the Frog* and also the fact that the French were oftentimes referred to as frogs because they were known to eat frog legs. Luckily, Jean-Luc did not take offense to the stereotype. Instead he laughed, reminding me that Americans were oftentimes referred to by the French as pigs. I much preferred princess.

"What have you told your tadpoles about me, *ma grenouille*?" I asked, teasing Jean-Luc with the French word for "frog."

"I thought I was your *prince charmant*," said Jean-Luc.

"Maybe. But I haven't kissed you yet."

"As I recall, you did. Twenty years ago. Remember the stairwell leading up to my apartment in Paris?"

Boy, did I. Before I got all flustered, I changed the course of the conversation back on track. "And the kids? Have you told them anything about me?"

"Well, *princess*," said Jean-Luc with a laugh, "Maxence was very concerned as to why I was calling and writing a person named Sam so much, especially after he saw your letter. So he asked who you were."

"And you said—"

"I explained that Sam was a very good friend from America. And then Max asked me with a very straight face, 'Papa, are you a gay?'"

"Oh no."

"Oh yes. I explained your name was Samantha, but they didn't believe me. Like me, a scientist, they wanted proof."

While we waited for our laughter to settle down, a thought popped into my head. We hadn't really discussed his divorce much as of late. "Any news on Natasha?"

"She's found an apartment, which I'm helping her out with until our divorce is finalized. I'm hoping she'll be moved out when the children and I return home."

"Will the kids miss her?"

"Honey, they've only asked if she's taking the cat."

My heart ached just thinking about their estranged relationship with this woman. "Well, you'll just have to get them a new one."

"I'll leave that up to you and the kids." Even without seeing me, Jean-Luc was already trying to include me in his children's lives. He let out a labored breath. "I think Natasha's found somebody new. Some women are like monkeys. They won't leave quietly unless they've got a firm grip on another branch."

"I'm nothing like a monkey," I said. "And if you're a branch, it might break. We haven't seen each other in twenty years."

"We're going to change that."

My heartbeat quickened. "Are we?"

"Could we talk about August? It's a good time for me since the children will be at their grandmother's. I checked my Air France miles and I have enough to afford you a round-trip ticket from Los Angeles to Paris."

We'd touched upon the subject of seeing each other, but no real plans had been set. Could I do this? Could I fly over five thousand miles to visit a man I hadn't seen in twenty years? The answer came quickly. I may have made many mistakes in the past, but I wasn't an idiot. Twenty years ago, I left a chunk of my heart on a train platform at Gare de Lyon. Now I had a chance to reclaim it. And I had a plan.

Right after I got off the phone with Jean-Luc, I was going to cash in my dwindled-down retirement account, which would give me five thousand dollars. According to Fidelity's website, all I'd have to pay was a 10 percent fee. With this money, I could pay my credit cards down, making the payments more manageable, leaving a cushion of two thousand dollars.

"I can buy my own ticket," I said.

"No, Sam, I'm a man. I can't let you."

"But I—"

"You don't even have a job."

"I walk dogs…"

It was a lost cause, and I wasn't about to beleaguer this point with him. Really, if he wanted to use his frequent-flyer points on me, so be it. Judging by the tone in his voice, there was no way he was going to back down. "You're sure you can use the miles?"

"I've already reserved the ticket. All I need to know is if the dates of August second to the twelfth work for you and then I'll book it."

I was going to dare to follow my heart. "My schedule is wide open."

"That's a yes?"

"Yes!"

"Do you want to hear what I have planned?"

"No, I want it all to be a surprise. *Amène-moi n'importe où.*"

Take me anywhere.

The moment we hung up the phone, I called Tracey. Before I could utter a word, she said, "You won't believe this!"

"What?"

"I found the photo album from our trip. I mailed it out yesterday, along with a few other surprises." She laughed her hyena laugh. "So, what's up with you?"

My next sentence spilled out of my mouth in one breath. "Jean-Luc wants to fly me to Paris. And I'm thinking of going," I said, even though I'd already verbally committed to the trip. Perhaps a part of me wanted Tracey to talk me out of this insane decision.

"When?"

"The beginning of August."

"Oh. My. God. You're *so* going to Paris. If you don't, I'll kill you. This is incredible. Jean-Luc, I think he's the one and always has been. He's your soul mate."

Was he? All signs seemed to be pointing to yes. Then again, I wondered: Why did I have to fly all the way to France to find *mon âme soeur*? Later that evening, out of curiosity I pulled up a dating site. It was time to investigate. Were there other men out there like Jean-Luc?

You are: woman

Seeking: men

Age range: ?

For scientific research, the laws of attraction, and whatnot, I had to think about the last one to give an honest answer. Much younger was out of the question. I couldn't imagine myself carrying on with somebody who would get carded at a bar. And what if somebody mistook me for said dude's mother? As for older men, I didn't need a father figure who wanted me to put my tiny hand in his. After giving it some thought, I plugged in the ages of thirty-seven to forty-seven, a ten-year spread seeming reasonable, not too old, not too young—Goldilocks right.

First guy: wanted women in between the ages of eighteen and forty-five. Errr, potential pedophile or serial killer. Second guy: spent time on the beach. That's nice, but shouldn't he be working? He also wanted women between the ages of eighteen and thirty. He was forty-seven. This was a total reality check. Oh yes, the older guys wanted their women younger—much, much younger.

Next.

And next.

I clicked through men like they were shoe listings on Zappos .com to realize none of them would be the perfect fit for me. I knew exactly the kind of person I was searching for if I was lucky enough to find love again, and yes, after not understanding what it was for so long, I did want to find love. I wanted a man who was open to the possibility of having children and who wanted, no, *needed* to have them with me. I didn't need a rich man, but I did want stability. I wanted to be attracted to him physically, intellectually, and emotionally. I wanted to be able to communicate openly, not feel as if I was walking on eggshells. I wanted a man who didn't need to be mothered. My thoughts gravitated to Jean-Luc. I had it pretty good with my sight-unseen Frenchman.

The fantasies playing around in my dreams had turned increasingly vivid and erotic. Take the one where I'm wearing a short summer dress with nothing on underneath it. That's right—no bra, no panties, nada. And we're in a public place, either a park or a dark alley, and he presses me up against a tree or a stone wall, and his hand slides up my thigh, and his breath warms my neck, and his body is pinned against mine, and...

What could I say? I'd been repressed. Either that, or I'd fallen asleep to an airing of *Emmanuelle* on Cinemax. At any rate, one day I woke up needing to hear Jean-Luc's voice, but it was too early to call. Our correspondence had evolved from friendly to romantic to dropping sexual innuendos to sexually charged, so I decided to send Jean-Luc a one-line email using some "dirty" French slang I'd learned on a website.

J'ai la trique pour toi.

I clicked on send, thinking this surely would impress him, because it was definitely not the kind of French one learns in school, definitely not what he'd expect to hear from me at this juncture. Enter, stage left, a forward and very brash—when hidden behind a computer screen—American. I was proud of myself for making the first move until I received his response a few minutes later.

Your sentence *"J'ai la trique pour toi"*? I laughed, but I'm a bit scared—especially for my ass. Don't forget I'm virgin at this point. So if you have *"la trique,"* I think I'll need to walk with my backside to the wall. Plus, I'll never pick up the soap when I shower with you! Please, Sam, protect my virginity! Kiss.

Clearly, this was not the response I'd expected. What had I lost in translation?

I pulled up the site and came to the realization that while yes, this little line, this simple little thought, was slang for being horny, the literal translation was "I have a big stick for you." Which would imply I had a hard-on! Before I scared the guy off with my big stick, I wrote him back.

Zut alors! Sorry! I read somewhere that *"avoir la trique"* was slang for feeling horny. I guess it's only for guys. Rest assured, your virginity is safe with me. Now, go ahead, laugh! Laugh all you want.

To which he instantly replied:

You are incredibly funny and beautiful. I'll call you in five minutes, just enough time to drink my coffee. *Tu es superbe*, Samantha.

I waited for his call, rereading our exchange, cringing with embarrassment. Five minutes later (as promised), the phone rang. I stared at it, dreading to answer. On the third ring, I made my move. Might as well not beat myself up. Just roll with it, Sam. *"J'ai la trique,"* I said.

Jean-Luc couldn't utter his response, he was laughing so hard. And it was infectious. Through my gasps and wheezes, I assured him, oh yes, just give me some time, because this will be the first of many faux pas I will surely make. Bodhi greeted me with one of his big kisses, his tongue sticking to my chin and slurping upward to my eye. "No, no, no," I squealed. "If you heard the heavy breathing, that wasn't me. It was Bodhi, my parents' golden retriever. I dropped the phone off my bed."

"You sleep with dogs?" He sounded shocked, maybe even disgusted.

The moment he said dogs, Bodhi jumped back onto the bed, taking his place with the others—Ike, Jack, and Gunnar. Yes, my bed was one giant fur ball of varying sizes and colors.

"No," I explained. "I only sleep with Ike. The others all come up to my bed in the morning." Or in the middle of the night. Or whenever they felt like it.

"Oh," he answered with a sigh.

"Please don't tell me you don't like dogs."

"Oh, I like dogs," he began. "But…"

"But what?"

"Animals don't belong in your bed."

Admittedly, my entire family spoiled their animals beyond explanation. Did I dare tell Jean-Luc I took the dogs out for hot dogs and beach days? No, I'd have to break Jean-Luc in one fur ball at a time. And that time wasn't now.

"How tall are you?" I asked.

"Changing the subject?"

Yes. "No, it's just that I don't remember. Tracey has all the pictures."

"At least you had pictures." It was his turn to laugh now. "I had nothing. No letters, no pictures. Nothing. You just left me standing on the train tracks, never to be heard from—"

"Hahaha. Should I break out the violins? Because that's the saddest story I've ever heard. And besides, I apologized."

"Twenty years later."

"Oh, you didn't even remember who I was." We'd found a natural groove with teasing banter, but my question had been left unanswered. "I'd really like to know. How tall are you?"

"Around one point seventy-six meters."

He'd given an American girl his height in meters? Meters? I didn't have time to Google the conversion. So I did what any woman who doesn't want to make a fool out of herself does; I went quiet.

"How tall are you?" he finally asked, breaking the uncomfortable silence.

"I'm five foot five."

He sucked in his breath. "*Oaouh, oaouh, oaouh,* I didn't remember you being so tall, almost the same height as me. You're like a model."

"Not really," I answered, wondering how short French models are. And wait a second. He was the same height as me? I thought I could get over this—intelligence and a sense of humor were more important—but it was really going to limit my shoe selection. "I suppose, when we meet, I shouldn't pack my three-inch heels—"

"Honey, of course you can. You'll walk in the street, and I'll walk on the curb." He laughed, heartily this time. "Are there any other measurements you want to know?"

A blush prickled my cheeks. My face went hot. "No. There aren't any other measurements I want to know." I rolled off the bed onto the floor, wheezing in hysterics. "Oh my god! I can't believe you just asked me that."

⟳

Because of the way Jean-Luc and I had connected in the most serious of times and also the most humorous, my gut instinct told me to make the most of the time I had with my parents, especially my mom. Since she lost out on her youth taking care of little me, my mom was reliving her twenties again, earning her the well-deserved nickname of Party Anne-imal. Much to my dad's chagrin, she now had me to go out with, and Wednesday evening was karaoke night at one of Malibu's hot spots. So my mom invited some of her friends to meet up with us, and I invited Stacy. We got to Malibu's Wine Barrel early to grab a table and a bite to eat. I'd never been there before, and I had to admit, the place was nice. With dark wood walls, a nice bar, it was the kind of place you'd find in downtown

Chicago, save for the fact it was located next to a Bank of America in a strip mall.

Over a tray of cheese and a sinfully delicious Pinot Noir, I'd soon find out my reputation had proceeded me. Thanks to my mom, everybody in town knew about my story with my Frenchman, which also meant I was the center of attention, especially with all the newly single ladies. One of my mom's friends introduced me to a girl from New York named Rainbow, who was also going through a divorce. We bonded immediately.

A crazed Belgian, trying to show some Malibu flash, bought fifty bottles of champagne, sending them to every table in the place. He ran around the bar telling everybody he was the heir to a famed children's books author's fortune, that he owned all the licensing rights. Funny, I'd always thought this particular author was from England. After he tried flirting with all the women at our table, to no avail, he finally left our corner, and the conversation went immediately back to Jean-Luc.

"When you go to France, can you bring me one back?"

"What does he look like?"

"Does he have a brother?"

"Do you have any of his letters with you?"

Here I stood, in the midst of change with an exciting and very hopeful adventure in front of me. And I realized how lucky I was to be falling in love.

9

Let the Love Adventure Begin

Perhaps it was because we are inundated with sexy girls with pouty lips in sexy poses—ads for pole-stripping classes, the Victoria's Secret catalogue, not to mention all those racy Facebook profiles. Perhaps it was because I wanted to turn up the heat in my already boiling relationship with Jean-Luc. Perhaps it was because I wanted to feel sexy too. Perhaps it was because, little by little, fear was leaving my system. In any case, no matter what had inspired me, I decided to send Jean-Luc some provocative pictures of myself, something I'd never had the courage to do before.

My MacBook had a built-in camera. So I sat on my bed in varying poses and in varying states of not quite being undressed, my blouse hanging off my shoulder, a little lace of my bra showing, taking one picture after the other. When I was finished, out of hundreds of photos, I deleted all but three. And there was no way in hell I was sending them to Jean-Luc. At least not the way they were. I opened up Photoshop and reduced each photo to the size of my index fingernail and put them in one file, a triptych of sorts. Happy with my creative endeavor, I attached the photo and sent it off. The phone rang a couple of minutes later.

"Sam, the photo you sent was so little, now the screen of my computer is like a contact lens. Someone from my work walked in—"

"Oh my god. They didn't see anything?" My voice shook with panic. I finally garnered up the courage to do something like this, and now the entire world, or at least Jean-Luc's office, was probably laughing at me, the American girl who can't even get sending a provocative picture right.

"How could anybody see anything? The more I enlarged it, the worse the quality got, all pixilated into a bunch of fuzzy squares."

"This whole seduction thing is foreign to me."

"You can only imagine how badly I want to see you. You're beautiful, Sam."

Commanded by his confident voice, my nerves settled down immediately. Maybe it was the French accent? Maybe it was the smooth, sexy inflections in his tone? Whatever it was about him, it worked, and he always knew the right things to say. He tipped my Libra scales right to the middle, in perfect balance.

"I've got some bad news."

My heart raced. He'd been buttering me up. "What is it?"

"My car blew up."

What? It blew up? Maybe his soon-to-be ex was behind it? Maybe she was after him? From what he'd told me, she was a little off kilter. "Someone bombed your car? Natasha?"

"Don't be ridiculous. It was an old car—a BM *DoubleV*. It just died. There was nothing that could be done." I waited for him to yell, to complain. He didn't do anything but sigh. "Don't worry. This won't mess up our trip. I've already checked into booking a rental car."

"Oh."

Being pragmatic, or maybe paranoid, I wasn't about to fly over five thousand miles without some kind of a back-up emergency plan. So many things could happen. First of all, Jean-Luc would be driving over seven hours from Toulouse to pick me up at Charles de Gaulle in Paris. His car could "blow up." Again. Plus, my worries didn't stop with mechanical issues or fatal accidents. What if we didn't recognize one another? Or, as the perfect revenge for my twenty-year silence, at the last minute he might change his mind, not even bother picking me up, leaving me in Paris all alone.

What if the pictures he sent me weren't even of him? What if I hadn't been corresponding with the real Jean-Luc? I had seen Liam Neeson's movie, *Taken*, where the Albanian Mafia kidnaps and drugs women, ultimately selling them off as sex slaves. The traffickers targeted their prey in Paris, at Charles de Gaulle, the airport I'd be flying into.

Yes, I knew my imagination was in overdrive, racing down the speedway of paranoia at three hundred miles per hour. I knew what Jean-Luc would say: don't be nervous. But saying and doing were two different things. I played out every scenario in my head, no matter how outlandish. Since my knight in shining armor wouldn't ride into the baggage claim on a horse, I needed to be cautious. Maybe a little more so than usual.

"Jean-Luc, I have a small favor to ask of you."

"Anything, princess."

"Do they have those cheap pay-as-you-go cell phones in France?"

"Yes, my daughter has one for emergencies."

"Could you please buy me one and send it to me with a prepaid card?" I wondered if this was a rude request. "Of course, I'll pay you back. I'd just like a means to get in touch with you. You know, in case something happens."

"What could possibly happen?"

With great patience, he listened to me explain all the reasons I felt the need for the phone. As the words tumbled out of my mouth, I realized how ridiculous I sounded. To cover up my tracks, I told him how my sister teased me about how he could be a human trafficker for the Albanian Mafia. The more I babbled, the deeper the hole I dug.

"Honey, honey, honey, I think it's a superb idea." I was now convinced Jean-Luc knew the golden rule: a man always agrees with a woman, especially when he wants to stop a ludicrous rant. "I'll send you our spare phone tomorrow."

I breathed out a sigh of relief.

"Honey, before I leave you, I do need your advice on one topic. Tell me your preference, where do you want to spend the last night? In Versailles or in Paris?"

Seeing as I'd never seen it in person, Versailles, the wealthy suburb of Paris famous for its decadent castle, was tempting. However, I thought it would be utterly romantic if Jean-Luc and I stayed in Paris, the place where we first met. Together, we could retrace our steps—eat at Dame Tartine, grab a glass of port at an outdoor café on the Champs-Élysées, and walk by his old apartment. Then again, we could create a new memory, an even better one.

"Surprise me," I finally said. "It's completely up to you. I'm in your hands."

"I can't wait," he said.

Neither could I.

The next two weeks were a blur of dog tails and a haze of hot Malibu summer days. Two days before I was to leave for Paris, I invited Stacy over to take a dip in my parents' pool—an added bonus of living at home and a welcome relief from ninety-degree weather and the unrelenting canyon sun. So my new friend (and boss) was with me when Jean-Luc's package arrived. In addition to a green cell phone, dried lavender and roses tumbled out of the box, presumably from Jean-Luc's garden.

Her jaw dropped open. "Who does that? I mean, it's just so romantic."

Must be the French touch.

"It is romantic, but this isn't." I handed a second envelope over to Stacy.

"Is this what I think it is?"

"Yep."

She threw her arms around me. "Congratulations! You're a free woman!"

I gulped. Free or not, seeing my divorce decree in its finality was a bit disconcerting. This wasn't just some kind of weird fantasy; it was real. I was excited for the future, but I was petrified for it too. I was still a dog walker, Jean-Luc and I hadn't even reconnected face-to-face, and I was still living at home with my parents. The sweat from walking dogs was nothing compared to the sweat of fear of the unknown. It was time to jump in the pool, to try to calm down my nerves.

After a quick dip, Stacy took off and I walked back to the house, wondering if I knew what the hell I was doing. As if to answer me, another package wrapped up in brown paper rested on the front stoop. It too was addressed to me, from Tracey. Inside it was the photo album from our European adventure. Additionally, Tracey had sent her travel journal filled with schoolgirl ramblings and ooh-la-las, plus the letters and postcards Patrick had sent to her. For the moment, I set those aside. I needed to see the pictures, one in particular. And there it was: the photo of Jean-Luc and me standing on the steps of Sacré-Coeur, me with a wide crazy grin, wearing a hot pink T-shirt and jean shorts, him holding on to my arm, looking ever so handsome, wearing a white button-down shirt and black slacks, his beautiful bow-shaped lips pulled into a half smile. A new rush of memories slammed my brain upon seeing the photos, feelings long forgotten but stored somewhere inside.

I ran into the house, packages in hand. Instead of telling my mom about the divorce decree or my emergency phone sent along with dried lavender, I screamed, "Tracey finally sent the photo album! Jean-Luc is taller than me!"

I didn't get an answer. Apparently Mom was off teaching a yoga class at the VA. Which gave me plenty of time to scan all the photos into the computer, email Jean-Luc, call Tracey, and finish packing. Heaven forbid I forget anything. I must have been packing and unpacking, checking and rechecking, for at least three weeks. The night before I left for Charles de Gaulle, I stood out on the balcony off my bedroom, searching for one last push, one final sign that I was doing the right thing by flying to Paris. I didn't find anything inspiring, so I emailed Jean-Luc.

From: Samantha
To: Jean-Luc

Subject: A message…

It was a beautiful night so I decided to drive down to the beach and take a walk. I tried looking for the infamous space station, the one with the message written on it, but for the life of me I couldn't find it. As chance would have it, I had a glass bottle, a piece of paper, and a pen in my purse. So all alone under the stars, I wrote you a message. You'll just have to wait to see what I wrote, because yes, I put my letter in the bottle and I threw it into the Pacific. Maybe the next time you're at the beach, you'll find it.

Samantha

From: Jean-Luc
To: Samantha

Subject: re: A message…

Honey, I don't think your message will reach me. I could get scientific on you and tell you about trajectory patterns and the like, but I'm sure it would bore you. I'm sorry, but the bottle will not make it here. Or is my funny girl trying to get me back for the space station?

Big kisses—more today than yesterday, but less than tomorrow.

From: Samantha
To: Jean-Luc

Subject: re: A message…

I forgot to tell you—it's a magic bottle. To find it, all you have to do is follow your heart.

Jean-Luc had understood my odd brand of humor. I got my sign!

Before I knew it, my mother was driving me to the airport. "Are you excited?" she asked.

I stared straight ahead, hands clasped in my lap. "Stop asking me that. You're making me nervous."

"Call me the second you land. I want to make sure you get in okay."

"You just want to know what happens when we see each other."

"Can you blame me?"

"No," I said. She'd been living this love adventure vicariously through me since it had begun a few months ago. Of course she wanted to know what happened.

"So are you excited?"

"Please, you're really making me nervous."

A pause.

"You must be excited."

Two hours later, I was crammed into a window seat, right above the wing, my heart racing. What was going to happen when the plane landed? Sure, Jean-Luc and I had connected twenty years ago. And we'd connected over the phone and in hundreds of emails. But what if the man behind the screen and the phone wasn't the man I'd thought him to be? What if the physical attraction between us wasn't as strong as the emotional bond we'd established?

Over the loudspeaker, the safety instructions came, first in French, then in English—both languages incomprehensible, muffled murmurs pulsating in my ears like one of the adults in a Charlie Brown special. Dizziness set in. A drop of sweat trickled down my neck, pooling in the small of my back. The woman seated next to me whispered something to her husband, shifting her weight away from me. I averted my gaze and stared out the window, begging for a torrential downpour, lightning, anything. But it was just another beautiful day in sunny Southern California, not a cloud in sight. The plane lurched backward. Seriously, what was I thinking? Leaving the country with a heart filled with hope and a few measly dollars?

I had to get off this plane.

But how? I was bright enough to know that if I screamed "Bomb!" at the top of my lungs, some undercover air marshal would drag me to prison, kicking and screaming with a stun gun pointed at my neck.

Maybe I could feign a heart attack?

A stewardess dressed in a fitted blue suit caught my attention, graceful fingers pointing out the emergency exits, the bathrooms. She was perfectly coiffed, wearing the newest shade of red Chanel lipstick. Pretty. Taking the comfort route in yoga pants and a T-shirt, I wasn't exactly the epitome of style. And I was headed for the fashion capital of the world.

The woman seated next to me shot me a concerned look. "Afraid to fly, huh?"

Her voice was smooth, calm.

Mine, when it squeaked out, was not.

"No, I fly all the time." I immediately read the confusion on her face and decided to share my dilemma. "You see, I'm about to meet up with this guy I haven't seen in a while—a long, long while. He's, uh, err, French. I met him in Paris." Her mouth twisted. I thought it was my cue to carry on. "I met him twenty years ago. We're both divorced now. Well, not exactly. Mine just went through a few days ago. He's still working on his…"

And why was I telling her all this? I needed diarrhea medication. For my mouth. Although I'd been living in Malibu where the crazed blond, blue-eyed look was all the rage, I was certain I'd scared her to death when she leaned as far away from me as humanly possible. The focus needed to switch from me to her fast. "Paris is a really romantic city, don't you think? I've been there three times. Have you?"

"Of course we've been to Paris, but we're on our way to visit family in Armenia. We only have a layover at Charles de Gaulle." She went back to reading her gossip rag. "Good luck."

Under normal circumstances, I'd find her behavior rude, but I wasn't surprised when she didn't press me for more information. Had our situations been reversed, I would have wanted all the juicy details. I'm built that way—an American woman who can't help but glance at the tabloid headlines in the supermarket or over the shoulder of the person seated next to me.

My stomach nearly dropped into my uterus as the plane lifted off. I leaned toward the window and pressed my forehead to the glass, taking slow, deep, purposeful breaths. Below, Los Angeles became a tiny speck, the Pacific Ocean glimmering like a beautiful blue velvet dress worthy of the red carpet. Once we were in the air, an overwhelming rush of freedom surged through me. My hands released the armrests and my lips curved into a smile. If Jean-Luc was as amazing in person as he was on paper, and if we connected the way we had the first time twenty years ago, then this love adventure was worth the risk.

The long flight gave me plenty of time to "Play it again, Sam," to think about the first time I'd met Jean-Luc in 1989, to think about the man whose letters inspired seven blog posts and a two-decades-late apology, the man who now inspired me. Soon, instead of being seated on a plane, my thoughts gravitated to Paris, to that hot summer's night in 1989, right to the very first time I'd met Jean-Luc, the memory playing in my head like a movie.

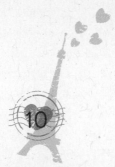

Two American Tartes
at Dame Tartine

The second night of my two-week European adventure way back in 1989 had all the ingredients for a clichéd romance. A crowded café? In Paris? A handsome Frenchman? Check, check, and, considering there was not one but *two* Frenchmen, double check.

Tracey had a much better view of their table. I had to crane my neck and peer over my right shoulder, making an effort not to be too obvious. But I was. My eyes locked onto a sexy man's eyes across the crowded restaurant. It was love at first sight, or, as the French would say, *un coup de foudre*—a bolt of lightning, a shock to the system. Before I tipped over in my chair, I pretended to grab something out of my purse, a blush prickling my cheeks.

"So, which one do you want?" asked Tracey, as if we could just order the two Frenchmen right off the menu.

"That depends. Should I ask the waiter if the guy wearing the green shirt comes with a side of fries?"

"Oh, thank God! I was just about to call dibs on the darker-haired one. White shirt." Tracey licked her lips. "This could be the best restaurant in all of Paris."

It might not have been a Michelin three-star, but Dame Tartine was turning out to be a very tasty choice. We'd discovered the trendy café in front of this crazy fountain—the Stravinsky Fountain by the

Centre Pompidou in the Beaubourg. The café was, in our American eyes, so very French, from the red awning with gold lettering right down to the heavily glossed red wooden chairs and the handwritten sign displaying the daily specials. Even the waiters wore the requisite white shirt, black tie, long black apron, and snobbish Parisian attitude. As it was priced right for our limited budgets, we figured there was no better way to take part in Parisian café society than sitting outside people watching, surrounded by wisps of cigarette smoke, the whimsical fountain of moving sculptures gurgling in the background.

Turned out, everybody else had the same idea that balmy summer's night; the outside terrace was packed. Too hungry to look for another place, we agreed when the host offered to seat us inside. Little did we know the view from our table would be much more…captivating.

"Tracey, stop staring," I said through clenched teeth, trying to keep my lips from moving. As if—with my back facing their table—the guy in the green shirt could tell I was talking about him. I straightened up in my seat, sure that even my posture gave me away.

Tracey didn't even try to hide her ogling. Her brown eyes sparkled with something I can only describe as crazed lust. I shifted my body to block her view. "I'm serious. You've got to cut it out. They're going to think there's something wrong with you."

"I can't help it, Sam. It's like I'm hypnotized. The darker-haired one is so gorgeous, he's like a French Tom Cruise." She paused. "But way, way better looking."

Although I was tempted to turn around and see if her comparison rang true, I was still reeling from the jolt to my heart. Instead, I leaned forward, placing my elbows on the white butcher paper-covered table, crumbs from crusty, flaky bread digging into my skin. "What are they doing now?"

Tracey's brows furrowed. "I think they're leaving."

No, no, no! The romance I had created in my head couldn't end even before it began. The Frenchman wearing the green shirt, the one with the sexy lips and penetrating gaze, he and I were *supposed* to fall desperately head-over-heels in love. We'd have a wild affair, vow our undying love, and then, once I graduated from college, I'd move here: to Paris.

Wasn't that every American girl's dream?

But surely these two guys had better things to do than pick up nineteen-year-old American tourists and cater to their unrealistic fantasies. They probably had sexy French girlfriends, the kind of women Tracey and I had been seeing all day long—the sultry ones with long shiny hair and perfect pouty lips, the ones whose style could only be called Parisian, whether they were wearing sundresses or the chicest of Chanel. Yes, these girls were the kind who could lower anybody's self-esteem with one calculated stare from their smoldering, black-lined, almond-shaped eyes.

Tracey and I had tried our best to blend in, in a feeble attempt to look sophisticated and sexy, but we were out of our league in Paris. Our T-shirts with huge shoulder pads ate up our small frames. Add in the giant black belts with a huge silver buckles, the black mini-skirts, the black patent leather kitten heels, and you had two late-1980s fashion disasters.

This minor setback didn't faze my friend in the slightest. She brushed her hair off her shoulder and broke out into a wide grin. Her long, silver earrings swayed back and forth, a soundless metronome counting in time to the beat of my disappointed heart.

"Why are you smiling like that?" I frowned. "In fact, why are you smiling at all? They. Are. Leaving."

Besides raising her eyebrows, Tracey didn't have to say another word. I made another lame attempt to pass a surreptitious glance over my shoulder to find our two Frenchmen approaching our table, a confident step in their swaggers.

The air was electric.

Before I knew it, one of them was standing right behind me. "American?" asked a deep, accented voice.

Pardon?

Seriously, what had tipped them off? We may not have been as put together as the French girls who haunted our vision at every turn, but with Tracey's dark hair, brown eyes, and angular features, she could have easily passed for Spanish, Italian, Greek, maybe even French. Was it my blond (or slightly orange-ish) hair (blame Sun-In and a hairdryer) and blue eyes that gave us away?

Tracey managed to sigh. "Yes, how'd you know?"

Took the words right out of my gaping mouth.

The guys positioned themselves in front of our table. Tracey's French Tom Cruise pointed to our bottle of wine, and they both laughed. "No self-respecting French woman would ever order a bottle of wine sans *un bouchon*."

Regardless of the sexy accent, my fantasy took a nosedive. Had they come over to our table to insult us? What the heck was a *bouchon*? Only one way to find out. "*Bouchon?*" I'd asked, meeting amused gazes and quickly looking away.

"Without a, ummm, a cork."

"Oh, well then," I said, my tone more defensive than I wanted it to be. "What should we have ordered?"

"A carafe would have been, um, more *ac-cep-ta-ble*."

We were young American girls, clueless about how to order wine, and who better to point out our crass error than two young Frenchmen? And they were laughing. Laughing at us. Because of the screw top. Were Tracey and I progressive or what?

Note: In France, it's still un-ac-cep-ta-ble to order wine with a screw top.

Eyes cast down, I mumbled, "It was the cheapest."

French Tom Cruise nudged his friend in the side and said something quickly, too fast for me to pick up a single word.

"We'd like to propose you a good bottle of wine," said the object of my affection, his English amusingly formal but perfect. "But on one condition. If you would allow us the honor, we would like to join you at your table."

Tracey smiled so big, I'm surprised her face didn't crack. That was all the encouragement they needed. The fantasy was back on.

"Permit me to introduce myself. I'm Jean-Luc," said my Frenchman, pulling up a chair and taking a seat next to...Tracey?

French Tom Cruise sat next to me. "My name *eez* Patrick."

Pa-treek.

"I'm Tracey." She pointed at me, daggers of confusion shooting out of her eyes. "And that's Samantha."

"Samantha," repeated Jean-Luc. "It's a very pretty name." He turned toward Tracey, brushing me off. "Where are you from?"

Wait one little second here.

What was going on?

Clearly, the whole thing with the wine had been a well-played pickup line, and Jean-Luc and Patrick were masters of "the neg," long before shows like *The Pickup Artist* aired or books like *The Bro Code* were published, but I'd thought Jean-Luc and I had shared a moment.

I may have been smiling on the outside, but inside I was screaming.

Maybe a Mime Can Point Us in the Right Direction

Jean-Luc called the waiter over with a confident flick of his wrist. I found it impossible not to stare at his beautiful bow-shaped lips as he spoke to the server. He could have said anything and I would have swooned at the melody, the beautiful French language rolling off his tongue. A dark emerald green button-down shirt complemented his hazel eyes.

Eyes that I'd thought had been for me.

It wasn't as if I didn't find Patrick attractive. He was a perfect specimen of a man with movie-star good looks, his hair was dark brown, almost black, and he had beautiful crystalline blue eyes. Like Jean-Luc, he also had beautiful lips and a sexy cleft in his chin. Yet something about him was too perfect—for my tastes, at least.

The only thing Tracey and I could do was to try to put this potentially awkward situation behind us—although we'd never been in one quite like it before. In high school, things always worked out in our favor. She dated one guy. I dated his best friend. I dated one twin. She dated the other. After an amicable breakup, I even set her up with one of my exes. She'd dubbed him the Pac-Man kisser after an eat-your-face-off make-out session in which he almost dislocated her jaw. Good intentions aside, *that* relationship was short lived. Yes, guys had come and gone, but our friendship had always come first, with no boy ever breaking our bond.

Resigned to our fate, I smiled at Tracey with a shrug. She smiled back. Things could have been worse. After all, we were sitting at a café with not one but two handsome Frenchmen in Paris. Who were we to complain?

Our waiter returned with a menu, handing it over to Jean-Luc.

"Have you girls taken something to eat?" he asked. "I'd like to match your selections with the wine."

Normally, I was the kind of girl who talked a mile a minute, the kind of girl who thrived on attention, flirted with the best of them. I wanted to answer, but I was so nervous that it was hard enough speaking English, let alone French. Odd. I'd been stunned into blushing silence.

"We both ordered the co—chicken with wine sauce," said Tracey, coming to the rescue yet again. "What about you?"

I stifled a laugh, certain that Tracey didn't want to mispronounce the word "*coq*" in *coq au vin*. Jean-Luc popped his lips, as if to say, "No problem."

"We've already had our meals. The wine is for you."

Great. I didn't know if my nerves could take it. They were going to watch us eat? Either I had some kind of social anxiety disorder or first-date nerves had me on the edge of my seat. Would he think I was a pig? Would something get stuck in my teeth? Like a piece of spinach? Or some black pepper? Tracey, on the other hand, was still smiling away like a fool. The waiter tapped his pen against his pad impatiently. With a flourish of hand movements, Jean-Luc pointed to something on the menu, and I could make out the words *vin blanc*. White wine. The waiter, with typical Parisian flair, rolled his eyes and said, "*Bon choix.*"

Jean-Luc shot me a sexy wink. "I think you'll like my selection." His eyes told me what his lips didn't say: he'd felt the connection too. "What brings you to Paris?"

His gaze didn't leave mine. Tracey took the opportunity to flirt her way over toward Patrick—a slight repositioning of her chair, a flip of her hair, and she was set.

It took me a second, but I managed to find my voice. "Well, my family moved to London last year, so Trace and I are doing the whole Eurail thing while we have the chance." I paused. Lest he think I was some spoiled American, spending Daddy's money, I needed to make something clear. "I worked three jobs over the summer to pay for the trip—waitressing and an internship."

"And when you're not traveling the world, waitressing, or interning?"

"I'm an art major at Syracuse University. Advertising design."

"Ah, art. Plenty of that in Paris. Have you been to any of the museums?"

"Well, today, we went to the Louvre, Musée de l'Orangerie, and the Musée Picasso. Yesterday, we went to Notre-Dame, took a boat ride down the Seine on a *bateau mouche*, visited the Eiffel Tower, and—"

"How could you visit all those museums in one day? The Louvre should take a week to visit in itself."

Did I dare tell him Tracey and I had run through the Louvre in an hour, right past Delacroix's *Liberty Guiding the People*, past the Rembrandts and the Caravaggios, the Renoirs and the Van Goghs, and right up to the *Mona Lisa*, only to be disappointed to find the famed painting displayed behind plexiglass and surrounded by camera-wielding tourists? Or that we'd spent a good fifteen minutes mimicking armless Greek sculptures by stuffing our arms inside our T-shirts? No, some things were better left unsaid. I had to put my best patent leather kitten heel forward and pretend I possessed at least one ounce of sophistication.

"You know how it is. It's our first trip to Paris. So many things to see and do, so little time."

Jean-Luc held me captive in his gaze. "And do you like what you've seen?"

Blushing, I nodded. Instead of playing along with an enticing quip, my idiot-mode kicked in. "We went on this huge Ferris wheel in the Jardin des Tuileries last night. It was amazing. Once we were at the top, we could see all of Paris. The Tour Eiffel looked like a Christmas tree, there were so many lights on it!"

Good God, I sounded like a child, babbling on about a Ferris wheel and sparkling lights. Next, I'd probably launch into some diatribe about how badly the mimes near the Louvre freaked me out, blocking my path with their painted faces, striped shirts, suspenders, and red berets.

"Ah, yes! You chose the best time to come to Paris. It's the *Bicentenaire de la Révolution Française*—a party all summer long. It's too bad you weren't here for the *quatorze juillet*. Beautiful artificial fires lit up the night. There were performances in the street, right on the Champs-Élysées."

Et voilà. It was time to impress him with some knowledge. "Bastille Day, right?"

"Oui, c'est ça, but a very special one. The two-hundredth anniversary."

Perhaps somebody suggested that Patrick should teach Tracey a few French phrases? Maybe the guys went to the bathroom and switched seats upon their return? No matter how it occurred, a game of musical chairs had been played and the awkward situation had been rectified. Somehow I found myself sitting next to Jean-Luc with him enlightening me with the history of the French Revolution, which I only found interesting because of his excitement for his country's past. And because he was hot.

Naturally, I tried to impress Jean-Luc by speaking my mangled French, better known as *Franglais*, much to his amusement. Funnily, he insisted on "practicing" his English, which was already close to perfect. As for Tracey, who didn't speak French, save for a few words like *bonjour* (bong-or) or *au revoir* (or-ree-vor), and Patrick, who only spoke a little English, well, their conversation was a little more animated—like those dreaded mimes outside of the Louvre, there were a lot of hand movements going on.

"I have to be honest," said Jean-Luc. "I found the confidence to come and talk to you by approaching Tracey first. Your back was to me. And, she, *et alors,* how do I put this, seemed friendlier."

My heart stuttered a few beats.

Glancing across the table, I couldn't help but think about the first time I'd met Tracey my freshman year of high school. When she'd introduced herself, she'd stuck out her hand, said, "Shake," and when I'd reached for it, she'd pulled it away and did this bizarre Copacabana shimmy shake with her shoulders. Her dark brown eyes met mine and she'd said, "You look like fun. I know we're going to be friends." Then she turned on her heel and strutted down the hall like she didn't have a care in the world. After that, it had been my intention to avoid the girl at all costs. But I guess I couldn't shake her. I laughed silently at this memory, wondering how Jean-Luc knew Patrick. So I asked.

"We did our tour of duty together in the military—officers' training in Salon-de-Provence, in the South of France." He puffed out his chest proudly and said something sounding like "I was a lwhetnut."

"A wet nut? Could you spell that, please?" I asked. And he did. "Ohhhh, a lieutenant. So, you're an officer and a gentleman?"

"And a doctor too." He laughed. "But not a medical doctor. I'm finishing up my PhD."

My God, this guy was every girl's ultimate fantasy. Every mother on the planet would approve. *My* mother would have approved. Jean-Luc went on to explain how at the age of twenty-six, he had come to work at the French equivalent of NASA and spoke four or five different languages, including Russian. Heck, even though Jean-Luc was French, my retired colonel *Great Santini* of a grandfather, Poppy, would have given Jean-Luc his stamp of approval. Officer status trumped anything.

I was over the moon. Until my insecurities came crashing down like a rogue meteor.

Earth to Sam! Come in, Sam!

I wondered: Why in God's name was Jean-Luc wasting his time with me? He must have been after something, right? After all, we American girls had the reputation of going *Girls Gone Wild* when traveling Europe, lifting up our shirts and dropping our thongs for any handsome stranger who crossed our path. With nothing better to do on a Monday night, maybe he and Patrick were out trolling the streets with the hopes of getting laid.

"So do you and Patrick make it a habit of picking up American girls in touristy cafés?"

A flash of understanding sparked in Jean-Luc's eyes. "Aha, but this is Paris in the summer. Tourists overtake the city—every museum, every street. They even tour our sewers. No café is safe." He raised a brow and popped his lips. "Just so you know, you're the first American girl I've ever met."

"Yeah, right."

"It's true. And now I don't believe what they say, the stereotypes."

"And that would be?"

"Americans are rude."

"I've been on my best behavior." I smiled. "What else?"

"They're uncultured."

"Do I have to remind you about the bottle of wine with the screw top?"

"You speak French."

"*Pas bien.*"

"At least you try. And you have a passion for art."

"It's my major."

Jean-Luc took my hands. "You're unlike any other girl I've ever met."

"Please tell me that's not an insult."

"*Et alors*, not only are you beautiful, you're smart and you're funny. It's hard finding all three traits in one person." Intensity and truthfulness shone from his eyes. "How long are you in Paris?"

It may have been a crock, but I was done for. I gulped. "We leave tomorrow."

"Then tonight can never end."

And the Night Never Ends

The "first date" nerves finally settled down.

I made it through my *coq au vin* without any embarrassing food catastrophes, not one stray piece of chicken or peppercorn trapped in my teeth. Of course, I'd reminded myself not to inhale my dinner like a starved pig at an overfilled trough and not to speak with a full mouth. But whether I was using the right fork or not, the company at our table overshadowed the meal, and the conversation, along with the new bottle of wine, flowed.

Eleven thirty rolled around. Closing time. We'd overstayed our welcome at the café. The waiters lifted chairs onto tables, giving us dirty looks. Even though they hadn't dined with us, Jean-Luc and Patrick paid for our dinner and suggested we head over to the Champs-Élysées for a *digestif*. I had no clue how we got to Paris's most illustrious boulevard. For all I knew, we could have teleported. We were with a rocket scientist, after all, and all of a sudden, we were just there.

The bar they'd chosen had a distant view of the Arc de Triomphe, aglow in a golden hue, the Parisian nightlife twinkling. Patrick and Jean-Luc ordered drinks. Transfixed with Jean-Luc, after glancing at the Arc de Triomphe, I didn't take in much of anything else. Laughing with my best friend and two charming Frenchmen, I thought, *Life, it just doesn't get any better than this.*

In front of Tracey and Patrick, the waiter placed two glasses filled up a quarter of the way with a golden yellow liquid and one or two ice cubes, which were not quite winning the war with the summer heat. On the side, he placed a small carafe of water. Two small glasses filled with a heady red wine were placed in front of Jean-Luc and me.

"Usually," said Patrick, his accent thick, his words slow and purposeful, "pastis is served as an *aperitif, mais*, it's also a good drink on hot summer nights." Patrick poured some water into their drinks, diluting the concoction to a sickly yellow hue.

"What is it?" asked Tracey.

"An anise-flavored liqueur," answered Jean-Luc.

Tracey smelled her glass and took a hesitant sip. "Mmmm, it's, um, strong." I could tell by her expression that she didn't like it. She held out her glass. "Here, Sam, it's really good, try it."

"No, thanks. I think I'll stick with the wine. Don't want to mix."

"It's not wine," said Jean-Luc. "It's port. Have you ever tried it?"

"No. I'm in a sorority. At the fraternities, we're inducted into Beer Drinking 101."

Jean-Luc's mouth pulled into a grimace. "I don't really like beer."

I took a sip of the port, rich and thick. "Come to think of it, neither do I."

Soon, it was two in the morning and closing time for our new haunt. But why stop our Parisian love adventure, right? Tracey and I didn't want to go back to our youth hostel after having our drinks on the Champs-Élysées, and Patrick had a membership at some private club.

From what I can remember, the taxi ride was both scintillating and terrifying. We raced through the streets of Paris, the historical stone facades and pedestrians a blur. Wherever it was that we were going, I wanted to make it there alive. Good lord, the way Parisians drove—similar to crazed taxi drivers in New York, but worse—frightened me to death. In the backseat, one hand covered my eyes and the other rested on Jean-Luc's thigh. His aromatic cologne—citrusy and spicy—floated up to my nostrils. Sophisticated, yet subtle, the attraction to this scent was instantaneous. So very French. Intoxicating. The sexual energy between us was palpable, but besides stroking the top of my hand with his thumb, he hadn't made his move…yet.

We finally made it to our destination: La Bas, an exclusive establishment that, as we were told by Patrick, mostly catered to the illustrious fashion crowd and bourgeoisie Parisians. As we walked into the club, the bass of eighties dance music thumped in time to my beating heart. *Thump. Thump. Boom. Thump. Thump. Boom.* Patrick led us to a bank of leather couches, tucked in a dark corner away from the flashing lights of the disco floor.

The club was empty, save for one or two other couples. It was dark. The DJ played the popular hit of the day, Kaoma's "Lambada." Jean-Luc pulled me in close, his hands on my back, my hands on his shoulders. A little dirty dancing turned into a kiss. Once we started, we didn't stop. Total PDA, but who cared? This wasn't your typical college hookup or make-out session. It was an intense, complete, and utter out-of-body experience. I can't speak for them, but I think Tracey and Patrick were having a good time themselves.

Hey, if *Risky Business* had taught us anything, it was that every now and then you have to say what the…French kiss—at least until the club closes. Which, of course, it did. At six in the morning, we were booted out of the *boîte*, the blinding sun already in its place on the horizon, Parisians bustling down the cobbled alleyways, making their way to work and starting their days. Not leaving us to walk alone, Jean-Luc and Patrick escorted Tracey and me back to our youth hostel.

The hostel was a beautiful vine-covered building, complete with a cream-colored stone facade, located in the fourth arrondissement, right in the heart of the Saint-Gervais district—an area known for its narrow streets, private mansions, and townhouses. We couldn't beat the location—in walking distance to Notre-Dame, the Seine, and, of course, Le Centre Pompidou, where we'd met Jean-Luc and Patrick. Our room may have been bare bones minimum, nothing but two sets of bunk beds, but it was clean and it was cheap. The only downside was having to share our quarters with two perky blue-eyed, blond-haired girls from South Africa.

Jean-Luc smiled. "This is one of my favorite streets in Paris. I come here to escape. I love the history here."

In silence, we took in our surroundings. A cobbled brick path led up to the beautiful Église Saint-Gervais, which was the oldest church on the right bank of the Seine. Traditional iron street lamps hung off the sides of the buildings. Bicycles with wicker baskets were parked in front of the local café, its facade painted blue. The four of us stood in front of the carved wooden doors to the hostel, right under the Juliet-style wrought-iron balconies with our very own French Romeos. Parting, indeed, was such sweet sorrow. But the romance couldn't end. Not now! We still had fourteen hours left in the city of love! Patrick pulled Jean-Luc aside. Tracey and I leaned against the wall, talking in hushed whispers.

"Do I look disgusting?" I asked. "Like a Parisian sewer rat?"

"Your hair is a bit funky, but you're fine." She paused. "What about me?"

"You never look bad."

A group of girls bounded out of the youth hostel and stopped midtrack. They gazed at our two handsome Frenchmen and then caught sight of Tracey and me. Daggers of jealousy shot out of their eyes.

"Did you see those girls checking out Jean-Luc and Patrick?" I asked.

"Do you blame them?"

Not one bit.

Jean-Luc and Patrick turned to face us. "Patrick and I both have days of vacation we're able to use. With no sleep, neither of us can go to work. So we'll collect you in a couple of hours, show you some of Paris." He paused. "If that's okay with you."

Was he kidding? Both Tracey and I beamed.

"*Dors bien, ma belle,*" said Jean-Luc. "We'll pick you up at noon."

Jean-Luc and I shared one last kiss and then he and Patrick twisted around the corner and they were gone. Tracey and I staggered up the steps to our room and flopped down together onto the lower bunk, goofy smiles stretched across our faces.

"Oh my god," said Tracey. "I think I'm in love."

I propped myself up on my elbows. Love? She couldn't be falling in love. More to the point, *I* couldn't be falling in love. It was just lust, that first chemical reaction sparking both the brain and the body. Right? I was still in school in upstate New York. Jean-Luc lived here, in Paris. It would never work out. But my God, if I'd had a list for everything I'd ever dreamt for in a perfect man, Jean-Luc would have had a check in every box.

I huffed. "Don't be ridiculous. We just met them."

"Sam, didn't *Auntie Mame* teach you anything? 'Live! Life's a banquet and—'"

"'Most poor suckers are starving to death!'"

We broke out into giddy laughter as I finished the quote from Tracey's all-time favorite movie.

"What did you and Patrick talk about, anyway?"

"Music, the Beatles, American culture, stuff like that."

"So you could understand one another?"

"There was some confusion, but we managed." She yawned, making no attempt to cover her mouth. "Sam, I'm so tired, but I don't think I'll be able to sleep. My heart is still racing."

"Well, we should try."

I crawled up the wooden ladder to the top bunk. Lying there, staring at the ceiling, I thought, *No. No way in hell could I be falling in love. No, not me. There was no way I was falling in love.*

I awoke to the sound of somebody pounding on the door to our room. I looked at my watch. Twenty past eleven. Twenty minutes past check-out time. Forty minutes until Jean-Luc and Patrick's arrival. We hadn't packed, hadn't showered. I scurried down the ladder, opened the door, and yelled to Tracey, "Wake up!" She didn't budge, just kept snoring. A stout woman with a tight bun pursed her lips and put one hand on her hip. Her other hand held a mop.

"Please, *s'il vous plaît*," I said. "Can we have fifteen minutes—*quinze minutes*? We overslept." I pointed to our still-unpacked suit-cases and then brought my hands to prayer position, in case there was any confusion. "*Quinze minutes? S'il vous plaît?*"

The woman frowned. Surely, she was going to say no. So she surprised me when she didn't. "*Quinze minutes. Pas plus.*"

She turned on a flat heel, making her way down the hall.

"*Merci,*" I called out before running over to Tracey and shaking her awake. "Get. The. Hell. Up. We overslept. We have five minutes to shower. I'm going in first. Start packing."

Tracey sat upright. "Shit."

I bolted to the bathroom. Soon, we were two wet Tasmanian devils whirling around in an explosion of clothes, makeup, and shoes. Not quite the backpacking types, both of us had small suitcases with wheels. And not wanting to risk bed bugs or other strange creatures that may bite in the night, we'd even brought along our own blan-kets. Our suitcases barely closed.

"Sit on it," I said. "And I'll pull the zipper."

Twenty minutes later, out of breath, Tracey handed our room key to an aloof male student type behind the counter. He didn't look up from his magazine, just kept reading. We made our way downstairs to put our luggage in the basement's storage area. With a bounce in our step, exactly at noon, we headed down to the lobby expecting to see our Romeos waiting for us. They weren't there. Five minutes turned into fifteen minutes. Giddiness turned into sadness. Fifteen minutes turned into forty-five minutes. We paced the lobby of the hostel, feeling like the figure in Edvard Munch's painting *The Scream*—pure agony, trembling with anxiety.

It felt like high school all over again—waiting for the call that never came, the feelings of utter rejection, the humiliation. Less than eight hours after meeting me, Jean-Luc had managed to shatter my heart into tiny little pieces. I didn't blame him. He had nothing to gain from getting to know me. Tracey and I were leaving that night.

"I can't believe they blew us off," said Tracey.

I looked at my watch. They were now over an hour late. There was no way they were going to show up. "Let's just go grab a coffee."

"Does it come with a side car?"

"Oh, does Auntie need fuel?"

But now, not even quoting *Auntie Mame* could make us smile.

The Train Leaves the Station

"Tracey!"

"Samantha!"

We heard their shouts the moment we were about to head toward the small dining hall. Our heads twisted around so fast I'm surprised Tracey and I didn't get whiplash. There, at the bottom of the landing, Jean-Luc and Patrick stood with sheepish grins on their faces. Both Tracey and I smiled even bigger. Our Frenchmen bounded up the steps and swung us around in their muscular arms.

"Sorry we're late. The traffic was *horrible*."

"*On y va?*"

"It's time to see Paris."

Heads spinning, we headed for Patrick's car, the anger and humiliation melting away. Jean-Luc opened the car door. He wore nice slacks and a button-down white shirt, complete with a black tie. And here I was in a candy-pink T-shirt, high-waisted jean shorts, and white Keds.

"Where are we going?"

"Montmartre," said Jean-Luc.

"Am I dressed okay?"

"You're fine." He smiled. "Just fine. It's me who is overdressed."

Was he trying to impress *me*?

On the car ride, once again, I tried speaking to Jean-Luc in my mangled French. Unfortunately, in high school they'd taught us expressions, not actual conversational skills. Really, how many times could I have said, "*Je sais ce que c'est, mais je ne sais pas comment le dire en français*"? (I know what it is, but I don't know how to say it in French.) Jean-Luc told me my accent was very good, although I was pretty sure he was just being polite. He still insisted on "practicing" his English.

"Are you hungry?"

We hadn't eaten anything since dinner. "Actually, I am."

"I know just the place."

We parked the car and traversed the cobbled streets of Montmartre, passing art galleries with scenic oil paintings and watercolors displayed on the sidewalk in waves of colorful bursts, and made our way to a small café for crêpes—which aren't technically crêpes when filled with meats and cheeses, but a saltier pancake called a *galette*. They weren't quite the two-dollar bargain of a baguette with a slab of pâté, the lunch Tracey and I had the day before. In fact, the prices on the menu were a bit over the top.

"You're being tourists for us," I said. "Thank you."

"You don't have to thank me. It's my pleasure." Jean-Luc shrugged. "You know there's more to the French people and our food than just Paris."

"Where did you grow up?"

"La Ciotat—a small town on the Mediterranean Sea in the South—close to Marseilles." He laughed, a twinkle lighting his eyes. "I'm just a boy from the beaches of Provence. My father worked at the shipyards. Maybe one day I'll be able to take you there, show you a different side of France."

"That would be nice." Much as I wanted to believe in the idea of seeing him again, something deep in my gut told me it would never happen. It was now past three o'clock; my time with Jean-Luc was ticking down. "Tracey and I are headed for Nice tomorrow. I'm excited to see more of France."

Jean-Luc's smile turned into a frown. "Couldn't you stay in Paris a few more days?"

My eyes shot from Tracey's, which pleaded, to Jean-Luc and Patrick's, which looked hopeful. Tracey and I couldn't just deviate from the plan because of two guys, could we? Guys we'd only met the night before? I liked Jean-Luc, *really* liked him, but I couldn't fathom throwing away my one and only opportunity to see Europe.

Tracey piped up. "Sam, maybe we could. Maybe just one more night?"

I shook my head. "It's not possible. We've booked one-way non-refundable tickets, not an open-ended Eurail pass." It wasn't just our train tickets that were a bit pricey; the most expensive part of our trip was flying back from Athens to London. Sighing, I looked at Tracey. "I'd love to, but if something happens and we don't make it to Greece, we're totally screwed."

Tracey's face was so illuminated with happiness, an actual light bulb may have popped up over her head. "Maybe they could come with us? To Nice? We'll be there for three days."

We all looked to the rocket scientist for the answer.

Jean-Luc rubbed his temples. "It's summer in Paris. The trains to the South are definitely booked. And I have an important project I have to finish up tomorrow. My thesis."

The table went quiet, everybody deep in thought. The clock was tick, tick, ticking down. It was three-thirty. Our train left in five and a half hours. We threw a few more ideas around but couldn't find a solution to our dilemma.

Putting doom and gloom aside, the four of us walked over to Sacré-Coeur, its glorious white-domed basilica reaching high into the cornflower blue and cloudless summer sky. The towering white church reminded me of a fluffy wedding cake, layered not with icing but intricate Romano-Byzantine designs—each glorious detail more intricate than the next. In awe, I took in my surroundings, which included a sweeping view of Paris. Apparently it was mandatory to take your picture on the steps of Sacré-Coeur. So we did just that. A souvenir of the moment.

"Sacré-Coeur is the highest point in the city. But that's not the reason I wanted to bring you here." Jean-Luc pointed to the esplanade filled with artists behind easels with paintings tourists could purchase displayed at their side. "I know you enjoy art. I wanted you to see this. All the artists you love—the impressionists, the surrealists, the cubists—used to come here. They probably even ate at the very café where we ate."

The names of my favorite painters ran through my head—Monet, Dali, Van Gogh, Picasso, Pissarro, Lautrec, to name a few. To think they probably stood at the exact spot where I was right now was mind blowing. To think some of the artists painting before us could follow in the steps of master painters was inspirational. To think Jean-Luc actually remembered everything we had talked about the previous evening made my heart beat just a little bit faster.

"The area," Jean-Luc continued, "has quite a crazy history. In the early 1900s, none of the *bourgeois* Parisians would dare come here at night for fear of being mugged by a gang that called themselves the Apache. However, artists, poets, and writers all settled here, choosing the low rent and bohemian lifestyle—painting by day, drinking by night."

"At the cabarets. Like the Moulin Rouge."

"*Exactement*, but the Moulin Rouge is technically in an area called Pigalle. It's just down those stairs. After we're done here, we'll take a tour, yes?"

I nodded my head vigorously, the colorful poster of Toulouse Lautrec's can-can girls coming to mind.

Tracey tugged on the sleeve of my pink T-shirt. "Patrick wants to take me to visit the arrondissement he lives in, show me his family's home, and then we'll meet you back at Jean-Luc's around six thirty." She whispered excitedly, "I'm going to meet his mom."

His mom? Wait, what? And since when was going to Jean-Luc's place part of the plan?

Sneaky, sneaky. The guys were trying to get us alone—probably their plan along. This, of course, led me to doubt Jean-Luc's true intentions. It wasn't the threat of going to his place that had my mind reeling; it was the threat of what could potentially happen there. I watched Tracey and Patrick as they left, hand in hand, until they disappeared from view, my heart racing.

"Did you want to walk by the Moulin Rouge?" asked Jean-Luc. "After that, there's a wonderful cemetery I'd like to show you. A lot of famous artists, writers, and poets are buried there."

I could only nod.

We walked by what I thought was a pet store, due to the rabbits and geese displayed in cages. I stepped toward the cages to stroke a floppy-eared bunny. "Oh, they're so cute."

"Didn't your mother ever teach you not to play with your food?"

I whipped my body around to face Jean-Luc. "What?"

"*Lapin à la moutarde* is a, um, *une spécialité* in Paris."

I'm sure you can imagine the horror on my face when I noticed the word "*Boucherie*" prominently displayed in red, painted in flourished letters on the shop's window. Not a pet store. This was a butcher. "Rabbit with mustard sauce?"

Jean-Luc grabbed my waist, pulled me in close. "It's really quite good."

We kissed. A long, long French kiss. Rabbit? What rabbit?

One very heated taxi ride filled with kisses later, hand in hand, we strolled by the *Cimetière de Montmartre*. Its ornate tombs, I would learn, were home to the souls of poets, musicians, artists, writers, scientists, dancers, and composers—a few of the names familiar to me. Offenbach, Foucault, Degas, Dumas. We didn't walk into the cemetery but just took a quick peek into the entry, a glimpse at the towering stone mausoleums, and we were off, making our way back to Jean-Luc's place. I stared up at his Haussmann-inspired apartment building, both dread and anticipation rocking my body.

"It's beautiful," I said, regarding the luxurious architecture and craftsmanship of days gone by.

Jean-Luc laughed. "Well, the first five floors of apartments are very nice—very bourgeois. And it is a beautiful building, but…"

"What floor do you live on?"

"The sixth. I live in what's called a *chambre de bonne*, or maid's quarters." He shrugged. "But unlike some of the other apartments on my floor, I do have my own toilet and shower."

So foreign was the concept, I could only parrot him. "Your own toilet and shower?"

"After doing my tour in the military, this was the only place I found in Paris I could afford."

We stepped into the marble foyer.

"Where's the elevator?" I asked.

"There isn't one."

He took me by the hand, leading the way up the marble steps. After the taxi ride, I wanted to feel Jean-Luc's lips on mine again. We barely made it up the steps to his place. Young, nubile bodies tugged at each other's clothes, pushing each other against the wall. Frantic kisses. Sex was in the air. He opened up the door to his studio apartment, where the only piece of furniture was a mattress on the floor. Soon, we were sprawled out on the bed. Things were heating up, and quickly. The chemistry between us, between our bodies, was undeniably hot.

"I can't," I said, pushing him away before things went too far—yet still wanting more.

Jean-Luc rolled off me and onto his back, gasping out in frustration. "*Mais, pourquoi?*"

"Why? Because I like you."

Seriously, only a woman would understand my reasoning. And I didn't mean to sound so *Mickey Mouse Club*. Nobody, save for Tracey, would ever find out about this one-day stand. But I wasn't stupid. If I had given myself to him then, I knew we'd never see each other again. A part of me wanted to believe that we would meet up somehow in the future.

I lay on the mattress, breathless, debating my decision. Regardless of what my body was telling me to do, for once my head had made the right decision.

"It isn't my intention to push you into something you don't want to do," he said. "We can take our time. London isn't so far from Paris." He sat down next me, pulling me in close. "We have to see each other again. I don't want to lose you, Sam. I've never met anybody like you before."

Wrapped up in his arms so perfectly, I exhaled a deep breath. In the hallway, Tracey's laughter could be heard, loud and clear. She banged on the apartment door and yelled, "Samantha, we've got a train to catch!"

I glanced at my watch. It was eight o'clock in the evening. We had less than one hour to get back to the youth hostel, grab our bags, and make it to Gare de Lyon. The guys were still trying to convince us to stay, but how? There was no time to figure out a solution. All we could do was go.

⌒

Patrick pulled his car into a cramped space, one wheel up on the curb. The parking gods may have been on our side, but we only had five, maybe ten minutes to make our train. We were two blocks away from the station. Jean-Luc and Patrick grabbed our bags, carrying them instead of rolling them, and we ran.

Breathless, we made it to the platform with sixty seconds to spare. Jean-Luc and I shared one final kiss. "Stay in Paris, Samantha," he begged. "We need more time. There's so much I want to show you, do with you."

The only words my lips could form were the same ones I'd used just one hour before. "I really like you, but I can't."

"We have to do everything we can to save this passion between us." He gripped my arms and pulled me close. "I was serious when I said now that I've found you, I don't want to lose you."

The train whistle blew. I stepped into the passenger car. "This isn't a good-bye," I said.

The train lurched forward. I watched Jean-Luc until he became a tiny speck blowing air kisses in the distance. Tracey and I looked at one another and said the same thing: "Maybe we should have stayed."

But we didn't. We stuck to the plan.

As the train rolled along, insecurities chugged into my head. Jean-Luc was too perfect, too smart. He was seven years older, ready for a relationship. I was too young. The timing was wrong. Like a skilled surgeon, Jean-Luc had meticulously opened up my heart. If I didn't want to get hurt, it was up to me to close it again. We hadn't even reached our next destination, and my good-bye had already turned into the more permanent *adieu*.

Our European journey continued. Tracey and I made it to the South of France, visiting the beaches of Nice, Monaco, and Cannes. Then it was on to Geneva, Florence, and Greece, where I had too many shots of ouzo and too many plates broken on my head (literally). But no matter how hard I'd tried to convince myself Jean-Luc was wrong for me, it didn't work. I returned to my studies at Syracuse University to find six of Jean-Luc's letters awaiting me. I tried writing him back, but my words came out wrong, sounded stupid, could never match the passion found in his.

By the time the seventh letter arrived, guilt had rendered me numb. Instead of listening to my heart and writing Jean-Luc back, I tucked his letters into a blue plastic folder and got back to college life.

I wouldn't think about Jean-Luc again for many years.

Now, after a two-decade hiatus, I was actually going to see him again.

Letter Four
Paris, August 6, 1989

My Lady,

I am enjoyed one more time to write to you, to create this invisible link between you and I. All these letters are the hours we didn't have to get to know one another. So since I can't talk to you, I put my words down on this paper like a crazy writer straight from the Bukowski world. But I am not drunk, well, maybe a bit buzzed with the pictures of you in my head.

When I am with a girl, my blood boils, and when I love this girl, all my blood is vaporized and I can climb at the curtain (French saying). It's perhaps the picture of the expression "love gives you wings" - do I try to fly? I can write you for hours, to catch the time we didn't share. I hope through these letters you would be able to draw a certain picture of me. A positive one.

Samantha, someone in Paris misses you as darkness can miss the sunshine. Every star you see in the sky shows the sparkling of my eyes, created by your meeting. If you were Juliet, I would like to be your Romeo, but don't forget to send me the ladder.

Your Latin Lover,
Jean-Luc

14

Le Coup de Foudre Strikes Again

Despite the two glasses of red wine I'd drunk with the hopes of knocking myself out, sleep eluded me. Over the loudspeaker, the captain's voice lilted with a French accent, reminding me I was on a plane, getting ready to spend ten days and nine nights with a man I had spent only twenty-four hours with, twenty long years ago. So many things could go wrong. Then again, so many things could go right.

When I was twenty-four, a guy I was dating took me to Hawaii. I wasn't sure how I felt about him. He was kind of uptight, didn't quite "get" my sense of humor, but I was like, why not? Maybe we'll connect. Plus, it was cold in Chicago. So I went with him, expecting paradise and a little romance. What I got was my idea of hell— tropical rainstorms, a cat-sized rat lurking around on one of the rafters in our room, and a guy I couldn't stand to spend more than two seconds with. Thanks to the hotel's lending library, I must have read thirty or so crappy books over five torturous days. Finally, it was time for us to part ways. When he finally dropped me off at the airport, I bolted out of the rental car, never once looking back.

I'd told Jean-Luc this story over the phone, and he'd laughed and urged me to pack books instead of clothes, just in case. I was beginning to wonder.

I slouched down in my cramped window seat, flicking through

the movies. My heart nearly stopped when I saw one of the choices: *Je l'aimais*, based on the novel by Anna Gavalda, which Jean-Luc had recommended I read. I laughed to myself, apparently out loud. The woman seated next to me shouldered closer to her husband. At that point, I didn't really care if she thought I was crazy.

Jean-Luc's recommendation of *Je l'aimais* had been a small but mildly amusing disaster in our relationship. First, when I'd popped over to Amazon.com to read an excerpt, I'd read from the wrong book, that title being "*Je voudrais que quelqu'un m'attende quelque part,*" *I Wish Someone Were Waiting for Me Somewhere*, a collection of short stories. Even worse, I'd sent Jean-Luc some nonsensical email about how I loved Gavalda's style, how I couldn't wait to read what happened between the woman, a literary type, and the handsome stranger she randomly encountered on boulevard Saint-Germain, and how these types of encounters were called "meet-cutes" in the movie world. And then I screwed my head on straight.

No, *Je l'aimais* wasn't about a random encounter between two strangers. It was about how a man, Pierre, comforted his daughter-in-law, Chloe, shortly after his son left her and their two young daughters for another woman. On that night, Pierre shared something that had haunted him for over twenty years—his secret love for a woman named Mathilde. With much remorse, he confessed to Chloe how he had chosen the safer route, how he was a man who dared not. Now his life was filled with regret for casting aside the only woman he'd ever truly loved.

As I watched the movie, tears dampened my eyes. I could have been Pierre. *Je l'aimais* could have been me. I was reminded of why I was on that plane. I was following my heart. I was a woman who dared.

Adventuress or not, the moment the plane touched the ground, my nerves set on fire. I was there, in Paris. We were supposed to wait until we reached the gate to use portable electronic devices, but my French emergency phone found its way from my purse into my hand, and I turned it on. I was a rebel about to suffer a complete nervous breakdown, and I needed to speak with Jean-Luc to make sure he had made it to the airport okay.

I could barely focus from the lack of sleep, the tiny buttons on the phone blurring. I dialed Jean-Luc's number and it just rang and rang and rang, and then, for good measure, it rang one more time before going to voice mail. Clearly, I must have dialed wrong. But no, oh no, his sexy and sultry French accent teased me on the voice mail message.

"Hi," I said. "It's me. I'm here. I just landed. Um, call me back…okay?"

Finally, the phone buzzed to life, vibrating in my hand. I stared at it with horror. Usually, I was quite tech savvy. Not today. The cramped coach seat closed in on me. What I wouldn't have given for an oxygen mask. In a total freak-out moment, I couldn't figure out which button to press, so I pushed them all, ultimately missing his call. Thankfully, Jean-Luc called again. That time I chose the right button.

"Sam? Sam? Are you there?" Worry filled his tone.

"Uh, uh, uh…"

"Sorry, honey. I see I missed your call."

"Uh-huh."

"I was parking the car."

"Mmph."

"Are you okay?"

No, but I finally managed to get a coherent thought out. "You're here at the airport." It wasn't a question but a breathless, almost accusatory statement.

"Of course. Where else would I be?" He paused. "When you come out of customs, go left, not right."

"Me-a-ow." Wait. Did I just meow? I meant to say okay. My tongue stuck to the roof of my mouth. "I'll thee you apter cuthoms. To da laft."

"Are you, um, okay, Sam?"

Although his voice was filled with genuine concern, I couldn't help but think he probably wanted to bolt right out of there, probably worried he was about to meet up with the Elephant Man's speech-impaired twin sister. Before I screamed, "I am not an animal! I am a human being. I am a woman," a thought relaxed me. His voice may have oozed with a quiet confidence, but he was probably a wreck too. He had to be just as nervous as I was.

"I'm fine," I said. "Just a little tired."

"Okay." He didn't sound convinced. "I'm waiting for you. To the left," he said before the line went dead.

The plane pulled into the gate. *Ding.* The seatbelt sign was turned off. Passengers stood up, but I didn't move. Quickly, I ran through the contingency plan in my head. If I wasn't attracted to Jean-Luc on a physical level, I was supposed to kiss him on both cheeks, to "*faire la bise,*" the typical European greeting. Of course, we had never discussed what I was supposed to do if I liked what I saw. Shake his hand? Kiss him on the mouth? Or was Jean-Luc supposed to lift me into his arms and twirl me around? Then again, what if he didn't like the way I looked? Would he just leave me standing there? Would he turn and run?

The August heat seeped into the cabin. My pants stuck to my thighs, my hair to the nape of my neck. I had to get to the bathroom stat—to change my clothes, brush my hair, my teeth. The couple next to me finally pushed forward. I was barely able to get out of my seat to stand—or rather, wobble—in the aisle. I attempted to grab my bag from the overhead bin. Before it fell onto my head, a man caught it. I mumbled out a thank-you. Impatient passengers pushed this blond zombie down the tight aisle.

My ten-minute makeover would have to wait though; there was the matter of having to pass through airport security first—the police, not to be confused with customs. Even when they smiled, there was something ominous about their demeanor, something that said no matter who you were, no matter where you were, if you hadn't committed a crime and been busted for it yet, there was still time. I stood rigid in line. The stale scent of body odor—not mine, I hoped—permeated my nostrils, making me feel just a tad bit queasy. A uniformed officer sitting behind a plexiglass kiosk called me forward.

"Bonjour," I said with what I thought was a smile.

"Passport, please." The guy lifted a brow. I handed over my passport and nervously watched him scrutinize every page. His dark eyes locked onto mine, forcing me to meet his gaze. I wanted to tell him the only thing dangerous about me was my breath, but I didn't. Humor and *la police* just don't mix.

A woman wearing a magnificent headscarf with swirls of dark purples and browns was being grilled one kiosk over. An infant clung to her chest. The moment the guard stamped her passport, her head lifted higher. Everyone has a story. I wondered what hers was.

I wondered where mine was going.

"Madame?" My interrogator interrupted my thoughts. "And your business in Paris, Madame?"

"I'm not here on business. I'm here for pleasure." *Pleasure.*

Satisfied with my response, the guard scanned my passport, stamped it, and handed it back with a frown. "*Bienvenue en France. Bon séjour.*"

I raced to the ladies' room. In a smart move, I'd brought a poly/lycra blend dress, not one wrinkle on it. It was a white midsleeve number with a navy baroque pattern and a couple of sparkles, cute and curve fitting. Sexy but not over the top, the hem rested about three inches above the top of my knee. Just enough leg. I scrambled out of my T-shirt and yoga pants, wiped my body off with a baby wipe, put on deodorant, and threw the clean frock on. I pulled my white wedge cork heels out of the bag and slipped them onto my feet. Sunglasses to hide my sleep-deprived eyes. There, I almost felt human again. For a moment, I debated if it would be possible to wash my hair in the sink.

Before I'd left, I'd tried to convince Jean-Luc to pick me up at some hotel near the airport, where rooms are rented by the hour. Given my situation, I'd wanted to look my absolute best, maybe take a shower. Always a gentleman, he'd agreed to my crazy plan. Then I reconsidered. First, I would have had to take a bus a half an hour away, and with my French, I could have ended up in Timbuktu. And second, because this bears repeating, it was a hotel where they rented rooms by the hour.

My hair, I decided, had weathered the journey fine—not as greasy as I had anticipated it would be after nearly twenty-four hours of traveling. I smoothed it out with a brush. I touched up my lipstick, checked myself out one last time. Considering I hadn't slept, and even though I felt like hell warmed over, I didn't look nearly as bad as I'd thought I would. Tired passengers limped by as I made my way to baggage claim.

Forty-five minutes passed and the bags still hadn't made their appearance on the conveyer belt. Too many languages floated in the air. I didn't understand a thing, and my head felt as if it could explode. I was not looking forward to bending over in a dress to pick up a fifty-pound bag. I was wearing a thong. I was getting angry, impatient, and paranoid. A ringtone startled me. I was so distracted I barely noticed that it was the phone I'd been gripping like a lifeline in my hand. "Hello."

"Honey, did you get lost?"

"No, the bags haven't come out yet. I'm sorry. There's nothing I can do to speed things up—" As if it was cued, the conveyor belt churned to life.

Jean-Luc breathed out a sigh of relief. "I'll see you soon. I can't wait."

Sooner turned out to be later. My bag was the last one out.

A sea of saris, bright blues and greens glistening with silver paillettes, billowed around in the hot breeze. There must have been about thirty people milling about, blocking my view, and speaking in a foreign tongue. It wasn't French and I wondered if I had made a mistake, if I had actually arrived in, oh, I didn't know, India. Finally, the crowd parted and I saw Jean-Luc standing amid the cocoa-colored bodies. I sucked in my breath. Wearing a blue and white striped shirt and jeans, he was undeniably French. He was also hard to miss, really handsome—much better in person than in pictures.

His beautiful bow-shaped lips curved into a smile, warm and sexy, offset by charming dimples. He might not have had a full head of hair, but he worked this look well. His nose was imperfect, a little crooked, but this only added to his charm. And I loved the cleft in his chin, the square shape of his masculine jawline, his perfectly sized ears.

My sister, who had demanded I forward her the pictures Jean-Luc had sent, called the triangle of hair under his bottom lip a "flavor saver," which was a pretty disgusting term, but I thought his soul patch was damn sexy, especially when combined with the well-manicured sideburns. I walked closer toward Jean-Luc and his smile widened, making him even sexier. My heart jackhammered against my ribs.

My pace quickened. I was one foot in front of Jean-Luc when my body lurched forward. Before I fell, he took me into his arms, strong and muscular. We gazed into each other's eyes, his soft caramel with hints of green, dreamy. Needing to end any kind of awkwardness right away, I went for it and planted a big kiss on his lips. It was an instantaneous attraction, a chemical reaction.

He hugged me tighter. "Now that I've found you, I don't want to let you go, not again."

"Correction," I said. "I found you."

"Honey, oh honey, love isn't a competition."

Our lips met again, and then our tongues. *Soyez la bienvenue en France* with a real French kiss. Lightning struck. It had been so long since I'd been kissed—truly kissed—like that. Jean-Luc wheeled my suitcase and threw my carry-on bag over his shoulder. On the way to the car, we passed a young couple seated on a bench whose lips were locked together. They just carried on with their make-out session, unaware of anybody or anything, just each other.

Jean-Luc whispered in my ear. "*Soupe de langues!*"

"Tongue soup?" I raised my brows inquisitively as I translated his words. "The French really do have a way with words."

"That's not the only thing we have a way with."

All of a sudden, Jean-Luc and I were making out like teenagers in the middle of the parking garage. The kiss was so long and so good, chills ran down my spine. Somehow we made it to the rental car with me sitting in the passenger seat, not in his lap. We were driving somewhere. Anywhere. The bizarre, nervous sounds emitting from my mouth were not my own.

I regarded Jean-Luc, admiring his quiet confidence, his style. With one hand dangling over the steering wheel, the other one on the gear shift, my Frenchman was a relaxed driver, zipping in and out of traffic, coming close to the bumper of the red Deux Chevaux in front of us. Me? I was using my invisible brake in the passenger seat.

"Does my driving make you nervous?"

His voice was sexy, low and tender. "No. Why do you ask?"

He laughed. It was melodic and warm. "You know, there are no brakes on your side of the car."

On the highway, Jean-Luc's hand found its way from the gear shift to my knee. Goosebumps puckered my neck, my arms. I cleared my throat. "So, did you get any sleep last night?"

He had driven over seven hours from Toulouse to Paris to pick me up.

"I pulled over at a motel midway and took a rest and a shower."

His hand became more courageous, finding its way to my thigh. Silence hung in the air. My heartbeat pulsed in my ears. I couldn't help but wonder how soon was too soon? We'd been communicating with each other for well over three months, writing hundreds of letters, speaking for two to three hours on the phone a day. Now I was actually with him. "Were you nervous to see me?" I asked, breaking the silence.

Jean-Luc turned his head toward me and laughed. "Why would I be nervous?"

"Oh, I don't know. Maybe because we haven't seen each other in twenty years."

He squeezed my thigh. "Because you never wrote me back—"

"Yes, I did."

"Twenty years later."

"I can assure you if I had written you back then and we saw each other again, things would be a lot different now."

"Because I was…what did you call me?"

"A player. I called you a player. And from what you've told me about your past, it's true," I teased.

"Honey, I have to be honest with you."

Here it comes. He was going to drop a bomb, like he had twenty girlfriends, all of whom he loved, all of whom were under the age of thirty. One word squeaked out of my mouth. "Yes?"

"I was a little nervous to see you, like a school boy getting ready to pick up his first date."

My lips curved into a grin. "You were?"

"Yes, but I'm a man. I'm not supposed to admit fear to you. But we promised we would talk about anything. There will be no secrets between us. Ever."

Something deep in my gut told me that Jean-Luc and I would be together for a very long time. I could sense it. This was not our first date. Everything was already so natural between us. We had already professed our feelings for one another, whispered I love yous and *je t'aimes* during our late night telephone calls. It was then I decided to let my inhibitions go, to drop my guard, and let passion lead me. I twisted my body toward him. His hand stroked my inner thigh, grazing the lace separating flesh from fabric. I gulped. "How long is it to the hotel?"

"Two hours." He pulled his hand out from under my dress and grabbed my hand again, squeezing it. "We've waited twenty years. Two hours won't kill us."

"Where are we going? Paris?"

"No, not Paris. You've already been to Paris. You'll see."

An Instant Connection

Perhaps I was suffering dementia from lack of sleep. Perhaps years of being sexually repressed had built up. Whatever the reason, we'd barely stepped foot into the hotel room before I threw Jean-Luc onto the bed, straddling him. His fervor immediately matched mine. In a matter of seconds, our clothes were on the floor, and since I'd been starved for love, a feeding frenzy began. I was ravenous.

Apparently, so was he. When we made love that first time, an intensity shone from his eyes. In fact, his gaze never left mine. Breathless, we lay in bed, me wrapped in his arms.

"I don't understand," said Jean-Luc.

"Understand what?"

"*Alors*, I don't understand how somebody could ignore you for so long. Did you tell me the truth?"

I rolled over on my side, balancing on my elbow and stroking his chest with my free hand. "I've never, never lied to you. When I told you Chris and I made love six or eight times a year, it was the sad truth."

"That's nothing. Nothing." He sucked in his breath, stared at the ceiling. "Sam, you're a very sensual woman, not a piece of furniture. I don't understand how you let it happen."

This was what I was missing out on? "Well, it did."

"Life isn't worth living unless there is passion." He flipped me onto my back, grinning wickedly. His eyes locked on to mine, intense. "We have to make up for lost time."

Three orgasms, a toe-curling, leg-shaking, close-to-hyperventilating escapade, and one and a half hours later, I learned that Jean-Luc was an insatiable and very gracious lover.

"Where are we?" I asked dreamily.

"In Chartres."

"What's the name of the hotel?"

"Best Western."

I knew this brand to be a decent hotel chain in the United States when you were on a road trip and didn't want to stay in a fleabag motel, but this place was nice. Really nice. With hues of chocolate and beige and white, the decor was cozy and elegant—wainscoted walls, plush bedding, a charming antique desk in the corner, thick carpet and lovely curtains, even a chandelier.

"You're kidding."

"Are they not like this in the United States?"

"Not even close." I closed my eyes. Maybe things were just better in France?

"Just wait and see what else I have planned for you, princess." He kissed me on the nose and rolled out of bed. His body was perfect, chiseled. "Don't go to sleep. Get up and take your shower. We have places to see."

"But I need sleep," I pleaded.

"You'll mess up your schedule. You have to stay awake." Jean-Luc walked over to his suitcase and retrieved a few small packages out of it. His butt was cute, round, not flat. Perky. His shoulders were broad and strong, his back angling into a perfect *v*. "Besides, sleeping girls can't open presents."

"I like presents." I sat straight up in bed, the sheet draped over my body. "I have some things for you too."

From his bag, he handed me gift after gift. A gold-dipped neck-lace with matching earrings from a village in Provence. A bottle of Violette perfume from Toulouse. A cashmere scarf purchased on his trip to Scotland. French soaps—*Savon de Marseille*—a rainbow of colors and scents, for my mom.

This guy was good. Real good.

The French have a reputation for being the world's best lovers, which included not just the physical act of sex but everything else that went along with it—the passion, the romance, the whole nine yards. Jean-Luc certainly lived up to the reputation and then some.

And I had bought him a book on fish, a hat, and a few stinking T-shirts from Malibu for him and his kids? Granted, everything was tied in to his love for scuba diving, but compared to his gifts, I felt like one crappy present giver, save for the sexy black baby doll negligee and hot-pink corset I'd picked up at Victoria's Secret before I'd left, which of course weren't really for him.

True to his word, Jean-Luc would not let me go back to bed after my shower. Instead, we were to head over to the Cathédrale Notre-Dame de Chartres, considered to be one of the greatest achievements in Gothic architecture and also the reason we were in Chartres, the town bearing the same name. Jean-Luc took me by the hand, leading me through a park and then through a maze of smaller streets. I didn't bother asking him how he knew the way. His stride was one of purpose. Stumbling in my wedges, I tried to keep up with his pace.

After twisting through the cobbled brick streets, passing by restaurant after restaurant, we stopped. I blinked the sleep away from my eyes. There it stood in all its glory, its sand castle–like spires reaching into the blue skies, calling up to the heavens, a direct line to God: Chartres. The sculptures and carvings were magnificent, not to mention the flying buttresses. Oh yes, the terminology from art school was all coming back to me. A tired woman of very few words, I could only mumble, "Wow."

The ceiling soared above my head. Stained-glass windows spilled jewel-toned colors onto the floor, offering depictions of biblical stories. I was immediately drawn to the Blue Madonna, wise, regal, and wearing an elusive Mona Lisa smile. I drank in my surroundings, immersed in a world of color and light—magnificent blues, reds, greens, and purples.

Jean-Luc took me by the hand again. "Do you want to see the tower?"

I could tell by his schoolboy expression that he wanted to show it to me. So I went with the flow. We purchased our tickets and began the harrowing climb. Right from the first step, I regretted the decision, each step becoming more labored than the next. I envisioned myself tumbling down the hard limestone stairs.

"How far to the top?" I placed my hands on my knees, stopping to catch my breath.

"Three hundred steps."

I echoed him. "Three hundred steps?"

"Honey, we don't have to go to the top. There are plenty of viewpoints along the way."

"No, no, no," I said, although my tired body was pleading to turn around. "My dad raised me to respect the dollar. You paid seven euro for each of us. We're going up."

Once we got to the top, my gaze leapt from the weathered pale green rooftop to the gargoyles offset by a darkening blue sky to the village and wheat fields below us, hues of yellows and reds. There was history here. Real history. Jean-Luc stood behind me, his breath soft in my ear, his hands on my hips, and standing in this historical site, I felt as if I had known him for centuries. Exactly as he had promised two decades earlier, I was seeing France through the eyes of a Frenchman. The church bell rang seven times, its melody filling the air, reverberating in my body and my heart. It was then I decided seven was my lucky number. I also wondered what else fate had in store for us.

"We better go before they lock us in," said Jean-Luc.

Outside the cathedral, the town of Chartres was full of beautiful winding streets and romantic stone bridges, a surprise waiting around every corner. Music echoed in the streets. We followed the melody and found ourselves in a large square, a band playing center stage—a singer, a drummer, a guitarist, and two accordion players. Like one giant party, a dozen or so cafés surrounded the stage, all with outdoor seating, every table filled with people smoking and drinking and laughing. The band played a dizzying, frenetic song with varying tempos, the players theatrical in their movements. As hypnotic as the music was, people danced feverishly in front of the stage, spinning and clapping.

"Is this gypsy music?" I asked.

"No, not really," said Jean-Luc. "This is music from this region, very old French mixed with a bunch of different influences—some gypsy, some tango—basically folk music."

"It's great." Tired as I was, I couldn't help but find my foot tapping along to the beat. Yet as soon as I expended the extra energy to do so, I stumbled into Jean-Luc. He caught me, supporting me by the elbows.

"Let's get you some food. And then we'll get you to bed."

With wicked intent, I raised my brow in what I hoped to be a seductive manner. "I'm looking forward to that."

"*Tu es une femme gourmande*," Jean-Luc whispered hotly in my ear, his hand sliding up my back. "A very, very, very greedy girl."

My knees gave out from underneath me.

He draped his arm over my shoulders and we made our way to a restaurant we'd passed by earlier. Chic but comfortable, the room was beautifully decorated, romantic even. With the blue and white checkered curtains, the decor was country French in some ways but exotic in others. Moroccan influences were everywhere—beaded lamps, tiled tables, pillows, and scrolled iron partitions. Jean-Luc ordered us a lamb and vegetable *tajine*, a dish named after the clay pots our meal would be served in, and a carafe of wine.

There was no need to speak, and I smiled at my good fortune. Jean-Luc stroked my thumb with his. We'd only been together a short while, but we'd already found our groove. In what seemed to be just a minute later, the server placed a very large clay pot in front of us, flatbread resting by its side. A medley of mouth-watering scents enveloped the table. Complex and aromatic, the ingredients tick-led my senses—apples, pears, apricots, olive, lemon, almonds, and a variety of spices like cinnamon, saffron, ginger, and pepper. The meat practically melted in my mouth and the vegetables—zucchini, carrots, and onions infused in a tomato-based sauce laced with the flavors of cinnamon, paprika, cloves, and cayenne pepper—were delicious. Dinner was *almost* as spicy as our chemistry.

We inhaled our food and headed back to the hotel for "dessert."

Usually, I'd fall asleep on the opposite side of the bed as my part-ner, not wanting anything to disturb my sleep. But nothing about our relationship was usual, and it was as if we had been glued together, my head resting on his shoulder, my leg draped over his body. Even our breath seemed to be in sync. I woke up a few hours later, surprised to find myself still entangled in Jean-Luc's arms. Jean-Luc stroked my back with his soft fingertips. "You are beautiful, Sam, the prettiest rose in my garden. I've been awake for hours, just watching you sleep." He rolled on top of me, pressing his muscular body against mine, his attraction to me perfectly clear. "I love looking at you."

We had a second helping of dessert at four a.m.

Oh yes, I was making up for lost time.

A *prince charmant* who was making all this princess's dreams come true, Jean-Luc informed me our next stop on this rekindle-the-romance tour was the Château de Razay, a sixteenth-century châ-teau in the Loire Valley close to some of the most famous castles in France, where we would be staying for two nights.

In France, apparently, there are many types of accommodations to choose from, including motels, hotels ranging from zero to five stars, *gîtes* (a self-catered and furnished home), an *auberge* (an inn), luxurious *relais et châteaux* (actual castles), or a *chambre d'hôtes*. Comprised of twenty-nine rooms, the Château de Razay was the latter—basically an upscale bed-and-breakfast in a mansion. On the drive over, I was chatting excitedly about how beautiful the French countryside was with its rolling hills dotted with cows, when Jean-Luc said, "I think you need to practice your French."

"*Zut alors.* I haven't spoken it since my twenties."

"*C'est comme le vélo. Tu n'oublies jamais.*"

"It is *not* like riding a bike. I've forgotten everything."

He raised his eyebrows. "*Mais, tu m'as écrit des lettres en français.*"

I was busted.

"Yes, but I had help." I smiled innocently. "Google Translate…"

"Well, now you have me."

"*Sacré bleu,*" I said.

"Are you quoting a cartoon?"

"Why?"

"Nobody ever uses that expression anymore," he said, and then he laughed.

Over the next few hours, Jean-Luc spoke in French, updating me on modern French terminology, and I made an attempt to hold up my end of the conversation—but it was a real struggle, especially when every time I opened my mouth, he corrected me. No, he said, you never pronounce the last letter. For example, *devant*—note the *t*—was pronounced *devan*. My head was spinning. There was no zoning out or jumping back into the conversation when it suited me. We were driving on a small countryside road when, thankful for a distraction, I screamed, "*Arrête! Arrête!*"

A cloud of dust exploded in front of the window. Jean-Luc screeched the car to a halt on the side of the road. "Honey, *ça va? Tu es malade?*"

"No, I'm not sick. I'm perfectly fine," I said. "But just look at this field. Look how beautiful it is."

"I thought it was something serious, but it's only *des tournesols,*" he said, gripping his heart in a mock heart attack. "I suppose you want to take a picture."

He already knew me so well.

There is nothing more French than passing by an endless field of sunflowers in full bloom in the summer, ablaze in golds and yellows and oranges. *Tournesol*, the French word for sunflower, as Jean-Luc explained, meant to turn toward the sun, and the field we had pulled in front of was right out of my dreams. Lush yellow flowers tilted their happy faces toward the heavens, their tall stalks dancing in the breeze. Dotted with clouds, the pale blue sky provided a beautiful contrast to the hues on the ground. Camera in hand, I jumped out of the car. With a bemused expression, Jean-Luc watched me try to set up my mini tripod on the hood, but it kept tipping over.

"Come on," I said. "I don't only want a picture of flowers. I want a picture of us in front of them."

I placed my hands on my hips and tapped my foot until he begrudgingly exited the Ford. A few trials and errors later, I finally got my shot. Jean-Luc pulled me in for a passionate kiss. "*On y va*," he said. "Let's get going."

He opened up the passenger door, and one minute later, we were on our way. I shot Jean-Luc a sideways glance. Even his profile was sexy, with his chiseled chin, the sculpted sideburns. I could have stared at him all day. I was so giddy I didn't recognize this bizarre side of my personality. I wanted to kiss him—in fact, I wanted to do more than kiss him. Instead, I took his hand. When did I become *that* girl in love?

Finally, the château came into view and the place screamed, "Romance, romance!" It was reminiscent of a castle, with bright and vibrant rose-colored hydrangea surrounding the main house and cream-colored bricks with gray, peaked, tiled rooftops and scalloped plaster molding.

"*C'est magnifique!*" I exclaimed.

As we stepped out of the car and onto the gravel driveway, a giant black potbellied pig, which immediately lay down and squirmed on its back, begging for a rub, greeted us. Happily, I obliged, surprised to find its fur was rough and bristly. The human proprietor was equally warm and welcoming. She practically leapt down the steps to give us the old European double-cheek kiss and then motioned for us to follow her to our room. We left our bags in the trunk and rushed after her, the French running fast off her tongue. I just smiled and nodded. Inside the château, every wall was painted sunflower yellow, paired with red carpeting. Pretty, in a "look at me, I'm happy although I clash slightly" way, it was quite a contrast from the elegant and much quieter exterior, but no matter, because our room was absolutely delightful, complete with a four-poster bed with billowy white curtains. The woman handed us a key and exited, the smile never leaving her face. I eyed the bed and then raised my brows at Jean-Luc.

"Tsk, tsk, tsk. Later, my love. After this morning, I think we have to preserve you, and don't you want to visit le Château de Chenonceau?"

After seeing a picture of my dad standing in front of the historic castle in his twenties, I'd done quite a bit of research on the place. Known as the *château des femmes*, the castle sat in all her former glory, her stone cold beauty reflected on the River Cher, her beautiful gardens open to the thousands of tourists that visit every year. Tourists like me. She did not disappoint. Nor did the château we would visit after: Chambord, the largest castle in the Loire Valley. Although he'd been impressed with my knowledge of Chenonceau, it was Jean-Luc's turn to give the history lesson as we waited in line for tickets.

"Château de Chambord," he began, each syllable drawn out and pronounced in a way I could only describe as being very French, "is recognized throughout the world, not only because of its size but because of its impressive Italian Renaissance architecture." He said this proudly and his eyes lit up. "Built as a hunting lodge for François I…"

I eyed the magnificent structure, which was almost indescribable with the fantasy of its immense roof seeming to go on for miles, the turrets, the chimneys, and the well-manicured gardens. "Wait a second. This place was a hunting lodge?"

He shrugged and flipped his hands palms up. "What can I say? The French are extravagant, and this is a masterpiece of the Renaissance, a crowning jewel. *Incroyable!*"

Forget about the hunting lodge and its symbol of the salamander, Jean-Luc was the incredible one. I stared at him, expecting him to start bitching and moaning about how hot it was outside and how the line to get into the castle hadn't budged. He didn't raise his voice or break out into an angry rant. He just stood there, quietly, giving me a history lesson while calling me princess.

"You're not irritated with the line?"

"Should I be?"

"No, no, no," I said. "I'm just used to a different kind of reaction."

His eyes widened with understanding. "Honey, I never let the little things in life bother me, especially things I can't change. Understand?"

People operate on two levels: rational and emotional. Judging by the calm tone of his voice and his extra-cool demeanor, Jean-Luc thought things through before spouting off.

He snuck a hand up my dress, caressing my thigh. I swiped his hand away in one quick movement. He ignored my obvious embarrassment and pointed toward the castle. "It was at the young age of twenty-five that François showed the world what a spectacular vision he had. I'm proud to share it with you. I want to share everything with you."

So Many Castles, So Little Time

I was falling deeply and hopelessly in love with this man. Which scared me to death. Of course, I knew when I left on this trip that I had very, very strong feelings for Jean-Luc, but they hadn't seemed quite as well formed. He'd just been a man behind the words, but now he was very, very real, smart, sexy, and funny, better than I had imagined. Before we fell asleep after our day of discoveries, Jean-Luc whispered into my ear, "*Je t'aime, mon coeur. Avec tout mon coeur et mon âme.* I love you, my wife."

His words jolted me upright. "Did you just call me your wife?"

He shrugged and popped his lips. "It's the way I feel. *Je t'aime.*"

"Why?" I asked, not just for an affirmation, but because I was actually rather curious. Jean-Luc regarded me with a bemused expression. I asked him again. "Why do you love me?"

"I don't have a choice. I just do."

"*Je t'aime aussi.*" I snuggled into his embrace. Like two pieces of a proverbial puzzle, we fit. Still, doubt crept into my head. Things seemed too perfect between us, and I wondered when the other shoe was going to drop. I tried to think positively, but it was hard when my heart was on the firing line. I clung on to hope like a life preserver. This time I wasn't talking myself out of love; I was diving head first into it.

In the morning, after a light breakfast of buttery croissants and *confiture d'abricot*, we visited Château d'Ussé—reputed to be the inspiration behind both Charles Perrault's *Sleeping Beauty*—*La Belle au Bois Dormant*—and Walt Disney's iconic castle. A true fairy-tale setting, it was located on the edge of the Chinon Forest, on the banks of the Indre River, overlooking terraced gardens.

If I could have chosen one castle in all of France to live in, it would have been this one. Everything about the château promised enchantment, especially the architecture with its gray-blue slate roofs and dormer windows, not to mention its towers and turrets. It was almost impossible to imagine that at one point in time, the château was used as a fortress, complete with drawbridges and battlements.

Jean-Luc guided me through the gardens. "You really made me laugh in one of your letters."

"Which one?" There must have been at least two hundred shared between us.

"Your crazy letter, the one where you told me passion was like an old pair of socks—"

"I know, I know. Holes included." I slapped my hands over my eyes. "Please don't quote me."

"Life without passion is like the sky without the sun, the moon without the stars." He stopped, took me by the arms, and pressed me against a stone wall. "I cannot live my life without passion. Can you?"

"It's not as if I'd intended on living a passionless life."

His eyes locked onto mine. "Samantha, I want to give you everything. Everything I have. I don't have much, but what I have is yours. I want you to know joy. You're so special and so unique. I want to give you something you've never had. I want to give you the gift of a child."

Never before had I heard such words come out of an actual human mouth. I was breathless. A tear crept into the corner of my eye, slowly making its way down my cheek.

A couple walked by us, each holding the hand of their daughter, who must have been about three years old. They swung her up into the air, her toes pointing toward the blue sky. She giggled. And then she looked over her shoulder, peeking at me through a blue-bowed pigtail. Her grin got bigger, like she was sharing a secret with me, like she knew what Jean-Luc and I had been talking about, and she was urging me to consider it. The couple and their little girl walked on. I shuddered and ran through the logistics in my head. He couldn't be serious. "Now? You want to have a child now?"

"No, not now. But soon. By this time next year, we'll be married. We'll start then."

It wasn't a formal proposal, but a promise—one I believed would come true. There was no other way for us. We were meant to be together. I laughed, trying to keep my feelings at bay. "What are you? Some kind of prophet?"

"No, I'm a realist. And as I've said before, according to both our situations, we both have to be extremely patient."

"But we've just only met again."

"And now that we have, I never want to lose you." He stopped midstep. "Sam, you're the most unique and wonderful woman I've ever known." His face turned serious. "You do want to continue on the path we're on?"

Even before I could ask my own questions, he gave me answers. I couldn't imagine my life without Jean-Luc. I was so attracted to his intelligence, his passion, to everything about him. It didn't matter how things came to be, only that we were now together. Waiting another twenty years was out of the question. I glanced at Château d'Ussé. "Could we get married in a castle?"

Jean-Luc brushed a lock of hair off my face. "If there is one thing France has many of, it's castles, princess."

Oh, sugar plum trees and fairy-tale wishes, it seemed that all of my dreams were about to come true. I was floating on a magical cloud, trying to take everything in.

After a late morning excursion to yet another castle, Château d'Azay le Rideau, we hit Dinan, a medieval town unique in Bretagne, completely surrounded by ramparts—or in layman's terms, a walled village. History fascinated Jean-Luc. His eyes lit up. Mine were getting a little foggy.

"Honey," I said, interrupting him as he told me that the walls, nearly intact, were three kilometers long. "I don't want to be high maintenance—"

"High maintenance? What is this? Are you a plane?"

"What? No, I'm not a plane. I'm typically a low-maintenance girl, meaning I'm not demanding—"

"This expression, high maintenance, it's funny." I frowned. "Princess, what's wrong? Do you feel okay?"

My stomach grumbled loudly and I choked back some embarrassment.

"Honey, I love you, noises and all. We'll stop for something to eat in the next village. I didn't realize it was so late." Jean-Luc burst out laughing. "It was a very loud night with you."

My mind raced with all of the embarrassing ways I could have possibly been noisy. I sank into my seat and clenched my teeth, one hand hiding me from his loving gaze. Hopefully he'd just implied that I grind my teeth—not something else, like, heaven forbid, gas. Regardless of the love building between us, I still wanted to impress Jean-Luc. Jean-Luc just smiled and whipped the car down winding streets on a mission to find his princess some food before she suffered a hypoglycemic attack.

My man pulled through, finding a local patisserie, where he purchased a couple of tasty strawberry tarts with flaky crusts. Crisis averted.

We arrived in Dinan one hour later and checked into the hotel. By the way the woman at the front desk flirted and giggled with Jean-Luc, I could tell she was quite smitten with him. When her face flushed with a blush, I was certain of it. Suffice it to say, we'd been so wrapped up with one another, I'd never taken notice of the effect Jean-Luc had on other women.

"She likes you," I whispered as the woman turned around to retrieve our keys.

"Don't be silly."

"She's talking to you. And she's all but ignoring me."

Jean-Luc regarded me as if I was crazy. But I wasn't. We headed to our room and I straddled Jean-Luc on the bed, teasing him. "Are you sure you don't want to trade me in for your new girlfriend?"

He flipped me onto my back and pinned me down. "*Jalouse?*"

"No, I'm not jealous."

Sure, maybe the green-eyed monster did pay a visit, but it wasn't because the woman was attractive or young. It was because she could communicate with Jean-Luc in his mother tongue. Me? It seemed I had foot-in-mouth syndrome in not one but two languages. But regardless of language or cultural differences, I still had some questions that needed answering. In any new relationship, there were bound to be minor insecurities. Over the past few months, we'd had daily two- to three-hour-long phone conversations, no subject left unturned, both of our histories open books. And since the topic of other women had been breached, I had to get something off my chest now or forever hold my peace.

"Why didn't you marry the children's mother?"

"She didn't want to. We talked about it, but she was against marriage. After a while, things slipped between us, mostly because of me."

The French called these living situations *concubinage*. I knew many couples in France lived together without being married, and it was probably one of the reasons divorce rates were so low in their country. As a foreigner, I'd need a visa or a green card to live here, and to get that paperwork, I would need to become Jean-Luc's wife. Just living together and not getting married wasn't an option for us. If we were going to be together, we'd have to be 100 percent committed.

"So you left Frédérique for the Vietnamese girl…"

"For a year. When we got back together, I thought things would change. I thought we could work things out. And then the children were born. Things were great in the beginning and we tried, we really tried. And then—"

"You left her for Anya—Russian girl number one."

Jean-Luc looked up at the ceiling in remembrance. "Anya was younger, much, much younger. Very pretty—"

I wanted answers, not details. "May I remind you I'm also much younger than you. Seven years younger."

"Honey, I don't mean anything by it."

"Oh, come on, Jean-Luc, I'm a confident woman, but I don't need to know how pretty or young any of your exes were. Besides, I've already found both of their Facebook pages."

His eyebrows shot up. "What?"

"Didn't you ever wonder why I asked for their last names? I Googled them too."

"My little spy, you have been a busy girl."

"I was curious about them. Are you bothered I checked into your past?"

"No. I have nothing to hide from you. And I was just trying to make a point." He sighed heavily. "I had a crisis in my head. I thought being with a younger woman would give me what I wanted from life. But that was not the case and, as you know, my life turned into a living hell."

Old insecurities die hard, and I couldn't help but ask the one question that kept me from trusting him fully, the one starting this whole line of questioning in the first place.

"So what's to stop you from leaving me? Especially for a *much, much* younger woman."

A searing heat blazed from his eyes. He rolled off me, onto his back. Neither of us said anything for a minute or two. I didn't want to ruin things with Jean-Luc, but I knew better than to let things simmer under the surface. I'd learned that lesson the hard way with Chris.

Jean-Luc sat up. "Sam, I've told you before, with you things are different. I want to be the best man for you, the best person for you. I know what it's like to be unfaithful. All the lies, all the pain it causes. I want to be able to face myself in the mirror and be happy with who

I am. I've made many, many mistakes in my life, and believe me I've paid. I've paid." He paused, his breathing labored. "I've never wanted to call anybody else my wife. Just you. And I feel you are already my wife and I want to scream it from the mountains. Everything I've shared with you, everything you've shared with me, has been shared in confidence so we can build something solid together, something that will stand the test of time. Sam, I love you with all my heart and my soul." He grabbed me by the shoulders. "You have to promise to trust me. All relationships take work—both on physical and mental levels—and I think, together, we can do it."

I bit down on my bottom lip and shook my head. "Jean-Luc, I just needed to erase any doubts or reservations I have. Because you've told me so much about your past, it's been on my mind, not all the time, but a lingering thought picking into my subconscious. Now we've cleared the air and I can move forward without looking back. We promised each other we'd talk about everything and anything. No secrets, right?"

"Never. There will never be any secrets between us." He pulled me close to his chest and hugged me so tightly I could barely breathe. "Honey, I have to tell you something."

I sucked in my breath. "Yes. Anything."

"The hardest day I've ever faced was telling the children their mother died. They'd seen her suffer for years, but in her final days, she didn't want to see them. She was too sick and barely resembled herself. Sometimes, I think the children still have a hard time understanding why—why she didn't want to see them and why she died." His voice wavered. "You should have seen their faces when I told them…" I squeezed his hand and let him carry on. "Sam, two young kids should never have to see their mother die." He choked back his words. "I've tried to be the best dad I could be. Now that their mother is gone, everything in their world, in my world, has changed. I thought things with Natasha would get better, I did, but time would only show I'd been hoping for too much. Then you came into my life, and I saw I could have something different. I saw a better life."

"Jean-Luc, it's the same for me. I'd all but given up and thought I deserved no better. I'd settled. And then I found your letters, and now everything has changed."

"Everything." Jean-Luc squeezed my hand hard. "With you I see a kind woman, a wonderful woman with the heart of a child, a woman who will be good to my children—the ones I have now and the ones we will hopefully have together. So, Sam, I think I'd be the stupidest man on the planet if I ever messed things up with you. Just promise me one thing," he said.

"Yes, anything."

"You'll never make me feel like half a man. It's the reason I left the children's mother. I want to feel whole with you."

Ditto. We fell back into each other's arms and made crazy, mad, passionate love.

The Rekindle-the-Romance Tour Continues

The two nights we spent in Dinan passed without any hitches—save for the woman at the hotel cornering Jean-Luc every chance she got, which we both found to be pretty funny. At night we walked the steep cobbled streets, exploring the town and doing a little window-shopping. We ate *galettes* filled with *chèvre chaud*, warm goat cheese, accompanied by a *cidre brut*, a dry cider. We stopped by a local pub and people-watched while enjoying mint mojitos. Each evening ended with us making love. We began each day the same way.

We visited the fortified city of Saint-Malo, complete with its pirate flags, and enjoyed fresh oysters by the sea, walking along the rugged beaches. We hiked through the ancient town of Mont Saint-Michel, the former monastic settlement located in Normandy, which from afar resembled a giant sand castle floating above amber-colored fields of corn and wheat. When we arrived there, Jean-Luc warned me about the sea of never-ending tourists and also the fact that we had to leave before high tide or we'd be stuck, since the tidal island would be surrounded by water in a few hours.

We traversed the beaches of Normandy, the casino in Deauville, a town known as the French Riviera of the North. We ate *moules frites*, explored history, and drank fine French wines. We were a young(ish) couple in love and having the time of our lives.

The funny thing was, I'd never been a sentimental, heart-goes-all-a-flutter girl, and now I'd become the female half of the couple I used to make fun of—the ones with their hands all over each other, gazing longingly into each other's eyes. Normally, I would have said those kinds of couples never last, but each day I spent with Jean-Luc proved this theory dead wrong.

While we were checking into another château-turned-bed-and-breakfast, Château de Goville, just outside of Bayeux in the Normandy region of France, I found myself wondering how on earth I was going to be able to leave Jean-Luc in a few days. I watched him speaking to the owner and gazed at Jean-Luc proudly. He simply charmed this older gentleman, who, uptight at first, was now slapping Jean-Luc on the back as if they were old friends.

Too bad I had no idea what they were saying to each other, so I just took everything in as Jean-Luc booked our room.

French antiquities were displayed about everywhere, in every cranny, every room, and every nook—plates, textiles, porcelain roosters, and glass figurines. The atmosphere had an old-world elegance about it, as only the French could pull off. Jean-Luc still chatted with the owner, and I knew I had more than a few minutes to explore the grounds. I wanted to absorb the atmosphere, breathe it all in. I stepped outside, into a beautiful French garden with manicured bushes, roses, and a small gazebo tucked in the back. The exterior of the château was in a state of decay—the sandy limestone a bit cracked, the white shutters peeling—but that only enhanced its charm.

Jean-Luc had done it again; he'd found my idea of perfection.

A young couple rode up the gravel driveway on a motorcycle, the engine coming to an abrupt halt. Curious, I watched them take off their helmets. The guy was good-looking enough, in a broody sort of way, and the girl was quintessentially French, a permanent pout on her lips and gorgeous even though her long brown hair was a windswept mess. They walked by me, leaving the front door open, and headed up the stairs, each step echoing loudly.

Jean-Luc waved me back inside, and we were shown up the stairs and into our room.

Sage green brocade fabric decorated the walls. There was a beautiful mahogany writing desk in the corner and a round table with two chairs before the window, a place to take our breakfast in the morning. It was lovely—a strange, eclectic kind of lovely. We sprawled out on the canopied bed and the distinct sounds of a couple making love—a bed squeaking, a girl moaning—came from the room above us. Lights rattled. I was fairly certain I knew who was experiencing the passionate exchange, yet it was over just as soon it began. A door slammed. Footsteps clomped down the stairs.

"I think we have some competition," said Jean-Luc with a sexy wink.

"Competition? I feel sorry for the girl. It only lasted two minutes."

"Nothing wrong with a quick shot."

But there was. Time had passed by too quickly. We only had two days left. Two days left to tease one another. Two days left to make love.

In the morning, we drove three hours to the quaint seaside village of Étretat, a commune in the Haute-Normandie region, making it just in time for lunch. We'd sat outside in a tented restaurant, enjoying the sea-scented air and listening to the cries of seagulls, where Jean-Luc introduced me to a new treat called *bulots*—which were little sea snails served with an aioli sauce flavored with lemon zest. No stranger to more typical dishes like *escargot*, I'd trusted Jean-Luc to order and heartily dug the delicacies out of their mottled brown shells, eating one right after the other.

"Where are we off to next?" I asked.

"It's a surprise," said Jean-Luc. He peered at me over his Ray-Ban sunglasses. "It's my hope you'll love it."

Jean-Luc paid for our lunch and led me by the hand. We walked through town then across a grassy knoll. With each step we took, the view became increasingly breathtaking. I soon found myself over-looking chalky white cliffs and the dark blue waters of La Manche, which separated France from its neighbor Great Britain.

"I've never visited here, but I remembered you loved art, and mostly the French impressionists," said Jean-Luc, pointing to a stunning archway in one of the rock formations. "These are the cliffs Monet loved to paint. Do you remember seeing his painting at the Musée d'Orsay on your first trip to Paris?"

"Yes," I said, my voice catching in the back of my throat. Just like twenty years earlier, way back in 1989, when Jean-Luc had taken me to Sacré-Coeur to point out where my favorite artists had painted because he'd remembered our conversation from the evening before, he'd remembered my love for French artists, namely the impression-ists. Jean-Luc pulled me in for a kiss, the breeze blowing through our hair.

"Come," he said, pulling away from the embrace. "Let's explore."

We stood at the edge of the cliff, but I wasn't scared. I'd placed all of my trust into Jean-Luc's hands. Fear of love and being loved was really becoming a distant nightmare of my past. I wanted to take the leap.

⌒

Our last two nights were spent in Saint-Valéry-en-Caux, a short one-hour drive from Étretat. The fatigue from nonstop explo-ration had finally set in. One short walk later, we'd decided to take our dinner at the hotel, which was lovely and overlooked the rocky beach.

Again, I placed my faith in Jean-Luc. He hadn't done me wrong just yet. In fact, he'd done everything right. So I agreed when he suggested I try the *pot-au-feu de la mer*. The waiter placed the meal on my place mat. I'd expected mussels, shrimp, and maybe some calamari, not a bunch of fish—heads, eyeballs, and skin includ-ed—in a steaming bowl of cabbage soup. The explosion of various colors, combined with the pungent smell, brought an open-air fish market on a hot day to mind. Still, I couldn't offend Jean-Luc by sending it back, so I swallowed a bite of the unidentifiable fish back with a sip of wine, the only way to wash the mouthful of torturous tastes down.

"How's your dish?" asked Jean-Luc.

I shoved a piece of bread in my mouth and tried to keep from grimacing. "The, the, the shrimp are really good." They were too salty and difficult to manage with their shells on.

"And the other fish? They have a nice taste?"

"Mmmm-hmm. Delicious. Want some?" Like the one staring at me? He took a bite from my bowl, leaving a silvery skin behind. He motioned for me to continue eating with his fork. But I couldn't. Not without a chaser. There was just one problem. Only one set of glasses sat on the table and they were filled to the top with the house rosé. He'd think I was an alcoholic if I started chugging wine. I picked up the carafe of water. "Honey, can you ask the waitress for two water glasses? *Ou, j'ai besoin d'une pipe.*"

The couple seated at the next table over snorted into their napkins. Jean-Luc broke out into a wide, sexy grin. "You just said you needed a blow job."

"No, I didn't. I said I needed a straw." I sunk into my chair, mumbling as I corrected myself. Damn that dirty French site. "Which would have been *une paille*, not *une pipe.*"

Jean-Luc leaned forward, stealing a bite of something pink and slippery from my bowl. My lips twitched involuntarily. His eyes sparkled mischievously. "And you lied to me. You promised you would never lie to me."

"I didn't lie."

"Yes, yes, you did." He laughed. "You don't like your dinner. You hate it. It's like watching a small child squirm."

"So you knew this whole time? And you didn't say anything?"

"It's been very entertaining watching you eat. You make some very funny faces, Sam. Very funny."

"I didn't want to disappoint you," I said.

"You could never disappoint me, Sam. You are a treasure, one I intend to keep."

⁓

The days and nights blurred together into one. On the rocky beach of Saint-Valéry-en-Caux, we spread out a beach towel and tried to enjoy our last moments together with a bottle of wine, a slab of green pepper pâté, and a loaf of freshly baked bread. In the distance, a family paddled bright orange kayaks, circumnavigating a couple of fishermen casting their nets. The water was calm, smooth as glass. In contrast, my emotions rocked. A pit of dread replaced the butterflies of happiness fluttering around in my stomach. The following morning, Jean-Luc would be dropping me off at Charles de Gaulle. And I wasn't ready to leave.

"We've got some rough times ahead of us, and we need to be patient," said Jean-Luc, "but we can do this. We're laying the foundation for the rest of our lives. Now, all we have to do is build."

Besides my love and maybe some pretty words, I wasn't able to offer Jean-Luc much of anything. "What can I build on? I don't have a job. No money. All I have are the clothes on my back."

Jean-Luc laughed. It started off soft and got louder. I furrowed my brows. "What's so funny?"

He poked me in the ribs. "That's the saddest story I've ever heard."

"I'm being serious."

"So am I." He kissed me on the forehead. "I love you, Sam. I've said this to you before, and I'll keep saying it until you believe me. I want to share everything with you. Although everything I have isn't much. I'm a very simple man, living a very simple life."

A life less complicated sounded good to me. I was tired of running, tired of trying to keep up with the Joneses. I didn't need a fancy car or a huge house or designer clothes. When it all came down to it, nothing like that mattered at all, and it never had. All I needed was a life rich with love. And passion.

Oh yes, I needed passion.

In silence, we watched the sunset cast a yellow and orange hue on the white cliffs towering above us. A warm summer breeze brushed through my hair. Jean-Luc wrapped his arms around me, holding me tight as if I could blow away. The air smelled fresh and salty, clean, a promise of new beginnings.

Shifting my weight slightly, I turned my head so I could see Jean-Luc's face. His eyes reflected the color of the sky, so peaceful, so serene. I watched the seagulls swoop in the air and the waves crash onto the rocky shore, feeling as if I was in a perfect dream and I didn't want to wake up. In that perfect moment, I found the quietness and the peace I'd been searching for my entire life. Jean-Luc's heart beat against my back.

He got me, accepted me with all my faults.

I got him.

I settled into his arms, leaning my back against his chest. A single, silent tear rolled down my cheek. The following morning I would be on a plane. I didn't want to say good-bye. But of course, I had to.

From: Jean-Luc
To: Samantha

Subject: Mon Amour

I've just arrived home after seven hours of driving without my wonderful passenger. I often looked at the empty seat next to me, hoping to find you there. You cannot imagine how much I miss you, all of you—your body, your skin, your eyes, your mouth, your laughter, your humor. You're a wonderful woman, so tender and so nice, full of surprises. I never thought I'd find a woman like you. Never in my dreams. And yet you exist! The reality of you is beyond words. These ten days with you were fantastic, but a life with you, it has no qualifier; it's just the door of paradise. Yes, everything is beautiful.

Yours,

Jean-Luc

Meet the Parents

Minute by minute, hour by hour, the days crawled by. I was back in a holding pattern, a perpetual state of limbo. Besides Jean-Luc, nothing else had changed in my life. I still couldn't find work. My savings had dwindled down to nothing. Plus, my dog walking was only paying for the gas money needed to get me to the clients' homes, leaving me with about ten extra dollars each week. To add insult to injury, I was snubbed by a couple of ladies while walking a little Jack Russell Terrier puppy named Rocky at a local park.

"Oh, he's so cute," said one woman. She was wearing yoga pants and a full face of makeup, her hair and manicure freshly done.

"How old is he?" her Malibu twin asked with an unnatural smile. Her eyes were expressionless—probably a victim of Urgent Care, where the doctors actually give emergency Botox shots.

I shrugged. "I don't know. He's not mine."

Their once-friendly smiles morphed into utter disdain. "Oh, you're just a dog walker." They turned on their heels and sashayed away, leaving me standing on the dusty path.

I wanted to yell after them, "I'm not just a dog walker. I'm a former art director, just biding my time until I move to France." No such words came out of my mouth. Rocky, adding to my humiliation, pooped. I pulled out a blue plastic bag from my pocket and picked it up. Covered in sweat, I dropped Rocky back at his home and headed over to the next client's house to find three teenage girls lounging poolside under a striped cabana, eating strawberries.

"Oh, that's the dog walker. Just ignore her."

What if things with Jean-Luc didn't work out? Would I become the crazy dog lady living at home with her parents, shunned by Malibu's finest? Exasperated, I went home and checked my email to see if there was any good news from Jean-Luc—the brightest light in my life.

My mother walked into the kitchen. "Are you emailing that Frenchman again? You've got to get off your computer, meet more people."

"I don't want to. It's a moot point. He's the only one for me."

"Don't be ridiculous, Sam. You might have had a fantastic vacation together, but you hardly know him."

I needed to shock her into acceptance. We may have tiptoed around it, but sex wasn't exactly a taboo subject in my house growing up. At the age of sixteen, I'd asked my mom if I could go on birth controls pills to, wink-wink, regulate my period. My mother, as she would tell me many years later, wasn't born yesterday. I couldn't believe what I wanted to say, so I just blurted it out. "He's an amazing lover."

"Lover?" She choked on her English muffin. "What?" A blush crept onto my mom's cheeks and her jaw went slack. "Sam, I'm the mom. We can't talk about things like this." She pinched her lips together and shot me a sideways glance. "So how big was his junk?"

Coffee flew out of my mouth onto the glass table. His *junk*? Maybe I'd pushed things too far by even mentioning sex. "Mom, this reaches a whole new level of being so wrong it's not even funny."

But it was. And we couldn't stop laughing.

Since my mother and I seemed to share everything now, I decided to show her how Google Translate worked with one of my frog's French emails. I picked one of the shorter letters, which, at first glance, appeared "correct."

My love,

This morning during breakfast I really thought about you. We have today and tomorrow and I'm wild with joy to have you with me…it is the conclusion.

Lots of love for my little darling, my naughty little slut.

(*Plein d'amour pour ma petite chérie, ma petite cochonne.*)

My mom glared at the computer screen. "Why in the world is he calling you a slut?"

After I picked my jaw off the floor, I responded, "What? No, no, nooooo, he's not calling me a slut. *Ma petite cochonne* means 'my little pig.'" Which it did. But there was a sexual connotation when you call a woman a little pig—it wasn't a literal translation to slut. Thanks, Google.

My mother wasn't convinced. "Well, why is he calling you a little pig?"

"It's a term of endearment? Oink?"

"Then you should call him a *gros cochon*. A big pig."

"No, you can call him that to his face. According to his latest email, he'd like to visit in October. Of course, if that's okay with you."

She looked at me like I had three heads. "*Mi casa, su casa,*" she said. "And you don't have to ask. I'm dying to meet him in person!"

In the early evening, I sat on the balcony off my bedroom, Ike by my side, a chilled Chardonnay in hand. Outside, among the trees and birds, I could breathe. Being outside in nature always had a soothing effect on my soul. I loved watching the hummingbirds. What magical, fantastical creatures they were, zipping around from flower to flower, iridescent bodies sparkling in the sunlight, wings moving a thousand miles per hour. And then the most amazing thing happened.

One of the birds hovered two feet in front of me. His body was electric, a bright sparkling green, his neck a bright red. A little engine purring, his wings fluttered and hummed. The bird tilted his head from side to side, appearing to be just as interested in me as I was in him. I held my breath, not wanting to startle this magnificent creature. Not a moment later, he flew closer, now six inches in front of my face. His wings beat so furiously I could barely discern them. In a quick motion, he darted toward me. Afraid of being poked in the eye with his pointy, black beak, I jumped back. As if laughing at my fear, he buzzed over my head one more time before landing on a tree branch.

I laughed back.

This hummingbird, for me, carried a message from a higher power, telling me to be strong, to be patient, to appreciate my world, my new life. Jean-Luc knew my stance on religion; I was a believer, but the kind who accepted and respected all faiths. When I told Jean-Luc, always the scientist, of my experience in the yard, he launched into an explanation of how extraordinary hummingbirds were.

"They're an engineering marvel," he said.

Patiently, I listened to him explain how for years scientists in the aerospace field have tried to re-create the hummingbird's flight patterns, and I was amused by his excitement and passion for the subject. He marveled over how they are the only birds on the planet that can fly backward, true specialists in aerodynamics.

"Yes, yes, that's all interesting. But what do you think about the bird?"

"*C'est incroyable, mon coeur.* Like you," said Jean-Luc.

October snuck up like a surprise thunderstorm. My only hope was all the storm clouds would pass. Jessica came into town for a long weekend to celebrate my birthday—the big four-uh-oh. Somehow I'd managed to convince myself that forty was the new thirty. Bring on the bubbly.

My mom, Jessica, and I took the boat out with Ike and had an epic day. We were just cruising along, listening to Jimmy Buffett and drinking white wine, and a pod of at least forty, maybe fifty, dolphins swam up beside us, darting and rolling and playing in the foamy white wake. They were everywhere, swimming underneath the boat on their backs, showing off their white bellies by the bow, playing and jumping, orchestrating a show that would rival any Cirque du Soleil performance. Awesome and breathtakingly beautiful, the dolphins danced and swam, the water their stage. It was magic.

"Oh my God, do you see that?" screamed Jess. In fact, we were all squealing and pointing and smiling and laughing. But as quickly as they had appeared, the dolphins disappeared into the horizon. That day, I went home feeling content, but a few days later that sentiment would change into a melancholy sadness. This month was filled with too many good-byes.

I said good-bye to Jessica, who returned to her home in New York. I said good-bye to my thirties. Soon, it would also be time to say good-bye to my faithful companion, Ike. After he'd discovered Pet Airways had just launched, Chris had asked if we could share custody of the furry kid. I agreed.

I knew the day I put Ike on the plane would be hard and so would the days following it, but nothing prepared me for the pain of letting him go. When I dropped him off at Pet Airways, although I tried to convince myself otherwise, I had a feeling deep in my gut that it would be the last time I would see him. A lump formed in my throat, and it took everything in me not to burst into tears.

Like an overbearing mother, I warned the front desk about Ike's laryngeal paralysis. That if he started freaking out to please rub his neck and give him a Benadryl to calm him down. I handed the woman his bag with his food and medicine, his blankets and his favorite stuffed animal—a big brown monkey.

"His nickname is Monkey," I said. I pushed my sunglasses down from the top of head to cover my eyes.

She shot me a sympathetic smile.

I wanted to turn around and head back home, to forget about the deal I'd made with Chris. After all, Ike was happy. He had an excellent life in California—swimming in the pool, going to the beach, and eating barbecued hamburgers and hot dogs. But a promise was a promise. Ike was Chris's dog too.

I stooped down to give my furry best friend the hug of all hugs, throwing my arms around his neck. He licked the tears off my cheek. With a treat in her hand, the woman led Ike to the back room. Ike's tail wagged the whole time. And then he was gone. Once inside my car, I let loose. My body convulsed. My hands shook. I gulped back ragged sobs.

Back at the house, reminders of Ike were strewn about everywhere—stuffed animals, spare leashes, tumbleweeds of black fur rolling around on the ground. Bodhi, the golden retriever, followed me around wherever I went as if to say, "Stop being so sad! You have me!"

But losing Ike was like losing a child.

I couldn't stop crying.

I hugged Bodhi, the big lug, to my chest. And then I called Tracey. I could barely speak.

"What's wrong?" she asked.

"I just put Ike on a plane."

"Oh, Sam, I'm so sorry. You'll see him again though."

"No, T, my gut instinct tells me I won't. It felt like a final goodbye. He's not in good health. I should have kept him here. With me."

"Sam, chances are you're moving to France—"

"I don't know."

"But you love Jean-Luc and he loves you?"

"Yes."

"Look, I know he's coming to visit you soon, but after that, you need a test month or two. In France. You guys need to stop with the vacation fantasy and try things on for real. You need to see what his life is really like, what his kids are like." She paused. "And don't worry about Ike. You did everything you could for him."

"I know."

I was sobbing hysterically when I hung up the phone.

October 26 couldn't come soon enough. Jean-Luc's kids were staying at their grandmother's for the La Toussaint holiday, and my Frenchman was coming to town. The moment Jean-Luc exited baggage claim, I ran up to him and he swung me in his arms. Boy, did I miss those arms. I missed his smile. I missed his lips, his touch. We kissed, long, hard, and passionate. Before someone could yell "get a room," I led him across the street to the car. Fifteen minutes later, I pulled up to the marina.

"Where are we?" he asked.

"My parents' boat. I thought you'd want to freshen up before meeting them." I wiggled my eyebrows. "It's been two months since we've seen each other. I thought we could use a little privacy."

I got out of the car and walked to the docks before he could argue. Jean-Luc followed with his carry-on and we stepped onto the boat. He reached into his bag and pulled out a thin, black square box wrapped in a red bow. "*Joyeux anniversaire*, my love."

I tossed the box onto the counter and pushed Jean-Luc onto the bed. "All I want is you."

Two hours later, we showed up at my parents' house.

Outside the front door, I fingered the necklace Jean-Luc had just given me for my birthday. A beautiful, black Tahitian teardrop-shaped pearl hung from a v-shaped, pavé diamond-encrusted pendant, the chain white gold.

"Really, you shouldn't have."

"If I got you nothing," he argued, "I would never have heard the end of it."

"You came here. That's present enough."

"Hmmpf," he guffawed, narrowing his eyes into a teasing glare. "If there's one thing I know, it's women." His upper lip twitched. "I'm feeling a bit awkward meeting your parents."

"Why?"

"Because my divorce hasn't gone through yet." I could tell this really bothered him. But besides being patient, there was nothing either of us could do about it. "I would feel so much better if I was able to ask your father for your hand in marriage. Sam, I would rather have offered you a ring than a necklace."

My heart did a flip-flop.

His trepidation was palpable. He waved his hand in front of the door. "I'm a bit intimidated by all this. My house is much smaller than this. Much smaller. I can't offer you luxury or a pool or a boat. I can only—"

I kissed him lightly on the lips. "Jean-Luc, material things don't matter to me. All that matters is you. And I've told my parents everything. They understand. They do. I have a feeling you and my dad are really going to hit it off."

At least that was my greatest hope.

Checking Baggage

Unlike Jean-Luc and my mother, my adopted dad was raised in a life of privilege outside of New York City in a town called Rye. His family came from a line of bankers and lawyers whose history can be traced back to the *Mayflower*. In fact, two of his ancestors were original signers of the Declaration of Independence. His parents, whom I called Gram and Cracker, were quintessential WASPs. They shipped my dad off to an all boys' boarding school, Choate, at the age of eleven, where my father excelled in his studies and also learned to rebel. When it came time to choose a college, instead of opting for Yale and joining the Skull and Bones, like the two generations of men before him, he enrolled at Northwestern University in Evanston, Illinois. Unlike Yale, it was co-ed. It was also, gasp, a family scandal.

But just like Jean-Luc, my dad worked for everything he'd achieved; nothing was given to him. The start of his career was modest. He was living in a small rental apartment when he met my mom and drove an old red Jeep with a hard white top. But he was smart and made all the right moves, and it was no surprise his career in advertising took off the way it did. After all the traveling for his job, my mom refused to move anymore, and they'd settled into this California dreamin' life.

I moved to open the wooden Spanish doors with their iron fittings. Jean-Luc grabbed my arm and whispered, "What do I call your dad? His name is Livingston, right?"

I choked back a laugh. "Nobody has ever called him that. Just call him Tony."

"Tony?"

"I don't get it either. His dad, Livingston the second," I said with an over-the-top fake English accent, "was called Peter."

"I don't know, Sam," said Jean-Luc.

"Don't worry, you'll be fine. They're going to love you as much as I do."

And they did.

Jean-Luc and my parents connected instantly, helped by the housewarming gifts he'd brought from France—lavender products and candies and wine. In fact, I'd never seen my dad relate to somebody so well. I watched them talking together for what seemed to be hours, stunned, while my mother buzzed around Jean-Luc like a bee, laughing and smiling and joking.

With Jean-Luc out of earshot, my dad pulled me to the side. "Sam, you're really lucky. You must have a guardian angel looking out after you."

"I still feel like I'm reeling backward from one knockout punch, but I know what you mean. Along with all the bad came a world of good."

"Honey, everything will be fine. Bruises heal."

"So…what do you think about Jean-Luc?"

"It's nice having somebody I can talk to." He smiled. "I always thought you'd end up with somebody who had the soul of a poet. He's a great guy. And he's really smart. I didn't know he led a team of twenty-four scientists. It's very impressive."

"Yep, like you, he had to work really hard to get where he is today."

My dad and Jean-Luc may have come from different backgrounds, but they had a world in common. It wasn't like I expected them to be best friends or that I needed my parents' approval, but it sure was nice to have. Now I just had to have them compete in Trivial Pursuit or Scrabble, games my dad always won—a battle of wits, the American versus the French!

"If I haven't told you lately, I think you're great too," said my dad. "Whatever it is you want to do, your mother and I will support your decision, no matter what."

Should I drop the bomb then? Tell them I was probably marrying Jean-Luc and moving to France?

"I'm meeting his family over Christmas, Dad. He's going to book my ticket while he's here."

"He told me." My dad's eyes lit up. "The test month."

We all knew it was more than that.

I cringed. "It was Tracey's idea."

As I prepared dinner, a simple barbecue consisting of New York strip steaks and a big salad, my mom snuck up behind me and whispered, "He's so sweet. Now I know why you fell in love with him."

"He's so good to me."

"He's good *for* you. Dad likes him too. And don't forget the dogs! Even Jack likes him. And Jack doesn't like anybody. Everybody in Malibu wants to meet Jean-Luc."

"He's not a sideshow attraction."

"Come on! It'll be fun. Bring him to the Wine Barrel."

Singing karaoke at the Wine Barrel was not an option. I wanted Jean-Luc to see more of California while he had the chance. He had shown me practically all of France, and now it was my turn to play tour guide. The following day, Jean-Luc and I left for Palm Desert to stay with one of my oldest friends, Debra, for one night. After a two-hour drive, we pulled up to her house around noon, a bouquet of flowers and a bottle of wine in hand.

"Is this a hotel?" asked Jean-Luc.

I glanced at the beautiful Moroccan-inspired home. At over seventeen thousand square feet, it was enormous, the landscaping sheer perfection. "Nope," I said. "And if you think the outside is impressive, wait until you see the inside."

Ten-foot-tall carved wooden doors inlaid with brass opened at the press of a button. Debra greeted us. She was blond, beautiful, and with her impeccable taste, she even looked stylish in her beach cover-up. She kissed Jean-Luc on both cheeks. "It's so nice to meet you."

"Likewise," he said. "Thank you very much for hosting us."

"Come in, come in! I'll give you a quick tour and then we'll go have lunch at the club."

Behind his back, Debra gave me the thumbs-up, her mouth open, her head nodding in approval. Jean-Luc's jaw also dropped as we walked into her house. We stood in an open atrium, palm trees reaching up toward the sky. What I didn't tell Jean-Luc was that Debra hired workers from Morocco to build this masterpiece, with all the materials coming from Morocco too. The floors were intricately tiled. The brass lights were all hand hammered. The moldings were finely detailed, white and perfect, like the prettiest of wedding cakes. Jean-Luc took a step forward to peer over the balcony, where, downstairs, a full hammam spa awaited. Toward the back of the home, right off the gourmet kitchen, there was a hookah room, where at the press of a button, a twenty-foot-wide movie screen would rise in front of its stunned audience. Outside, there were two pools—one an infinity-edged lap pool, the other circular with built-in sun beds. It was paradise, a desert oasis of luxurious dreams.

At lunch, I watched Jean-Luc work his magic, marveling at his social grace. He didn't have to try to impress; being personable came naturally to him. When the check arrived, he reached for it. Debra stopped him. "It's a club. Only I can sign," she said. "Your money is no good here."

Jean-Luc glared at me. Debra laughed.

We spent the afternoon taking in the desert sun, listening to music, swimming in the pool, and drinking champagne. Debra and I sat on the outdoor couch, glasses in hand.

"Oh my god," she said. "We need to have him cloned. Stat."

"So you like him?"

"Like him? I LOVE him. He's adorable, smart, sexy…" She grabbed my knee. "Sam, I've never seen you so happy. You've really hit the jackpot with this one. He's really a great guy."

Jean-Luc waved to us from the pool.

"I agree," I said. "I agree."

Debra and I clinked glasses.

In the evening, we ate at the local sushi restaurant. Jean-Luc, as usual, was dapper in a smart black linen shirt, a black belt, and jeans. Again, I played observer, just listening in as he and Debra talked and laughed. At the end of the meal, Debra excused herself for the ladies' room.

"I want to pay for dinner," said Jean-Luc. "I didn't like not being able to pay at lunch."

"Then you better call the waiter over now," I said, and Jean-Luc did.

His face turned crimson when he found out Debra had already taken care of the bill.

"We'll just have to sneak out of the house in the morning and buy breakfast and lunch before she can catch us."

His mouth twitched.

Six days flew by too quickly. I knew that Jean-Luc would return to France and I'd find myself alone again. But rather than feeling empty, I was in high spirits. Soon I would spend one month with Jean-Luc in France—the test period. Who would be testing whom? We didn't know, although he had said that his kids could be a handful sometimes. That night, we sat on my bed with my laptop. Instead of booking my flight with his frequent-flyer miles, like I thought he was doing, he pulled up a site to Mauboussin, a French jeweler. He turned the screen toward me.

"When the time comes, I can't afford to buy you a big diamond. But diamonds are a dime a dozen. I'd like for you to have something different. Is there anything here you like?"

Wow. He'd really been thinking about rings. I shot Jean-Luc a sly smile and clicked through some designs. One design popped off the page: the *Fou de Toi*. It was a six-carat pale pink amethyst—a rose de France—set onto a delicate white gold band, offset by tiny pavé diamonds—a bonbon for any women's finger, total eye candy. I had no idea what Jean-Luc's budget was. The cost of this ring was two thousand euro.

"You like that one?" said Jean-Luc.

"I like the name. Crazy for you. Because I *am* crazy for you."

Jean-Luc clicked through the designs to another ring. It was white gold with a small diamond set into what looked like tiny butterfly wings, the band also inlaid with pavé diamonds. It was simple and elegant, charming. It also cost three hundred euro less. "What about this one?"

"It's pretty too." I read the name of the ring out loud. "*Moi aimer toi.*"

"You speak French like a cavewoman." He shoved the computer to the side and pushed me onto my back. "Me love you too."

My heart had gone from zero to ninety and all I wanted was to get a move on with my life, with Jean-Luc in it. And now he was gone. We spoke to each other every day, professed our undying love, and tried to support each other as best we could with oceans separating us. Of course, we also talked about marriage, but there were still so many unknowns. Like when would his divorce go through? And would his children like me? It was my greatest hope that they would come to accept me, but after what they'd been through with their first stepmother, they weren't exactly going to be running into my arms.

I'd thought about this a lot.

One thing I would never attempt to do was discipline Jean-Luc's children. This did not mean if they did something I didn't like, I'd let them walk over me. But I refused to play the role of the evil stepmonster, and hopefully they would come to view me as a friend, a person they could trust. I wanted to start working on gaining their confidence. I remembered the children were more brokenhearted over losing Natasha's cat when she left than they were over losing her. I needed to find a cat, a better cat, and stat. If anything, choosing a new pet together would help me connect with the kids.

A friend of mine had just posted a picture of her new Bengal kitten on Facebook, and the moment I saw him, I knew this was the breed I wanted to introduce the kids to. The search for a spotted, creamy and caramel-colored tiny panther began. After spending hours on Google, I found the name of a few breeders in my area only to learn that the kittens cost a minimum of twelve hundred dollars. Which wasn't going to happen. Upon further investigation, I discovered the mothers, or breeding cats, were usually sold for two hundred dollars or less, a much more manageable number. I ran the idea by Jean-Luc, and he suggested I discuss my idea with Elvire. After all, it would give us something to talk about woman-to-woman and a way for us to get to know one another.

So I emailed her.

Elvire, a cat lover, knew of the breed. Together, in French, we exchanged excited emails about how getting one for Christmas would be incredible, if Jean-Luc was agreeable. And so the research began. Elvire and I emailed back and forth, suggesting one breeder or the next. A few weeks later, after much digging, I was able to uncover *une éleveur* in the Bordeaux area—only two hours away from Jean-Luc's home. There were four kittens left to choose from—two boys and two girls. I asked Elvire to have Jean-Luc call the breeder for more information and then to have her papa call me. The phone rang a few minutes later.

"How much are they?" I asked, worried.

"Nine hundred euro."

Leave it to me to find one of the world's most expensive cats. "Honey, I told you. I could buy an older cat here," I said. "Two hundred dollars."

"They want a kitten."

"At a year old, they're kind of like kittens…"

"Elvire wants to pick the cat out, a female, and thanks to you, she now wants this breed. Maxence too."

Of course they did. The Bengal was like the rock star of cats. "I'm sorry."

"Honey, never apologize. Don't worry. I have an idea and the children have already agreed to it."

I listened to his solution, biting my nails. The kids, Jean-Luc, and I were going to split the cost of the cat. The children had some savings and they would pitch in one hundred and fifty euro each. Jean-Luc would pay for half. And I would be responsible for the remaining one-fifty.

"Uh, okay," I said.

"I always thought cats were free. You can find them anywhere on the street." Jean-Luc's laughter was met by my silence. His tone turned serious. "Honey, if you can't afford it, I can pay your portion, but I thought you'd want to be involved."

"No, no, no. This cat was my idea. I'll figure something out." Stupid cat. Me and my big fat mouth. "So what part will I own? The ass?"

A few days later, Elvire emailed me to ask if I had any ideas for names. Thinking of her recent obsession with Stephenie Meyer's *Twilight* saga, I suggested Bella. And so we agreed. Bella the Bengal cat it was. Expense aside, I was probably as excited for the cat as both the children were. Plus, it was a great way for me to break down some barriers with Elvire, whose raging hormones were about to kick in. Yes, with two tween-aged kids, I was about to dive into the fire headfirst.

The following morning, Jean-Luc called with incredible news. It wasn't about the cat; his divorce to Natasha had finally gone through. The drama was over and we could start planning our future—one big happy Franco-American family with a ridiculously expensive cat.

With the finalization of Jean-Luc's divorce, the inspiration to straighten out the rest of my life kicked me into motion. It was time to dig in, get rid of all the problems I'd been avoiding, tackling them head on like a linebacker, crushing the big ones first. One: I needed to meet with a bankruptcy attorney to figure out if chapter 7 was a viable option for me. I wasn't going to burden anyone with my debt—not Jean-Luc, not my parents, not anybody. Two: I needed to sell whatever I could. There was a jeweler in Santa Monica on Montana Street with a sign stating, "I buy gold," so I raced there.

The shop was nice, filled with beautiful pieces, all glittery with diamonds galore. A few eternity bands in a black display case caught my eye. But no, I wasn't there to pick something new out; I was there to sell. The owner of the shop held up a loop and inspected my wedding rings. He was young, around thirty-five, fairly good-looking with long brown hair that came down to his shoulders. He, like most men in LA, wore a funky outfit—two-hundred-dollar "cool kid jeans" and a button-down oxford with an embroidered dragon on the back. He placed the rings on a scale.

"I'll give you fifteen hundred for both."

I wasn't sure if I had heard him correctly. I felt like I'd been punched in the stomach. Some linebacker. I wanted to sink to my knees and vomit and then cry like a baby. "What?"

"First of all, the diamond is pear-shaped. Nobody buys pear-shaped rings anymore. It's pretty much useless unless I turn it into a necklace. Second, there's a chip in it." He pointed to the top of the diamond. "It needs to be sanded down, which will cost me a couple hundred and diminish its size. The platinum setting is only worth its weight. You have thin fingers so—" He cut himself off, probably noticing the tears welling up in my eyes. "How much did you think you could get for them, anyway?"

The words gurgled out of my mouth. "My ex told me the diamond was worth eighteen thousand."

"Not on this planet." The jeweler laughed. "While the quality is decent, it's not that good. Retail? You'd be lucky to get three or four for it."

"Four is good," I said. "I'll take four. Plus the value of the platinum."

"Honey, I don't buy retail, I buy wholesale. And as I told you, nobody is buying pear-shaped." My knees felt like they were about to give out from under me. The jeweler's half smile was filled with pity. "Look, I saw you drooling over the case. If you want to do a trade-in, I'll give you a better deal."

I shook my head numbly. I couldn't sell my old wedding rings to buy new ones. And although we'd discussed marriage and things seemed to be headed in that direction, Jean-Luc hadn't technically asked me yet. "No, that would be bad karma."

"It's just money," he said. "If it makes you feel any better, I'll buy the rings from you, hand you the cash, and then you give me the cash back and choose something else."

Was he kidding? Insane? I glared at him. "That doesn't make a difference."

"Up to you." He handed the rings back to me. "Really, I'm not giving you a lowball offer. It's fair. Think about it."

I mumbled, "I will," and headed for the door. My hands shook as I put the keys into the ignition. I visited three more jewelry stores who all told me more or less the same thing. Panic set in. I'd joked about it before, but it finally hit me that I really had nothing but the clothes on my back.

At home, my mother suggested I contact an estate sale agent she worked with a few years back, so I called and set up a meeting. In addition to the rings, she said they also could help me sell a silver-plated tea set I'd been trying to unload for years. Even in France, I couldn't see myself throwing a formal tea party. I'd have to be patient, the estate agent explained, but she thought she'd be able to sell everything for around five thousand dollars, less 35 percent. With no other options, I agreed.

As for bankruptcy, since I didn't know anybody who had gone through the process, I pored through websites looking for an attorney who (a) didn't look like Slick Willy the used car salesman, (b) didn't advertise a chapter 7 special for $795/all the litigation you need, and (c) wasn't an ambulance chaser. This took some time. Finally, after much research, I settled on a woman named Shannon Sugar who also practiced family law. After I filled her in on my situation and went over the disastrous state of my finances, I asked if she foresaw any problems.

"Well," said Shannon, "your finances are close to poverty level. You're definitely under the means. But there are no guarantees."

"Great," I said. I was a pauper. Just great.

"So I've told you about all the risks and you understand them."

Yes, I knew I'd ruin my near-perfect credit score, something I was bizarrely proud of. Yes, I knew there was a chance I wouldn't be discharged from my debt. Yes, I knew my finances were a brand-new shade of pathetic. Yes, I knew it would take about three months from start to finish. And yes, I knew, if I was lucky enough to sell my rings, the funds I'd make would cover the attorney's services, leaving me with little extra. Yes, I understood the risks.

"When did you want to file?" asked Shannon.

Want wasn't the exact word I'd have chosen. I didn't *want* to do this. Nobody in his or her right mind *wanted* to do this. I sucked in my sarcastic response. "I'd like to see how things go over the next few months. If my situation doesn't change, I'll need to start the process right after the New Year."

"Until then, don't use your credit cards. And don't pay any of your bills."

I was treading in an ocean of debt. I could do that.

Letter Five
Paris, August 13, 1989

"The pen runs faster than the tongue."

My heart,

This is my fifth letter. God needed seven days to create the world, so maybe I will need more than seven letters to build something as great as world creation is with you. The days are passing by and I'm still thinking of you with the same strength of the beginning. No news from you since you left Paris. I don't know, but tonight I am a bit troubled in my mind.

Samantha, even if you are just a shooting star who has crossed my life in such a marvelous way, I will still be able to keep our hours together as jewels. Of course, it is my hope that this shooting star won't disappear.

I want you to come to Paris soon. I miss you.

Soon, I will put this letter into the mail and I will wonder if I've written the best things to you. Perhaps I talked too much and you would be disturbed by my way of telling you my feelings. Perhaps you will take me as a crazy guy, like many "Frenchies."

But many things in my mind tell me to send you my words because we have to open ourselves up when we feel something so great as I feel for you. When you see your train at the station, you can't miss it. It could be the last. I do the same for my life. You belong to that story and I hope you felt and still feel the same.

I wish you were here tonight, by my side, giving moments of tenderness. Write me quickly. I need news from you.

Still yours,
Jean-Luc

The Test Month

For months, I did whatever I could to find a job. I scoured Monster.com and Craigslist postings, sending off résumés to here and to there, to basically everywhere. I stalked my recruiter. She brushed me off. There were no freelance opportunities. There were no jobs. There was nothing but my career as a dog walker with occasional overnights.

While taking care of two dogs, one horse, and a Shetland pony and sleeping in a guest room that had a collection of old dolls missing eyes and limbs staring me down from a shelf above the bed, I tossed and turned (flanked by the two dogs), and I reminded myself: at least the job would collect enough money to pay for my portion of the cat. But moving to France wasn't set in stone. Anything could happen. Jean-Luc's marriage with Natasha had gone sour because of her relationship—or lack thereof—with the kids. What if they didn't like me?

I'd find out soon enough.

December 19 arrived and I found myself back in France. I exited customs, about to meet my biggest critics. Jean-Luc ran toward me and gave me the biggest of bear hugs and an even bigger kiss. Maxence and Elvire peeked over his shoulder, staring at me—the oddity, the strange woman from America. Elvire was a delicate flower, thin with an ivory complexion and giant cat-shaped blue eyes, her auburn hair providing a stark contrast to the pallor of her skin. Maxence was her opposite. Small in stature, sure, but sturdy and tough, the ten-year-old's complexion was more olive toned, his eyes a blue green, and his hair a sandy brown. Both children had their father's perfect lips.

Before Natasha left, she told Jean-Luc he wouldn't find anybody to love his two horrible monsters. It may have been because it was Christmastime, but to me, they looked like little angels—nothing terrible about them at all.

"*Tu es plus jolie en personne,*" I said to Elvire, which immediately brought a big smile to her face. We kissed each other on the cheeks, and for good measure, I gave her a big hug. This process was also repeated with Maxence, but instead of telling him he was pretty, I told him he was *très beau.* Elvire's and Maxence's eyes darted from one to another and then to me. I could almost see their thoughts churning, wondering if I was as "nice as their father told them."

Jean-Luc took my bag and we walked to the car. "Ready to go home?"

Home. I was looking forward to seeing it.

"It's not much," said Jean-Luc. "But I do what I can. I had to buy it very quickly." He glanced at the kids. "Right after their mother died."

"I'm sure it's fine."

"There's a lot of work to be done."

"I'll help you." A do-it-yourself man, Jean-Luc had already prepared me for a few "issues," like the raw walls in the foyer that needed to be painted and the hole in the shower from one of his plumbing debacles.

"Sam, it's not at all like your parents' place."

"I know. I've already seen it." His eyes widened in horror. "Google Earth," I said by means of an explanation. "It's a cream-colored town house with a small front yard—two stories high with a green fence."

"When—"

"After you sent me the phone, I had your address on the package."

Jean-Luc was well aware of my curious nature. He called it snooping; I called it research. At least I'd been honest about my Mata Hari–like activities. "Ahh, my little spy. You have been a busy girl." He nudged my shoulder. "There's a box you might be interested in at home. I'll show you where it is."

We pulled up onto his street, which I immediately recognized from my Google investigations. A woman walking a rambunctious Pomeranian stared at our car. I lifted my hand in a friendly gesture. She glared at me and picked up her pace, practically dragging her dog down the street. Jean-Luc laughed. "People aren't as friendly here as they are in the States. They're, how do I put it, a bit more reserved."

He pulled into a parking spot. The kids jumped out of the car and headed for the white town house with the green iron gate. The small front yard was a bit overgrown with weeds, but I didn't say anything.

"I need your artistic sense to make the house a home," said Jean-Luc, fumbling with the keys.

"Didn't Natasha do anything?"

"No. I did everything—I worked on the house. I did the cooking and the cleaning, the grocery shopping, the decorating. Everything."

"But didn't she work?"

"For a while she did. Then her contract ran out and she collected unemployment. I have no idea what she did with her money. She never offered to pitch in for anything. When I'd ask her, she'd scream and cry."

"Has she called?"

"No, we haven't spoken since our divorce was finalized two weeks ago. We've only communicated by email."

"Has she reached out to the kids?"

"Not a word."

I huffed out my disapproval.

Jean-Luc opened the door. I was expecting "man taste"—a black leather couch with a big-screen TV, maybe a wagon wheel coffee table. But he'd been exaggerating about how much help he needed. Sure, the rooms could use a woman's touch, but he'd done a fine job decorating. The living room had natural-colored grass cloth wallpaper covering one wall, and the bare wall was painted a light beige. The dining room table, a solid, dark wood piece with four chairs, was of Asian influence, as was the sideboard on which the TV sat. The couch was chocolate brown, from IKEA, with just enough space for four. The room was narrow but comfortable and would benefit from some splashes of color—a rug, some art, throw pillows, candles, things of that nature. In the corner stood a Charlie Brown Christmas tree—a pathetic twig with four colored lights and a few pieces of multicolored garland thrown on it. It was clear that he was trying.

"When I bought this place, it had been abandoned. You should have seen it, Sam. It was horrible. Rushed to find something, I only had two weeks to make it habitable before the kids came to live with me. Thankfully, my brother helped."

I peered into the small kitchen with pine cabinets and a black-and-white checkered tile floor. Everything was spotless. Jean-Luc opened the door leading to the garage where I found a little alcove with a small laundry room. He pointed to the dryer. "I just bought that. For you. Merry Christmas, to my American girl."

"You're such a romantic," I said.

His beautiful lips pinched together in a smirk. "I am, Sam. Be patient. You'll see."

As he ushered me upstairs, I wondered what he was up to.

Jean-Luc had covered the entryway and the stairwell leading up to the second floor with brick-like tiles, but the work stopped midway at the landing, and the walls above the brick work were untreated drywall. He motioned to the bare walls and shrugged. "I know it needs to be painted. I just haven't had time to do anything yet. And I'd like for you to pick out the color."

I nodded, looking forward to lending a hand. "You've done a really nice job with the place. You should be proud."

"You're too kind. It's not perfect, but it will get there one day."

Elvire's room was wallpapered a pale sunflower yellow and

decorated with *Twilight* posters. In addition to her bed, there was a bookcase, a dresser, and a glass desk. It was total teenage chaos—an explosion of candy wrappers, papers, and clothes on the floor. Jean-Luc shook his head. "I told her to clean up, but she just doesn't listen." He yelled, "*Elvire, viens ici et range ta chambre!*"

"*Deux secondes*," came her reply.

Two seconds. I snorted, remembering what I was like at her age. Kids, whether in France or the United States or Zimbabwe, were all the same.

I picked up a photo of a much younger Elvire smiling with a woman with short dark hair. The woman had blue cat-shaped eyes, just like Elvire. Pink and blue confetti covered their bodies.

"Natasha asked Elvire to keep the pictures hidden away. Do they bother you?"

It wasn't as if they bothered me, per se. I felt like I was staring into the face of a ghost, a difficult feeling to describe—not quite jealousy, but an awareness. A little pit formed in my stomach. "Did Natasha want to compete with the memory of a dead mother?"

"No," said Jean-Luc. "She competed with Elvire for my attention."

"I'm more than happy to share you." Remembering the story he'd told me about his one ménage à trois, I kissed him and corrected myself. "With the kids, that is."

Jean-Luc ushered me into Max's room, which was wallpapered in cornflower blue. Unlike Elvire's, his room was neat and organized. Collectible trading cards were stacked in perfect little piles on his desk. His clothes had been put away. His toys were arranged. I smiled when I saw the blue robot my parents had given him for his birthday, which Jean-Luc had brought back for Max after visiting me in the States. A gray elephant trunk stuck out from under the navy blue duvet.

"That's Doudou. Max has had him since he was a baby."

"Oh," I said. Another remnant from the past. It was then that I told myself to leave snooping to the side. I knew everything about Jean-Luc and the kids that I needed to know.

"I have something else to show you," said Jean-Luc, guiding me to the balcony, which had been closed in with a big window. He smiled proudly. "I thought you'd need your own closet. I put the floors in myself, put up the walls. All you have to do is pick out the fixtures."

My heart beat wildly, happily.

Our next stop was the sparsely furnished master bedroom—only a bed and a dresser. "You look a little tired." He kissed me on the nose. "Take a rest while I prepare dinner."

I dreamt sweet dreams and didn't wake up until the next day. We made love in the morning, me trying to keep quiet with Max sleeping soundly right next door. For a while, we just lay there, wrapped up in each other's arms, legs intertwined.

"Do you think you'll be able to live here?" whispered Jean-Luc.

I rubbed my hand over his muscular chest. "It already feels like home."

Right after breakfast, Jean-Luc, the kids, and I were to head to the Christmas market in Toulouse. Nicknamed *La Ville Rose*, because of all its brick buildings, the "rose city" was the center for France's aerospace industry—and the reason Jean-Luc lived in the area. I was excited to see the rose city covered in a blanket of white, which, according to Jean-Luc, was very rare.

Dressed up in our winter gear—boots and jackets and hats and scarves—we drove twenty minutes to *Le Capitole*, the center of Toulouse, passing by snow-covered parks where parents pulled their children on plastic sleds and the Canal-du-Midi, which was now covered in a thin sheet of ice. We traversed up and down narrow streets flanked by beautiful buildings with iron balconies and carved wooden doors, finally arriving at our destination—a large square filled with little log cabins selling everything from clothes and shoes to spices to seafood and sausages. The stalls faced an enormous brick and limestone neoclassical building adorned with impressive sculptures. A bevy of cafés, complete with patrons sitting outside, surrounded the market.

"Once the market is finished, the square is empty. Sometimes performances or other events take place here. That's the city hall," said Jean-Luc, nodding to the *Capitolium*. "On its far right though, there is a theater. Do you like opera?"

The kids groaned. I laughed and said, "I do."

"And your favorite?"

"*Madame Butterfly*."

"One day, maybe we can see it together."

"I'd like that."

The kids ran ahead of us. Jean-Luc put his arm around me and we followed, giving them their space to explore but keeping an eye on them all the same.

Among the old and the young, we sauntered through the market window-shopping, just simply enjoying all the sights, smells, and sounds. There was a slight breeze, not enough to bring on chills, just enough to ensure the tip of my nose was cold. Max and Elvire ran up to a bonbon vendor, practically drooling over the sweets. Jean-Luc handed them each a couple of euro. Would they buy the sparkling, sugar-encrusted fruits—peaches, apples, and strawberries? Or chocolate?

"Honey, do you want a wine with spices? It's a specialty here." Jean-Luc tipped his head toward a stall a few feet away. I nodded an eager yes. He walked away, his strut confident. Again, I watched him yuck it up with the vendor. Jean-Luc was so easygoing; he made everybody smile.

Our eyes locked as he handed over a paper cup of *vin chaud*, and the scents of Christmas permeated my nostrils. I took a sip, the liquid warming my throat. Delicious. The kids soon rejoined us, crystallized sugar sparkling on their lips, and we walked on.

"Do you like the market?" asked Jean-Luc.

Like it? I loved the market. I loved the smells, the spices, cinnamon, and nutmeg permeating the air this time of year along with the freshly baked bread. Some of the vendors wore Santa caps and sang French Christmas carols, and the general feeling was one of festivity. The novelty of my new situation didn't look nearly as intimidating as it had upon my arrival.

Maxence pulled on the sleeve of my coat. "*Regarde! Un petit cochon!*"

In a box to our left, a small piglet ran around in circles squealing, the high-pitched sound sending dozens of pigeons into the air. The vendor was selling some sort of candy—the baby pig was obviously a ploy to attract younger customers. I smiled down upon Max. "*C'est toi?*"

"*Non, c'est notre dîner*," said Jean-Luc.

Elvire's eyes went wide. Maxence's laughter subsided. I punched Jean-Luc softly on the arm. "We are not eating piglet for dinner." I winked at the kids. "*Ton père, quel blagueur!*"

What a joker!

Maxence ran up to pet the pig. Jean-Luc placed one arm around me, the other around Elvire. "*Mes deux filles*," he said, and I smiled. Elvire's long eyelashes blinked the snow and any signs of mistrust away.

Miniature lace doily flakes covered the ground in a thin blanket of white, melting under our footsteps. The way the children looked at Jean-Luc, wide-eyed and worshiping, made my heart swell with pride, an overinflated water balloon about to burst. It was a winter wonderland. My wonderland. I was so happy I had to stop myself from spinning in circles in the middle of the street, arms flailing, tongue out to catch snowflakes, like the kids. We walked back to the parking garage with a bag of roasted chestnuts, leaving footprints behind us along the way.

It was time to meet Jean-Luc's friends.

Jean-Luc put on a classical CD and started up the car. The kids popped their earbuds into their iPods. "I've worked with Christian for about fourteen years now. He and his wife, Ghislaine, are as close to me as my own family is."

"What have you told them about me?"

Jean-Luc popped his lips. "Sam, you have nothing to worry about. I'm sure they're going to love you as much as I do."

But in typical Sam overthinking mode, I was worried. I clasped my hands together, imagining catastrophe. Like what if the kids told Jean-Luc's friends they couldn't stand me, couldn't wait for me to fly my American butt back home where it belonged? What if, instead of a straw, I asked for a blow job again? What if his friends were uptight, reserved folks who wouldn't get my sense of humor? What if we were being served *pot-au-feu de la mer* and I had to chug my glass of wine to wash it down?

Jean-Luc rang the doorbell. The door opened.

Turned out, my fears weren't justified. At all.

Christian had sparkling blue eyes, a huge smile, and like Jean-Luc, he came complete with an infectious laugh. He spoke a few words of English, which instantly put me at ease. Ghislaine, his wife, had a warm and cheerful face, cropped blond hair, and wore funky glasses with orange frames. Both of them, I guessed, were in their early sixties. With a rush of hand gestures, they ushered us into the living room.

From the moment we arrived, they didn't stop smiling. The aperitif—a sparkling wine—was poured. The kids entertained themselves with a book of magic tricks. Sitting by the fire, we ate small bites— cheeses and tortes—and made our best attempt to get to know one another through the language barrier. Jean-Luc translated when I didn't understand. I pantomimed helping Ghislaine in the kitchen, but she quickly declined.

Over dinner, a spicy Bordeaux wine was served. Jean-Luc recounted our 1989 romance, and how we reconnected twenty years later, and of our future plans to get married. I piped in here and there, speaking only in the past and the present in French. Nobody corrected me, because I was trying. We spoke of some of our troubles in our past relationships, him with Natasha and me with Chris. When we were finished, Ghislaine had tears in her eyes.

"*Je suis très contente*," she said and nodded her head toward the kids. "*Et je pense qu'ils sont heureux aussi. Ils ont besoin d'un morceau de bonheur.*"

It was then I noticed the children were smiling at me. I realized I didn't need a cat to give them what they'd been searching for, *un morceau de bonheur*—"a slice of happiness." All they needed to be surrounded with was love. Yes, all of us, we were all *très* content. Very happy.

In an attempt to warm me up even more to the regional specialties, tonight was all about *le canard*, or duck, and the various ways in which it was served. For starters, we indulged in *foie gras*, which I'd never tasted before and which was produced in this region of France. It was delicious, a delectable, buttery treat, and was followed by the main course, a *confit de canard*, leg of duck, served with roasted potatoes. Our hosts smiled and asked me if I liked the meal.

Indeed, I did. "*C'est fantastique!*"

No French dinner party would have been complete without a salad, a variety of cheeses, and fresh fruits, which, one course after the other, were served right before the dessert—a to-die-for chocolate tart decorated with candied kiwis and strawberries. By the end of the meal, I was stuffed and dizzy from all the rich flavors. Then fatigue set in. I could barely keep my eyes open, and I fought the urge to yawn. It was only ten o'clock, but after our busy day marketing and my jet lag, it felt like two in the morning. Jean-Luc eyed me and explained that I'd just flown in the evening before and he thought it would be a good idea to take me home. After all, we were leaving for Provence early in the morning.

"No problem! We understand!" our hosts exclaimed. A flurry of good-byes and double-cheeked kisses ensued.

On the car ride home, I couldn't help but think how much Christian and Ghislaine did, indeed, feel like family. I'd only spent a few hours with this fabulous couple, but their warmth and kindness made the notion of moving to France a whole lot less terrifying.

Rules of Engagement

If meeting Jean-Luc's friends had been nerve racking, it was nothing compared to how nervous I felt about meeting his sisters. Sisters were protective, the gatekeepers to the family—Lord knows mine was. We were staying *chez* Isabelle, the elder of Jean-Luc's sisters but younger than him by three years, setting off early in the morning.

Once again, I sat in the passenger seat, wringing my clammy hands.

An hour into the four-hour drive from Toulouse to Marseilles, the kids started arguing in the backseat, needling each other, punching, screaming, and yelling. Jean-Luc told them we wouldn't get the cat after the New Year if they didn't cut the crap. Either that or he would pull the car over. This last threat worked like a charm. He turned on the car stereo to a Top 40 station playing dance music—from both the United States and France. Elvire and I sang along to one of Lady Gaga's hits, "Poker Face"; Jean-Luc didn't quite retain his. He grimaced.

"*Les deux? Vous chantez comme une casserole.* The sound is worse than banging pots."

Elvire and I continued singing. Max put on his headset. Jean-Luc sighed.

Three hours and many songs later, we arrived at Isabelle's house. I was introduced to Richard (*Ree-chard*, soft on the *d*), Isabelle's partner of seven years, and her two sons, eighteen-year-old Maxime, twenty-three-year-old Steeve (with an extra *e*), Steeve's fiancée Laura, and, of course, Isabelle. Then I met Muriel, the youngest of Jean-Luc's sisters, her husband Alain and her two children, twelve-year-old Arnaud and eighteen-year-old Anaïs. Two large boxers, Leo and Juju, and a gray cat, Dolly, soon joined the party. Everybody, with the exception of the animals, kissed me on both cheeks, the introductions taking well over half an hour.

Both of Jean-Luc's sisters were drop-dead gorgeous, or *éblouissant*. Muriel was very slim and fit, with long brown hair and perfect posture. A raven-haired beauty, Isabelle was the curvier of the two, not to say she was heavy at all—probably a size four. Both sisters had that French attitude—a certain *je ne sais quoi* about them. I supposed it all came down to confidence, which both sisters wore well, and which also included their stylish outfits—effortless and chic, casual yet elegant. Glad to be wearing simple but stylish black boots, jeans, a black sweater, and a black scarf, I almost fit in. Almost. But I was definitely the foreigner. And with so many people talking at once, I was having a hard time understanding any French. My confidence was waning.

Isabelle and Muriel took me on a tour of the house, first pointing out the massive nativity scene in the living room. Some of the terra-cotta figurines, called *santons de Provence* and crafted right in the area, were hand-painted in bright blues, sparkling yellows, and vivid greens and reds, depicting the various characters of Provençal village life—fishermen, produce vendors, bohemian women, and shepherds with their sheep. All the villagers and animals stood within a beautiful arrangement of buildings and farms and stores, leading your eye to the *crèche*, where Mary, Joseph, and the Baby Jesus awaited, surrounded by angels and kings and, of course, more animals. Isabelle told me that she and Richard had both been collecting *santons* for years.

"*C'est magnifique*," I said. Admittedly, after I had seen Jean-Luc's Charlie Brown Christmas tree, I was a bit scared about how the French celebrated Christmas.

The sisters smiled. Isabelle excused herself and returned a few moments later with a small box. "Open. It's a small welcome to the family."

Muriel's grin widened. "From your new sisters."

I opened the gift to find a thin and very classic sterling silver bracelet from a store called Agatha Paris. While the bracelet was beautiful, I was more blown away by how warm these two women were, how kind everyone was. I was being welcomed into this country, this new life, with air kisses and acceptance.

"You like?"

"*J'aime beaucoup, beaucoup, beaucoup. Merci.*"

Seeing as they'd never been to the States, both sisters wanted to start planning a trip right away—and ASAP. And the perfect time was the marriage of Jean-Luc and Sam! They planned to come for two weeks, maybe three. It would be the trip of their lives! This was all news to me, and in one fell swoop, I saw my dream of getting married in a French castle vanish. I pulled Jean-Luc aside.

"What's all this talk about us getting married in California?" I whispered.

"I should have warned you how excited they were to finally have an excuse to visit the States."

Isabelle shot me a thumbs-up. The two sisters chatted, their voices rising in excitement. I could make out the words "Las Vegas!" "And California!" "The Grand Canyon!" "Area Fifty-One!" My mouth twisted and I sighed. "I'm no dream killer."

"Honey, if you want to get married here, we can. Don't change your ideas because of them." He tilted his head toward his sisters. They were still smiling. Somehow this seemed oddly planned out.

"Whatever. It's no big deal. I can always make my sister get married in a castle." I pulled my iTouch out of my purse and opened up the calendar. "When were you think…" I started, cutting myself off.

"My office is closed for two weeks at the end of July, and then I can take more days."

Wait one little second here. *Un instant.* Jean-Luc and I had talked about marriage, but he hadn't actually proposed yet. "But you haven't asked me—"

Muriel called Jean-Luc over before I could utter one more word. I heard the French words for "dinner," "help," and that was all I could discern. I eyed Jean-Luc curiously, but he held up a finger and said he had to look after the sauce.

Eleven pairs of eyes turned to me over dinner. This time in Franglais—a language I was more than familiar with—Isabelle asked, "Do *tu* and Jean-Luc wish *pour les enfants?*" For some reason I expected her to throw in the word *terrible*, but she didn't. She just watched me squirm in my hot seat, a smile on her face. Ah, what fun! Let's torture the American.

"We've talked about it," I said, stabbing a grape tomato with my fork. It split open, oozing yellow seeds. "But now is not the time."

The conversation was a little uncomfortable. I threw back my glass of wine. Unfortunately, all eyes still rested on me. With a bemused expression, Richard leaned over and refilled my glass. I could almost read his mind. "*Ahh, zis Americane*, she *eez* a drinker!" He may have even said it out loud.

"*Quand? Quand est-ce que tu veux des enfants?*" asked Muriel.

"*Après le mariage. Nous attendrons pour juillet*," I said, mustering up my best French. I sank in my seat, translating the words I'd just uttered. After the marriage? We'll wait for July? Why was I talking about a marriage that was just assumed? And having children?

The sisters, Richard, Alain, Steeve, Maxime, and Jean-Luc burst out in laughter. Isabelle grabbed her stomach. Muriel couldn't even look at me. Heart racing, I turned to Jean-Luc. "What? What's so funny?"

"Honey, you just said you were waiting to have an orgasm."

"No, no, no, I didn't say that. I said not until July. July!" My eyes went wide in confusion. The group's laughter came harder. Their eyes watered. They wheezed and giggled and snorted. I frowned.

Jean-Luc took my hand and squeezed it. "Sam, you didn't pronounce July right. You said it like the verb *jouir*, which means to have an orgasm."

Oh. No. I didn't.

But yes, yes, and OH YES, I did.

—◠—

The morning was dark and stormy, the clouds pregnant, threatening rain. Weather aside, we were on our way to Jean-Luc's hometown, La Ciotat, located on the edge of the Mediterranean Sea. After twenty minutes on the highway, we rounded a corner and Cassis, La Ciotat's neighboring seaside resort village, came into view. Breathtakingly beautiful, the colors of the magnificent landscape were especially vivid in the stormy light—yellow, salmon, and orange buildings settled among a backdrop of green. The town itself was nestled in a bay, surrounded by sheltered inlets known as *calanques*.

"Ahhh, this is the smell of home," said Jean-Luc as he rolled down his window. "Breathe it in."

The air carried the wet scent of salt and earth, and it was refreshing. We drove over rocky canyons and cliffs with jaw-dropping views of the waters below us toward La Ciotat. Scary and beautiful at the same time, the Mediterranean Sea churned and boiled, a whipped cream and frothy white.

"You must have loved growing up here."

"I did." Jean-Luc nodded and pointed to a bluff. "This is the highest point in all of Europe. Oh, we got into some trouble when we were young." He laughed softly to himself. "I never had to leave the town. Girls from all over Europe…"

"Simmer down, stud." I eyed the backseat. "There are children in the car."

"They don't understand English that well."

Laughter lit up Jean-Luc's eyes; I rolled mine.

La Ciotat was much bigger and more rugged than its dainty and charming neighbor, Cassis, but still beautiful. Taking a quick drive through town, we passed the old shipping port, the beach, and countless restaurants and shops—all of which seemed to cater to tourists. Besides the famed *calanques*, La Ciotat laid claim to hous-ing the world's oldest movie theater, the Eden, where the first movie screening took place.

"We have some time before my parents expect us," said Jean-Luc, which meant we were supposed to be punctual but not early. "So we'll grab a quick *café*."

We parked the car in a public lot by the beach and meandered the cobbled streets, eventually finding a *salon de thé*. We staked out a table for four next to a display of varying tea kettles—all with a very Japanese influence. The kids ordered two sodas and cookies. Jean-Luc and I opted for tea. Right after we placed our order, Jean-Luc pulled out his wallet. No cash. Before I could offer a *centime*, Jean-Luc got up, leaving me with the kids. "Don't even think about it, Sam. It isn't up for discussion. I'll be right back."

"*Où tu vas, Papa?*" asked Elvire just as the front door closed.

I held my hand up and rubbed my thumb against index and middle fingers, the universal sign: money. Elvire nodded her head in understanding. Suddenly, a ruckus came from outside, loud music and laughter. The kids eyed me. I nodded. We all jumped up from the table and headed out to find giant walking Christmas trees with big, googly eyes and men on stilts painted up like toy soldiers and giant snowflakes. Men in Santa hats played musical instruments—horns, drums, and trombones—while women dressed up in elf cos-tumes danced. It was madness of the best kind. I whipped out my video camera.

The mood in the courtyard was beyond festive, filled with laughter and, well, walking Christmas trees. A chubby tree covered in bright yellow balls, shiny ornaments, and big red bows bounded toward Maxence. Max's lopsided smile wanted to say, "I'm too cool for this," but the laughter in his eyes said otherwise. It must have been the floppy felt star on the Christmas tree's head. Immediately after this, one of the toy soldiers in candy-striped pants grasshopper-legged his way over to Elvire and stood right over her, his hands on his hips. His face was painted white, in contrast to his large Dali-esque swirling black mustache and goatee. Big round balls adorned his red suit, matching his jester-style hat. His eyes widened comically as he took a lock of Elvire's auburn hair, holding it high in the air, but not pulling it. Elvire burst into laughter before she ran away. The stilted man pretended to chase after her, dancing and shaking his fingers.

Jean-Luc walked up behind me. "What's going on here?"

"I have no idea." I'd been smiling so much that my cheeks hurt. "Is this what Christmas is like in the South of France?"

"*Évidemment.*"

A few moments later, the crowd of Christmas revelers dispersed to perform their merrymaking act on other unsuspecting persons. Laughing, we all headed inside the *salon de thé* to enjoy our mid-morning snack.

Jean-Luc's parents' apartment building was old, most likely built in the sixties, and a bit run down, a box without French charm—not quite what I expected, which Jean-Luc picked up on almost immediately.

"My father worked in the shipyards," he explained, "and was always afraid of investing money in real estate. A hard worker, he hung on to every franc he made. Now, even if they wanted to buy, the real estate in La Ciotat has skyrocketed to the moon, and they, like most of the residents here, wouldn't be able to afford prices accessible only to wealthy Parisians."

I shrugged off the initial shock. "Places don't matter. People do. I'm really excited to meet them."

The children bolted ahead of us and up a stairwell, their footsteps echoing throughout the corridor.

"There isn't an elevator?" I asked.

It was all a bit reminiscent of Jean-Luc's apartment way back in 1989 Paris.

"No."

"They have a bathroom?"

Jean-Luc grimaced. "Of course. It's not the middle ages."

One step at a time, we hiked our way up to the fourth floor. I was winded by the time we reached the top. The lights in the hallway flickered. Jean-Luc's brother, Michel, threw the door open and we entered a sunny three-bedroom apartment. Michel said *bonjour* by kissing both of my cheeks and then slunk into his room, closing the door behind him. This action did not go unnoticed by Jean-Luc's mother, who screamed something in angry French.

Jean-Luc whispered. "My parents are embarrassed by Michel's behavior."

I waved my hands. "*Non, ça va.* It's okay." Jean-Luc had already informed me about Michel's shyness. I took no offense.

Jean-Luc's father, André, was thin with a head of white downy hair, kind brown eyes, and a mischievous smile. At seventy-six, he looked fantastic, fit, and full of life. Jean-Luc's mother, Marcelle, came up behind him. She, like Jean-Luc had mentioned, was quite petite with beautiful green eyes, which offered an explanation for the color of Jean-Luc's—a mix of both his parents. She wrapped me in a big hug, much stronger than I would have given her credit for, and grabbed my face, kissing me on both cheeks. "*Bienvenue dans la famille,*" she said, and then more rounds of kissing ensued.

It appeared I was on my way to becoming part French. I may have had the kissing down, but it was time to improve those conversational skills. Then again, Jean-Luc hadn't asked me to marry him; he just assumed it would happen. In July, apparently.

I didn't even have time to breathe before we moved on again. Gilles, Jean-Luc's friend since childhood, and his wife, Nathalie, had invited us over for dinner, along with another couple, Claude and Danielle. Isabelle had already agreed to watch the kids. After the topic of conversation the previous night, I didn't know if I was in the mood to be hazed again, and from what Jean-Luc had told me about Gilles, I was a bit afraid to go. Gilles was the crazy one, the one with the wild eyes, the troublemaker. I was pretty certain we were in for it.

"I spoke to Gilles earlier," said Jean-Luc, "and he told me something quite funny." I grunted and he carried on. "On my wedding day to Natasha, he, along with a few members of my family, made a bet on how long the marriage would last." He chuckled softly to himself. "Half wouldn't give it six months. The others gave it a year."

I wondered what his family and friends were really saying about us behind our backs. What kind of bets were they making? I'd find out soon enough.

Jean-Luc stroked the top of my hand with his thumb. The action was nervous. There was something he wasn't telling me, something else on his mind. I shifted my body to face him. "What?"

He cleared his throat. "The reason the divorce with Natasha went so smoothly was because I had her sign some papers before the marriage."

"A prenuptial agreement?"

He nodded. "I never trusted her, but I do trust you. I thought she would change when we married, that the stability would make her more reliable. I'd thought wrong. She didn't get better. She got worse."

"I'll sign whatever you want me to."

"That's why I know we don't need this agreement. And when we are married, it will be for good."

"So we're getting married?"

"Of course," said Jean-Luc. "Is there any other way for us?"

"But—"

"Here we are," said Jean-Luc.

We pulled up to Gilles's house, large and modern with an infinity-edged pool. The front door opened and Gilles walked forward, his eyes wide, making him look a bit like Jack Nicholson in *The Shining*. I took a step backward, but before I could make a run for the hills, Gilles grabbed me by the shoulders, pulled me toward him, kissed me on both cheeks, and then picked me up and spun me around before setting me down. "Hello, Sam! Welcome!" he said in English. "Come *eeen* and have some champagne! Tonight, we celebrate your engagement! *Félicitations!*"

Gilles ushered Jean-Luc into the living room, slapping his butt. I followed with an out-of-place laugh. Nathalie exited the kitchen, rolling her eyes. She was dressed to the nines—another one who could pull off the "Who me? No, I just put this old outfit together" attitude. We gave each other a sly once-over, not too obvious but assessing one another nonetheless. Like most of the French women I'd encountered, Nathalie's makeup was minimal, just mascara, foundation, blush, and a smidgen of lip gloss. I noticed her pale gray suede boots immediately. They were perfection. She kissed me on both cheeks. "*Bonsoir, Samantha. Enchantée.*"

Then I was introduced to Claude and his wife of twenty-five years, Danielle. We sat on a brown couch—modern and reminiscent of Roche Bobois—and Nathalie served the aperitif—small bites of spiced cheeses, along with *kirs*. Gilles pulled a camera out from the pocket of his shirt.

"We all want to know why. Why, with all the men in the United States, all the men in the France, all the men in the world, why? Why are you with Jean-Luc?" The room shook with laughter. Gilles laughed maniacally and took my picture. He pointed to Jean-Luc and continued, "Just look at him. He's *orr-eeb-le*. A monster!"

In silence, I sat there, not quite sure what to do. Jean-Luc popped his lips. Nathalie and Danielle shrugged their shoulders. Having known each other for well over thirty years, this was all par for the course when these three cronies got together, I gathered.

"No woman in their right mind would marry him," agreed Claude. He tapped the side of his head twice. Gilles and Claude leaned forward. Gilles retrieved a pad of paper off the glass coffee table, as if to take notes.

"Tell us. Why?"

"I've never met anybody like him before. I love him."

Gilles's laughter echoed. He scribbled on his pad, and after flailing his arms around, said, "Sam, we need for you to be serious *pour un instant*. Why Jean-Luc?"

I took a sip of my champagne. I could roll with this, go with the flow, have a little fun of my own. "What's with all this talk about marriage?" I held out my left hand. "He hasn't even asked me yet. I don't see a ring on my finger. Do you? It could be one of those candy rings or plastic, for all I care."

Bingo.

Gilles and Claude gasped and clasped their hands over their mouths in mock shock. Danielle and Nathalie giggled. Jean-Luc sighed.

"*Zut alors*, Jean-Luc!" Gilles held out his camera with one hand and pointed to the ground with the other. "Get down! Get on one knee and do it now!"

The women clasped their hands with anticipation. Claude pulled Jean-Luc off the couch. And all of a sudden, Jean-Luc was on one knee in front of me. His friends chanted, "Do it! Do it! Do it!" Gilles took one picture after the other.

Jean-Luc grabbed my hand and said, "Samantha, will you be my wife?"

I opened my mouth to answer, but the collective groan filling the room cut me off. Gilles piped in while snapping pictures like a paparazzi photographer. "That was *or-eeb-ble*. Encore!"

Jean-Luc shook his head. "Samantha, my love, you are the only woman in the world for me, my brightest light, the prettiest rose in my garden. Will you do the honor of marrying me?"

"Not much better," said Gilles, "but it will do." He nudged my shoulder. "Aren't you going to answer him? Don't look at me. I already have a wife."

My gaze met Jean-Luc's. "Yes, I'll marry you."

Gilles, Claude, Danielle, and Nathalie chanted, "Kiss, kiss, kiss, kiss."

So we did.

"Where will this wedding be?" asked Nathalie.

Hint. Hint. Hint.

Jean-Luc and I answered in unison, "California."

Ringing in Christmas

We were back at Isabelle and Richard's, sitting on the bed, after having stuffed ourselves with more duck *chez* Gilles and Nathalie. If I ate any more *confit de canard*, I might have started quacking. Reclining on my elbows and kicking my boots off, I watched Jean-Luc pull out a circular, white box from his bag. A name, Mauboussin, marked the cover. He pulled the lid open. Resting inside was a white gold ring with a huge, and I mean huge, square, pale pink amethyst sparkling brilliantly among an elegant and feminine band of pavé diamonds. I gasped. The *Fou de Toi*!

"I wasn't planning on doing this tonight. But things have changed, and since Christmas Eve is tomorrow…What's one day?" Jean-Luc delicately pushed the jewel onto my left ring finger. "Since you already said yes."

Words wouldn't come to me. In awe, I gazed at the ring, about to burst into tears. "I wasn't joking when I said the ring could be plastic—"

"Honey, what's the matter? You don't like it? Did you like the other one better?"

Like it? Was he kidding? I looked up to Jean-Luc, tears streaming down my face. "Are you insane? I love it." I threw my arms around his neck and we kissed, his hands caressing my back. "Ring, no ring,

I love you so much." I laughed, eyeing my hand. "But this ring, truly, is something else."

"It is. Isn't it?"

I stared at the pink bonbon decorating my finger, smiling. Since we were now doing this by the book, I had an idea. "Please, you have to ask my dad for permission. It will mean so much to him."

"Let's call your parents now."

"I've got a better idea," I said. "We'll do it live."

I pulled out my computer, fired it up, waited impatiently for the start screen, and opened Skype. My parents' computer was listed as being online, and my mother answered on the first ring. "Hi, Sam!"

"Mom, put on the video and get Dad and Jess."

She yelled, "Tony, Jess, come here! Sam's calling from France!"

My grandmother's voice vibrated in the background. "Hi, Sam! I miss you."

The video screen came on and my mom's smile filled the screen. My grandmother peered over her shoulder. "Hi, Nanny. I miss you too!" I tilted my head to the side. "Nanny, this is Jean-Luc."

"Hello, Dottie," said Jean-Luc. "I've heard wonderful things about you."

"It's nice to meet you too, Jean-Luc," said Nanny, a look of confusion written on her face. "On Skype, I mean. I can't wait to meet you in person."

The whole family was on the computer screen now, talking over one another. Bodhi panted in the corner. All I could see was his wet black nose. I held my left hand up to the camera. My mom, Nanny, and Jess squealed.

"Oh my God."

"Congratulations!"

"Ahhhhhhhh!"

Once the ladies' excitement wore off, I jabbed Jean-Luc in the ribs. He straightened up, and while doing so, cut his head out of the view. I adjusted the screen so he'd be able to face my dad eye to eye, man to man.

"Hello, Tony, I'd like to ask for your permission to marry your daughter."

By the light in my dad's eyes, I could tell he appreciated Jean-Luc's gesture, even though it had obviously been prodded by me. "Of course," began my dad, but he was cut off.

The women in my family yelled, "Take her!"

Before I disconnected, my mom asked to see what a Provençal Christmas was like. So I marched my computer downstairs, showed her the tree and the *santons*, and along the way, introduced my sister, mom, and grandmother, who had come along on the tour, to Isabelle, Richard, Maxime, Steeve, and his fiancée, Laura, who were still up watching TV. They waved and laughed and all I could think was that this was so weird, being able to introduce my family to my new French family using a computer.

The second the screen dimmed, I called Tracey's cell phone, using my Skype call credits.

"Well, Merry Christmas," she said.

"To you too. Oh, and it's official."

"What is?"

"Jean-Luc and I are engaged!"

"Congratulations! I'm so happy for you!" She paused. "Are you, by chance, getting married in France?"

I sighed and explained the California decision.

———

Much as I loved my gray sweater with lavender sequins from Forever 21, I was no longer twenty-one, and it no longer fit me. So I gave it to Elvire. She smiled and thanked me, left, and two seconds later came back into the bathroom, wearing the sweater, and watched as I put on my makeup. She tilted her head to the side. I smiled. I could pick up the hint. She needed a woman in her life. I could feel it. And holy bejezus, if there ever was a time for bonding, it was now.

"*Est-ce que tu veux un peu de maquillage?*" I asked and Elvire nodded her head enthusiastically.

I chose all natural colors—a little brown eyeliner, a touch of cream eye shadow, a hint of blush, and some mascara. I handed her a lip gloss, which she applied. By the way her chin tilted up just a little higher, I could tell she felt pretty. Together, we plodded downstairs where Maxime and Steeve immediately gave her a catcall, which made her blush. She hit Maxime. "*Arrête!*"

"Your little girl is growing up," I said as I joined Jean-Luc on the couch.

He groaned.

"Hopefully, when she's older, she won't be like me."

"What do you mean?" asked Jean-Luc.

"Well, my family keeps trying to get rid of me, but like a boomerang I keep coming back."

For once, my humor translated. Jean-Luc took me by the arms and led me to the dining room. "I've caught you and I'm not letting you go."

"That's good," I said, "because I come with a no-return policy."

"*Tout le monde, venez à table*," came the call.

Everybody get to the table. It was Christmas Eve and time for dinner.

Alain, Muriel's husband, had brought over the main course for dinner, a wild boar. Someone said grace. My thoughts were elsewhere—primarily, *How the hell do I get out of eating this wild game in thick gray sauce without offending anyone?* My soon-to-be French family members, fourteen of them gathered for this feast, were speed talking one on top of another, and I wasn't able to take part in the very lively conversation because, once again, I couldn't make out one word. They could have been speaking in Swahili for all I could understand. Jean-Luc placed a piece of wild boar on my plate. My head spun. My stomach churned. I pushed a gristly piece with my fork, fighting back the queasiness roiling in my stomach. Jean-Luc piled a spoonful of thick sauce over the meat. I gulped. "Honey, I don't think I can eat this."

"It's good. You'll like it. Alain shot it himself."

Like that made it any better. "I know. But the sauce? It's gray…"

"Yes, it's delicious, incredible, made out of blood!"

Blood? I wanted to cry. Like the poor pig on my plate, I felt like I was being roasted. Everybody was laughing and talking as I held myself back from screaming in frustration. The more they laughed, the angrier I got. Insecurities pecked at my brain. This life, this world, was so very different from mine. I watched everybody eating and decided I must have horrible table manners; I didn't even eat right. Unlike me, when the French cut their food, they didn't switch their fork to their right hand before bringing it to their mouths. I stared at my ring. It hit me all at once. A new life? A new language? A new country? And two kids who would probably trade me for a pack of gum? Okay, maybe not a pack of gum, but a cat?

"Honey, what's wrong?' asked Jean-Luc.

"I don't know if I'm ready for this," I whispered.

"You don't have to eat the wild boar."

I forced a smile but didn't say a word.

Jean-Luc took the piece of wild boar off my plate and put it on his. Like kissing a scared child's wound, this simple action made everything all better. Instead of keeping secret the fears I'd had about changing my whole life, in hushed whispers, I told him about them. Jean-Luc understood my trepidation, and I realized that, even in overwhelming circumstances, I could conquer anything with him by my side. His old love letters, after all, had inspired me to change my life. So what was I so afraid of? Trying something new? All of this was new to me. Gathering up my courage, I ate a piece of that wild boar in the blood sauce. And it wasn't so bad. That night, I went to bed excited as any child on Christmas Eve. But my real Christmas gift was not the beautiful engagement ring, not our wild and passionate lovemaking, not the ridiculously expensive cat we would soon be picking up, and it was definitely not the clothes dryer; it was Jean-Luc and his kids.

"I know all of this is very different for you." Jean-Luc kissed the nape of my neck. "I'm just so happy to have you in my life. Together we can do this."

                    ⌒

My mother purchased green and red velvet monogrammed stockings from Pottery Barn for Jean-Luc, myself, and the kids, the latter of which I'd filled with a bunch of fun things—candy, T-shirts, games, lip glosses for Elvire, and temporary tattoos for Max. Both of their eyes lit up as they dug into the stockings, surprised to find more presents. As for Jean-Luc's Christmas gift, it was more sophisticated than a T-shirt or a plastic candy cane filled with chocolates. Immediately, he ripped his old watch off to put the new one on.

"How did you afford this?" he asked.

"Ancient Chinese secret," I said.

"Sam…"

"Jean-Luc, really, I bought it months ago when I had the cash."

"It's too much."

But it wasn't. Compared to what he'd done for me, it was nothing. "Well, I know you love scuba diving. And I know you needed a new watch."

I'd purchased the five-hundred-meter stainless-steel, blue-faced Swiss Army diving watch right when I returned home from our trip to Europe, months before the big bad wolf of bankruptcy came huffing and puffing and blowing my house down. When I saw the watch online, I knew I had to get it for Jean-Luc. And it was a bargain, since it was a discontinued model. It had taken great self-control to not tell him about it—especially since it had been hidden in my desk when he had visited me in October.

"At any rate, it was on sale and, like me, it comes with a no-return policy."

"Sam, it's too much," said Jean-Luc.

"Too late," I said.

After the family opened up their gifts, we packed up the children's things and drove the thirty minutes to drop them off at their maternal grandmother's, where they would be staying for a week. We pulled up to a small, fenced-in brick cottage. Across the street, chickens and roosters ran around in an open lot. A black-and-white cat came up to the gate. The children kissed us quickly on the cheeks, grabbed their bags, and jumped out of the car. They threw their bags down outside the front door and ran after the cat.

"Will I meet their grandmother?" I asked.

"No. She hates me, blames me for her daughter's death."

"It's not your fault Frédérique got cancer."

"She thinks so and there's no convincing her otherwise."

A gray-haired woman wearing charcoal pants and a white sweater came out of the house. I waved, but she didn't even bother to glance in our direction. She ushered the children into the house, never once looking over her shoulder or offering any kind of sign acknowledging our existence.

I gulped. This would be one hard problem to overcome. I made a mental note to try to figure out how to bridge the gap.

⌒

Since we were in the heart of Provence, Jean-Luc and I spent the remainder of the week at Isabelle's, and once again he became my own personal (and very sexy) tour guide. We visited ancient ruins and cathedrals and fortified cities—Marseilles, Aix-en-Provence, Saint-Rémy-de-Provence, and Les-Baux-de-Provence. But symbolizing my new life, I was looking forward to New Year's Eve. Gilles had invited Jean-Luc and me to stay at his cabin in the Alps.

We were well into the two-hour drive when Jean-Luc asked, "Honey, do you ski?"

The first time I went skiing was with Tracey and it was a nightmare. I'd never set foot on a mountain before, not that the slopes in southern Wisconsin were mountainous at all—more like man-made hills of solid ice. Tracey had given me about two seconds of instruction and we made our way to the chairlift, where it immediately knocked me over. I also fell getting off it. Tracey took me to the top of the hill and told me to "go for it." And go for it I did. Screaming, "Get out of my way! I don't know how to ski!" I went straight down, over a small jump, legs splayed, and right into some poor sucker who was stopped on the slope. From the top of the hill, Tracey said all she saw was a giant puff of white. Poof! Thankfully, I wasn't hurt, just had the wind knocked out of me. I also bent the guy's ski pole.

"I love to ski, but I'm thinking we should start me off slow, like the bunny hill. It's been awhile."

"Oh," said Jean-Luc. "It's like riding a bike. You never forget."

"Just like my French, right?"

Jean-Luc ignored my quip.

Another time I went skiing, once again with Tracey, I really hurt my knee and had to be carried down the mountain on a stretcher. I was beginning to wonder if this was such a good idea. Maybe I should just chill out in the lodge and drink hot cider.

"I don't have any ski clothes," I said, thinking I could get out of a probable visit to the emergency room.

"*C'est pas grave.*" No big deal. "Nathalie and her daughters have things for you."

"Great."

The landscape before us became mountainous and breathtakingly beautiful, jagged peaks stretching toward the sky. Gilles's cabin was situated in the Alpes-de-Haute-Provence in a ski community called Sainte-Anne-la-Condamine. Admittedly, it sounded pretty fabulous to be able to say, "Oh, I spent Christmas in Provence and then we went skiing in the Alps for New Year's."

The snow came down harder. It wasn't quite a blizzard, but visibility was definitely impaired. Focused on the road, Jean-Luc retained his always-cool demeanor. A couple of stray pine needles stuck to the window.

Finally, the sign for Sainte-Anne! Jean-Luc's knuckles turned white as he tried to keep the car under control. A bus was pulled over on the side of the road. There were no guardrails. One false move and we'd catapult over the side of the mountain. I closed my eyes until we were out of harm's way. And I prayed.

Twenty or so small wooden chalets dotted the hillside on our right. We turned down a narrow street and parked the car. Before exiting, I threw on a pair of Elvire's winter boots.

"Which one is Gilles's?"

Jean-Luc puffed out his bottom lip and shrugged his shoulders. He pulled out his cell phone from his jacket pocket, dialed, spoke quickly in French, and then headed for a small trail with a steep incline. "*Suis-moi.*" Follow me. "It's just back there. We have to be quick. I just spoke to Gilles and we're to meet him for lunch in ten minutes. Nathalie will show us into the cabin."

Placing one foot steadily in front of the other, I made my way across the road, which was covered in a thin layer of ice. The smell of smoke filled the air, a few fireplaces billowing white marshmallow puffs. With a big smile and cup of steaming coffee, Nathalie waved from the porch.

"*Coucou! Faites attention!*" Hey you! Be careful, said Nathalie. She grabbed me by the arm before I slipped down the steps.

We entered the chalet where a small living room and kitchen awaited. The bathroom was tucked in the back behind a curtain. Gilles's teenage daughters slept on the first level, which was an open room with a couple of beds and a bathroom. Nathalie pointed up to two lofted rooms with a small balcony. "*Ta chambre est à droite.*" Your room is to the right. "*On y va dans cinq minutes.*" I had five minutes to get ready. Natalie handed me a pair of black snow pants, a white ski jacket, a pair of gloves, a hat, thick woolly socks, and a pair of ski goggles.

Seemed I'd be nice and toasty in this sugar snow globe world.

Even if I broke a leg.

The moment we opened the door to the snack bar, the entire restaurant yelled, "Ahhhh, *c'est* Samantha *et* Jean-Luc," and everybody burst into song. A glass filled with two inches of pastis was pushed into my hand. I was kissed and I was hugged. And then I was kissed again. "*Félicitations!*"

I didn't know who these people were. But I already loved them.

Jean-Luc whispered in my ear, "Gilles told me most of these people here are vintners from an area called Nimes. They've all been coming here for years."

"Vintners?" I smiled so hard my cheeks hurt. "My kind of people."

I took a sip of pastis, which warmed my throat almost as much as my heart had been by this hearty and frenetic welcome. Then it was time to ski.

Unfortunately, Jean-Luc had confused "I love to ski" with "I can ski" and I ended up falling down, smashing my head, and twisting my knee on what was most definitely not the bunny hill. This did not stop us, however, from later dancing the night away to David Guetta's "Memories," featuring Kid Cudi, among other French and American hits, along with Gilles, Nathalie, and a wild crowd of vintners from Nimes—including a man by the name of Henri who I caught sneaking off with a magnum-sized bottle of pastis.

When the clock struck twelve, Jean-Luc kissed me on the lips while he had the chance. Apparently, in France, you have to kiss everybody in the whole place, and the people from Nimes throw in one more kiss for good measure—the southern French way, you air-kiss the cheeks three times. Right. Left. Right. Or maybe left, right, left. With news of our recent engagement, everybody wanted a piece of us. Jean-Luc and I managed to sneak out of the party early—at three in the morning—so we could ring in the New Year alone before passing out.

The following morning, we said our thank-yous and good-byes, leaving early to pick up the kids from their grandmother's and head back home. I was surprised when four people came out of the house to greet us—Thierry, the kids' uncle, his wife, Cristina, and their two kids, Thomas, who was the same age as Elvire, and Mathilde, who was Max's age. Jean-Luc and I stepped out of the car and completed the required double-cheek kisses.

It was through Thierry, who was once a close friend of Jean-Luc's, that Jean-Luc had met Frédérique. Naturally, after Jean-Luc had left his sister, their friendship had become strained. At the very least, Thierry made an effort to put his feelings for Jean-Luc aside for Max and Elvire, and this made me happy. The men teased each other about their hair, or rather, lack thereof. A final *Bonne Année* was exchanged, but even with the laughter and camaraderie, the air was heavier when the kids got into the car.

Max said something quickly in French. Jean-Luc's eyes darkened.

"What'd he say?" I asked.

"He said their grandmother and uncle teased them about you and me, saying my house must have a revolving front door. Which woman is coming? Which woman is going?"

"Well, hopefully one day, they'll see the light. You love the children. And you know what? I do too." I squeezed his hand. "I'm not going anywhere. And I'm removing the revolving door. We're on our way to becoming a real family now."

The French and American Paper Trail

Administratively speaking, we learned from the French consulate in Los Angeles that it would be much easier if we legally tied the proverbial knot in France and then had the family and friends ceremony in Malibu. In France, the only wedding that counted was the civil ceremony, performed at the local *mairie*, or mayor's office. An additional church or temple wedding was commonplace but didn't legalize the union. Before they would give us a date, we would have to supply the *mairie* with a marriage folder, and only then would they publish what was called *la publication des bans*, which was posted in a window for the entire town to see in case someone—a vindictive ex, for example—wished to challenge the marriage. A little reminiscent of the middle ages, yes, but it was the law. The paperwork was confusing and appeared to be endless.

The moment we got back to my new home, we headed straight to the Hôtel de Ville—a fancy way of saying the city hall—to pick up the list of required documents. We stepped into the mayor's building and sat on a rigid bench outside of the *état-civil* and patiently waited for our turn to be called. A few moments later, a stout woman with brown hair and dark eyes beckoned us into the office with a wiggle of her index finger. She sat behind a desk and motioned us to the chairs before her. While Jean-Luc explained the purpose of our visit, she eyed him curiously, her brown eyes flickering with recognition. The woman reached into a folder and pulled out an orange piece of paper, placing it in front of us. "*Vous avez des questions?*"

Her eyes said what her mouth didn't: you should know what's needed. Weren't you here last year? As we stood to leave, the woman caught a glimpse of my giant, candy-colored ring and glared at Jean-Luc. We were so doomed. I could sense it.

Jean-Luc's list was simple enough: his birth certificate, his divorce decree, proof of identity, and proof of residency. Mine, however, was a bit more tedious. In addition to the same documents, all of which would need to be translated by a certified translator, I'd also have to provide one of the following: a *certificat de non-remariage* or a *certificat de coutume*. The *certificat de non-remariage* was exactly that, a certificate stating I hadn't remarried since my divorce. The *certificat de coutume* was a legal opinion stating that, according to the laws in my country, I was legally free to marry and hadn't married since my divorce. "I think we should hire an attorney to provide both of the documents," said Jean-Luc.

"Why? It seems a little redundant. I mean, it says *or*. *Or* means *or*."

"I just have a feeling."

By the way the woman had eyed Jean-Luc at the *mairie*, I agreed.

"Have you told Chris about us yet?" asked Jean-Luc.

"Not yet. Have you told Natasha?"

"She doesn't answer my emails or calls. She doesn't care." He pursed his lips. "But Chris is still emailing you. It has to stop."

"I know," I said. "But things are different between Chris and me. We were together for almost thirteen years—"

"Sam, now you're with me."

"I'll tell him," I said. The only thing was that I didn't know how I'd conquer this fear, how I'd tell my ex I was happy. Finally. Happy.

While Jean-Luc was at work and the kids were at school, I spent my time looking for any potential freelance design opportunities back in the States only to find nothing, as well as trying to figure out the best way to get all the documents for my impending marriage, and soon. Although the French consulate's website listed attorneys and their areas of practice, finding one who could practice in both the United States and France proved to be a challenge. Jean-Luc and I gathered his documents together, but we decided it was best for me to collect mine upon my return to the States.

One week wouldn't hurt us, right?

Jean-Luc had promised me a glimpse of daily life with him and the children. And now that the holiday season had passed, daily life was exactly what I got. In the evenings, Jean-Luc taught me how to cook basic French cuisine, a skill he was more than familiar with, having been a single dad for such a long time. I'd open up a bottle of wine and we'd have a glass while he instructed me on the finer points of quiche making—the secret being premade crusts, tiny little pieces of ham called *lardons*, *crème fraîche*, *herbes de Provence*, and dijon mustard—the real kind. I'd cook up the *lardons* while Jean-Luc whipped the eggs with a whisk, a *fouet*. We'd meet somewhere in the middle and kiss—over a quiche, or a *pot-au-feu*, a *boeuf bourguignon*, or the even simpler "ettes"—*raclettes*, *tartiflettes*, or *galettes*. We worked well together, and I loved the fact that he enjoyed cooking as much as I did. One evening though, Jean-Luc was late coming home from work and I was preparing our meal alone when Elvire came into the kitchen, followed by Max.

"*On mange quoi ce soir?*" they asked, their expressions a tad fearful.

Jean-Luc had warned me about a food experience they'd had with Natasha. Apparently, she cooked a Russian meal loaded up with tons of mayonnaise and the kids refused to eat it, which sent Natasha into a temper tantrum. She ran upstairs crying, slammed a door, and wouldn't come out of the master bedroom until the next morning. She also refused to ever try her hand at cooking for the kids or Jean-Luc ever again. "*Ce soir*," I said with a big smile, "*on mange un magret du connard.*"

"*Connard?*" repeated Max.

"*Oui*," I said. "*T'aime le connard?*"

The kids broke out into unrestrained laughter, and I didn't

understand why until Elvire explained *connard* meant asshole in French, and that *canard* was duck. Whoops. Although my latest French faux pas had me cringing with embarrassment at first, it was a good one. For the first time, Max and Elvire were really laughing *with* me.

Over our duck dish served with a side of rice and French green beans, I glanced at the couch. It needed colorful pillows, some throw blankets. The living room floor needed a rug. Some art on the walls would have been nice too. The designer in me couldn't help plan everything out; not everything had to be utilitarian. Plus, I needed to put my own thumbprint on the place, to make this house a home. I made a mental checklist of what I needed to bring back from the States and what we'd need to register for. Like dishes and cutlery that matched, pots and pans that weren't warped, and serving bowls.

Thankfully, Jean-Luc agreed. He'd wanted to cheer up our home, but with his busy work schedule, he didn't have the time. I started out small, heading into town and picking up decorative items—on sale, of course—like two mercury glass candlesticks and a carved wooden tray.

As far as chores went, it seemed like the laundry never ended. Which was what happened when you had a tween-aged girl whose idea of cleaning her room meant dumping everything she owned into the laundry basket. I remembered those days. And I was thankful that Jean-Luc had purchased the dryer. I was an American woman used to modern conveniences, and I couldn't see myself hanging up clothes or sheets in the backyard in the winter using wooden pins like our neighbors did.

Friday nights were reserved for grocery shopping to pick up staples and Saturday mornings were spent at the local market to pick up fresh fruits and vegetables. On Sunday, Jean-Luc, the kids, and I cleaned together. Believe me, there is nothing sexier than watching a guy vacuum and mop, especially since I don't like to do either. I was more of a surface cleaner and an organizer. The only drama came when the children didn't listen to Jean-Luc or, like typical kids, they talked back. When that happened, I just pretended I didn't understand them. Until I was more settled in their lives, I wanted to stay out of it.

There was only one thing missing from our burgeoning Franco-American family unit: our kitten.

So we loaded up the car, drove the two hours to Bordeaux, singing the theme to *Happy Days*, to retrieve Bella from the breeder. The moment we all saw her, we fell in love. She was beautiful and her fur was incredibly soft, slick spun silk. She purred like the loudest of engines. Sleek and muscular, her stomach was spotted like a leopard and her legs were striped like a tiger. The markings on her face gave the impression that she wore a permanent smile. Her eyes were gigantic, a beautiful green and yellow, and she looked wise, almost mystical. The kids were beyond excited. I was too. So we may have purchased one of the world's most expensive cats, but just the sheer fact that it had brought me closer to the kids was priceless. We were like one big, happy almost-family.

It felt too good to be true.

And it really was, because once again, time passed by too quickly. We'd only just found our natural groove, the kids were just beginning to get to know me, and now it was time for me to leave. I gazed into Jean-Luc's eyes at the airport. He insisted on waiting with me in the check-in line, spending every last second with me while he could.

"Please, you have to tell him about us." By *him*, I knew Jean-Luc meant my ex-husband, Chris. "I can see it in your eyes. The guilt."

Before we had left for the airport, I'd made the mistake of checking my email to find multiple messages from Chris telling me how Ike's health was declining rapidly, which was more than worrisome. My gut instinct about my dog had proved right.

"Not now. It's not the time."

"Sam, I know how you are. You have a warm heart, but he's a toxin in your life. Poison doesn't kill you immediately. Little by little, it works its way through your system. You have to cut the poison out of your life before it damages everything. You have more important things to think about. You have me and the kids. You have to let go of your guilt and move on."

I knew he was right, but hurting Chris even more than I already had wasn't on my list of priorities—avoiding conflict was. "I promise. I'll do it."

"When?"

"I can't unload this on him now. Ike—"

"I understand about Ike, I do. But I also think he's using the dog to keep you in his life."

The woman behind the British Airways desk called me forward. Jean-Luc held my hand as I checked in, squeezing it. We only had a few minutes left together before I headed to the gate. A sadness hung over my once happy heart.

"Sam, I know you'll do the right thing." Jean-Luc whispered in my ear, "I need you here with me, fully."

"I'll do what I can. As fast as I can."

I broke down my life into manageable, bite-sized chunks, which made the issues I faced that much easier to swallow. First, the wedding. In regard to my birth certificate, which was the most important document on the list for the French government to approve our marriage folder, I needed to fill out some paperwork and send it off along with a notarized affidavit stating who I was and a check for fourteen dollars. Easy. I checked that off my list.

It was time to hire the bankruptcy attorney. To get rid of my debt, she'd cost me a hair over two thousand dollars. Before I took her on, I told her about my situation and how I planned on moving to France. This, she assured me, was not a problem. A few days later, I got word that my hearing was set for the end of February.

"Honey," said Jean-Luc on one of our daily phone calls. "If your bankruptcy doesn't go through, I'm here to help you out. We'll manage things together. I'll pay the monthly fees until I'm able to sell the studio apartment outside of Paris. I've been wanting to get rid of it anyway."

No way, no how. I appreciated his offer, but it wasn't going to happen. Not with my pride. "But that's your nest egg. It's your only investment. I'll take care of my financial mess on my own. It's not your problem."

Jean-Luc didn't have any debt, never had. When I'd first told him about the amount needed to pay off my credit cards, he didn't understand how I'd come to owe so much. He'd set the limit on his card to three thousand euro, and every month his card was paid off automatically. Sure, sometimes this left him in the "red," as he'd called it, but it was never for long and there were few bank penalties.

"Now I'm investing in you."

What a man. He would stick with me in any crisis.

Jean-Luc's tone turned serious. "Have you told Chris yet?"

"He's last on the list, but I'm getting to it."

"I'm proud of you," said Jean-Luc.

"Proud?"

"For being so strong."

At the time, I didn't see myself as strong. The stress was overwhelming and I was beginning to question my sanity. I wondered if I would be able to accomplish everything I needed to do to get my life back on track. My checklist was a mess of illegible scribbles. The more I thought about what I needed to do, the longer the list grew. I called Tracey, needing to hear a friendly voice.

"Can you come visit me before I move to France?" I asked.

"When were you thinking?"

"Well, I'm supposed to go back in April, so March?"

"I'll look into the tickets the second we hang up," she said. "I can't believe you're moving to France. It's crazy."

I gulped. This was all so crazy. Reality was beginning to sink in. Moving to another country was a daunting experience, to say the least. What was I getting myself into? Since I was in list mode, I decided to make one of all the pros and cons of marrying Jean-Luc and moving to France:

CONS
1. I would be far away from my family and friends.
2. I didn't speak the language that well.
3. I'd become an instant parent.

PROS
1. I'd spent the last year living at home with my parents, and France was only a flight away. I could always come back home when I wanted to.
2. I would make new friends. And all of my friends in the States were dying to visit me in France—especially my sister.
3. I'd be immersed in French society, so obviously my French would improve.
4. Jean-Luc's kids and I got along really well. I'm sure they had room in their hearts for me.
5. Moving to a new country would be an adventure.
6. I couldn't imagine a life without Jean-Luc. I loved him.

All of the pros canceled out the cons, and the revelation I'd had on Christmas Eve slammed my brain. I remembered I was fighting for love. If this was all crazy, let the crazy begin. I could deal with the stress, but the items on my to-do list weren't going to check themselves off. There was only one person I could rely on to pull me through the sludge of life: me and only me.

My bank account was just shy of being negative. I really needed money. I called Stacy to let her know I was ready and willing to do overnights, but that I'd only be able to walk Kira, the husky, since she was in my neighborhood and I was turning my car in. After hanging up with Stacy, I left a voice mail message for my recruiter—and then for good measure, I emailed her. I sent a couple of résumés off to a few more freelance opportunities I'd found on Craigslist. I called the bank and alerted them to my misfortune, letting them know I was going through bankruptcy proceedings and I would be surrendering my car. For the rest of the afternoon, I worked on my taxes. Because

I'd cashed in my 401(k) early, I watched my return go from being positive to owing three hundred dollars. My stomach plummeted too. Exhausted, I flopped down on my bed. I was just about to doze off to sleep when the phone rang. It was the estate agent who was working on selling my rings.

"Good news, bad news," she said. "What do you want first?"

I craved good news. "The good."

"Well, we sold the tea set."

"That's great." I sat straight up, wide awake. "And the bad news?"

"I spoke with my jewelry expert and she has an offer on your rings. It's not quite what you hoped for, but she believes it's as good as it's going to get."

The dollar amount was disappointing, but I wasn't going to press my luck, considering nobody in town wanted to give me more than two thousand. I did the math in my head. "I'll take it."

"I'll drop a check in the mail tomorrow."

I breathed out a sigh of relief so hearty it could rustle every leaf on every tree in the canyon.

While I still had the car and health insurance, I made an appointment with my doctor for my annual Pap smear. During the routine breast exam, she expressed concern over a few lumps she'd felt in my right breast. We scheduled a mammogram and ultrasound. Just like when I had found the lump when I was sixteen, I was constantly grabbing my breast, poking and prodding—more than worried. I wasn't sixteen anymore.

⌒

Two weeks later, two tattooed thugs came to pick up my car. I didn't make eye contact. I just handed over the keys and didn't say a word. A few hours later, I received the certified copy of my divorce decree, which was a blessing, but I also got a letter from the Los Angeles County vital record's office saying they didn't have records of my birth. I soon learned that because I was half-adopted, my records were sealed in Sacramento, and I had to contact the California Department of Public Health (CDPH), whose website stated it could take up to eighteen weeks to receive a birth certificate. Without a birth certificate that was issued and certified within the past six months, I couldn't get married to Jean-Luc.

Anger set in.

Damn that Chuck. Once again, my biological father had messed up my life. Had it not been for him, my birth certificate would be in my hand, delivered within two weeks.

Since I didn't have a car anymore, I stormed one mile up the canyon roads in the heat to walk Kira, hoping her owner, Barbara, an attorney, would be home. About my mom's age, Barbara was my favorite dog-walking client because she didn't treat me like lowly help but as a friend. Breathless, when I opened the front door, I was thrilled to find her sitting at the computer in the living room. With a quivering chin, I filled her in on my dilemma.

"It's election time, Samantha. You were smart to start by writing the CDPH. If that doesn't work, move on to big guys, like the senator or maybe even the governor. In fact, I wouldn't waste any time. Do it now. Their offices for constituents are just for that—to help people in their districts. It can't hurt." Barbara pumped her fist in victory. "Fight for your love. I'm rooting for you."

I wrote to every state official in California, begging for their help. Then I broke the news to Jean-Luc.

"Honey, don't get so upset," he said. "For now, we just have to keep moving forward with what we've got. Scan your old birth certificate and your divorce decree, send them to me, and I'll get everything translated while you track down the originals. And now that you have the decree, hire the attorney to execute the *certificat de coutume* and *non-remariage*. Don't stress. It will all work out."

But what if it didn't?

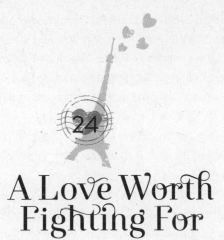

A Love Worth Fighting For

"Breathe in, breathe out. You can do this. You are a fearless adventuress," became my mantra. The three dozen orange and hot pink roses Jean-Luc sent on Valentine's Day solidified this new sentiment of power. And the email Jean-Luc sent later that day pushed me onward.

To: Samantha
From: Jean-Luc

Subject: Joyeuse Saint-Valentin

My Love,

Your first look this morning will turn to this message, and in my words you will see all the love that I carry for you. When we met, you were just a teenager and I was a young man, but a page of love was already writing itself—one page in a history book, our history with a capital H. This book was then closed as quickly as it was opened. Then one day in May 2009, twenty years later, the book was opened and the blank pages were filled with words of love…again and again.

This is what I did, what we did, every minute, every hour of every day since the month of May. I've got your heart in my hand and I will protect it as a priceless treasure. My words are never wasted when they speak or sing of My Love for You. The book is open today …Love…on this first Valentine's Day that we share for the first time. My heart beats for you as it never has previously beaten. I am faithful to your soul and your body. I am faithful to our oath. I'm faithful to my commitment. I am a man so in love, with you my princess, my beauty, my belle.

I love you. Happy Valentine's Day. Don't worry. Everything will work out. We will be together.

Jean-Luc, your man

Yes. I could do this. With love on my side, I could do anything, and I was fighting for it tooth and nail. Jean-Luc and I would be together, no matter the problems I faced.

The next item to check off the list was financial and extraordinarily stressful. My mother drove me to my bankruptcy hearing. I ran into the building to search out my attorney while she searched for a parking spot. Nausea set in. My palms perspired. My attorney waited for me in room number 110. Shannon rushed toward me. "You have your ID and social security card?"

My stomach dropped. "Social security card?" I held up my finger. A reminder email would have been nice. "Excuse me, I'll be right back."

Love wasn't going to help me out with this oversight. Then again, maybe it would?

I dashed into the hallway, scrambled for my cell phone, and called my mom, frantic. "Mom, please, can you go back home and get my social security card? It's in the white desk in the little drawer." I was practically hyperventilating. "They need it."

"Sam, Sam, it's okay. Calm down. I'm on my way."

I headed back to the room of doom and gloom where Shannon

handed me a piece of paper. It was an old unemployment stub, which listed my social on it. "I hope this will do. But who knows?" She pointed to a pair of stainless steel doors. "Follow me."

A man sat in front of a long metal desk, a woman typing by his side. Two tables faced them on either side of the room, like a capital letter *I*. There were about fifty chairs lined up in rows, some of them filled with people who all wore the same fearful expression as I did. I bit down on my bottom lip. Shannon led us to empty seats and motioned for me to sit down. She whispered, "When they call your name, you sit at the table closest to the door. I'll take the seat across from you." I nodded in understanding. "Just answer the questions honestly and it should be fine."

I looked at my watch. It was 11:30 a.m.—my judgment time. My name was called and my mom still hadn't returned. How did I overlook the social security card? The trustee spoke into a tape recorder, stating my name and case number, and that we were entering chapter 7 proceedings. Over his glasses, he peered at me and asked for my identification. I handed him my Illinois driver's license and my unemployment stub.

Shannon piped up. "She doesn't have her card with her, but we have a receipt for unemployment."

The trustee nodded. "Let the records show a government-issued document is being supplied for proof of social security."

The woman seated next to him typed away. I breathed out a sigh of relief as I was sworn in. The trustee flipped through the pages in my file. "You're including your car in these proceedings?"

"Yes. I voluntarily surrendered it last week."

"And your total debt, not including the car, is twenty thousand dollars?"

"Yes, sir."

"It states here you are a dog walker." I grunted out a yes. "And you bring in approximately one hundred dollars a week?"

"Yes, sir."

"Where do you live?"

"Right now, at home with my parents."

I sank lower and lower into my seat.

"You're recently divorced?"

I shifted in the hard, wooden chair. "Yes."

"You don't receive any support from your ex-husband?"

"No."

"And he can't help you with this debt?"

I choked back a laugh. The debt on Chris's cards was worse than mine. "No."

The trustee squinted at a page before him. "You receive about fourteen hundred a month with unemployment. It won't go on forever. When does it run out?"

"In one month."

The trustee scanned through the documents, shaking his head in disapproval, clucking his tongue. His eyes shot daggers in my attorney's direction. "With these sloppy financials, you have her coming in each month with a surplus of cash. Your projections are useless. Her unemployment runs out soon and she obviously won't be living with her parents forever."

Shannon's draw dropped. "But she comes under the means—"

"Means or not, in this sloppy financial statement, you don't project rent, utilities, her health bills, anything."

To qualify for chapter 7, my documents had to prove I didn't have enough disposable income to pay my bills, otherwise known as the "means test." Apparently, Shannon's projections were shoddy, and the mention of health care had me cringing with fear. Financial ruin wasn't my greatest worry. The previous week, my Pap smear had come back abnormal and my doctor wanted to perform further tests to rule out cervical cancer. I was trying my best to remain optimistic, but it was hard—especially when I was reminded of the mammograms, ultrasounds, and the cone biopsy I'd just scheduled and the fact that my temporary health insurance only covered a portion of the costs for these tests. My hand moved to my armpit.

"But she comes under the means. I show she—" interjected Shannon, but the trustee cut her off.

Everybody in the room stared at us, their eyes jumping from me to my hack attorney. I wanted to scream.

"I'm calling for a continuance so you're able to get your client's financial statement organized. In addition to this, I'll need to see proof of expenditures. If everything is in order when you refile, there will be no reason to appear here again." He scribbled something down onto a pad. "I expect all papers to be in my possession one month from today."

Before we parted ways, Shannon placed her hand on my back. "Don't worry. We'll fix this."

I forced a smile and, through clenched teeth, my words came out slowly and purposefully. I shrugged her hand off my body. "I'll get proof of my expenditures and estimates for everything else in the morning, including my recent doctor bills and estimates for the tests I'm going to have to go through."

Shannon shuffled out the door and down the hall. I went outside and called my mom, my hands shaking in anger, my body trembling with fear. Ten minutes later, I climbed into her SUV. "I'm sorry I sent you all the way home for nothing."

"It'll all work out, Sam. Seems the trustee was looking out for your best interests. And I've brought some good news with me."

Good news? Yeah, right, like maybe I won the lottery?

My mom handed over two letters, one from Governor Arnold Schwarzenegger's office of constituents and one from Senator Pavley's office, both offering assistance in helping me obtain my birth certificate. "Thank you. Thank you so much."

My mind went from pissed off and angry to floating in a state I called absolute euphoria.

Until the next bomb hit, when Jean-Luc called me.

"Honey, I've got some bad news," he says. "Every document needs to be certified by your government."

I hissed through my teeth, "But they *are* certified."

"Not with an Apostille."

I knew exactly what an Apostille was. I also knew they were not always required. Now I had to send each document to the Secretary of State of its issuing state to obtain a special seal certifying that my already-certified documents were true copies of the originals.

I squeezed my eyes shut. "I can't get my birth certificate certified with an Apostille when I don't even have my birth certificate. What if it doesn't come in time? We can't have a wedding celebration if we aren't even married. Maybe we should put off the friends and family ceremony until we know what's going on?"

"We can't," said Jean-Luc. "My entire family has already booked their tickets. It's the trip of their lives." He cleared his throat. "There's something else."

"What?"

"The *mairie* won't accept the documents we hired the attorney to draw up. Apparently, we need to pick up the forms at the consulate in Marseilles."

Hot tears of frustration streamed down my face. I gasped. "This is a nightmare."

"Honey, you're upset."

"Of course I'm upset! We're hitting one roadblock after the other. I just wish something would come easily for once. This is ridiculous." I paused. "Did you have this much trouble when you married Natasha?"

"No," he answered flatly. "Just you."

I flopped back on my bed. There was only one thing I could do: cross my fingers and hope for the best. "Send me all the documents back so I can take care of this."

Out of curiosity, I Googled Natasha to learn she'd gotten remarried sometime in February. I found a picture of her looking like a giant cream puff in a wedding dress, standing next to a skinny guy in a tux. She'd married another Frenchman. I emailed the link to Jean-Luc. Jean-Luc emailed back:

Good for her. She looks happy, my little spy. I guess this means I
should stop paying for her apartment.

I wondered why Jean-Luc and I were having so many problems.
Clearly, Natasha was free and clear.

Over the next few days, I received word from Chris that death
was knocking on Ike's door. He couldn't seem to bounce back from a
case of pneumonia and now his organs were failing. He wasn't eating
or walking and Chris had to use a special harness to lift him up. I
asked him to set up Skype on his computer so I could say good-bye
to my dog.

Ike's eyes were glazed and sad. He was sprawled out on the floor,
panting. I told him what a sweet boy he was, how proud I was of
him. And then I burst into tears. "You have to end his suffering," I
said. "This isn't the Ike I know. He can't even wag his tail."

"I know, Sam," said Chris. "But this is so hard."

He could barely speak.

"I didn't mean to send you a sick dog," I said.

"I know," he said.

"We did our best for Ike."

"I know," he said. "Sam, please tell me our marriage wasn't all bad.
We had some good times, right?"

"Of course we did."

"I wish we had been better to each other. I've got to go," he said.
"I can't—"

"I understand."

Trembling and holding back my tears, I closed out of Skype.

The following day, Chris sent a disheartening email, asking me to
call him again. Ike was unable to move, and his body just trembled
and shook. With my blessing, Chris scheduled Ike's euthanasia. He
wasn't living a dog's life anymore. Hard as it was, I had to support
this decision.

Chris and I talked and shared emails, grieving over the loss of
our furry replacement child. In a way, Ike was my last link to my

ex-husband. Now, before more damage could be done, it was finally time to tell Chris about Jean-Luc, about the kids, and our plans to get married. So I did.

"I've met somebody," I said.

"Oh."

"We're getting married."

He sucked in his breath. "What?"

"I'm moving to France"

We didn't say anything for a moment.

"Well, I hope you've found what you're looking for, that you'll be happy." His voice caught in his throat. "God, Sam, I wish I could have been that person, the one to turn the light on in you, not extinguish it. Whoever he is, he's a really lucky man."

He apologized for his past actions. I apologized for mine. We were both sorry. We were good—or as good as we could ever be. I could finally move on. Well, if the French government would let me.

Integration and Perspiration

I had to move forward, hopeful everything would work out, and so I threw myself into planning the wedding for family and friends in July. On Jean-Luc's side, there were nineteen people coming to Malibu from France, including Max and Elvire, of course; both of his sisters, Muriel's husband, Alain, along with the kids—Steeve and his fiancée Laura, Maxime, and Arnaud; Christian, Ghislaine, and their daughter Anne; Claude and Danielle and Gilles and Nathalie. Jean-Luc's parents and his brother wouldn't be able to attend, due to a health setback with his mother, but sent their best wishes. Richard, Isabelle's partner, couldn't take time off from work, and Anaïs, Muriel's daughter, had spent time in California the previous summer, so they were staying behind too.

On my side, I'd been trying to keep the list equal, but my mother kept adding people—some I didn't even know. In total, the list came in at around seventy guests, and there would be more if out-of-town family members decided the trip was affordable. I was only inviting a few close friends and counting on eight out of the twelve being able to make it. Because my mother was upping the wedding's cost with each person she added, my parents offered to split the cost for the wedding. Jean-Luc had given me a total budget of three thousand euro, one of the reasons both the rehearsal dinner *and* the wedding would take place at my parents' house.

For this, I counted my lucky stars. Jean-Luc and I could afford the big night.

My parents' backyard, even though it was primarily used as a dog run, was a magical place surrounded by wild white rose bushes and, ooh-la-la, French lavender. Overlooking the rolling canyon, Jean-Luc and I would exchange vows under a wooden arbor laden with white California jasmine. As I walked through the garden with my mom, who may have been even more excited than me, I filled her in on my ideas.

"I'm thinking of the theme 'garden by the sea'—the colors greens, blues, and whites," I said. "We'll keep the flowers simple—mostly chartreuse dendrobium orchids for the bulk and then three giant cymbidium flower heads sunken into vases with a wrapped leaf and a floating candle for the tables." I pulled out my spreadsheet. "I've gotten an estimate from a wholesaler, and if we do the arrangements ourselves, it cuts the budget big time. All we have to do is buy twelve vases from the dollar store, which you can keep after the wedding. What do you think?"

"Ooh, let's get submersible LED lights for the bottom of the arrangements. That would be so beautiful at night. And lots of candles. Lots and lots of candles." I nodded. My mom squealed, "This is so much fun!"

"I've ordered about two hundred Philippine starfish in varying sizes off of eBay to decorate with and also to make the keepsake gift." I showed her a photo of little silver Tibetan charms I'd also found. "I ordered seven hundred Tibetan charms for about forty dollars. Each one symbolizes something from the wedding—a fleur-de-lis for France, a dragonfly for the garden, a heart with a lock and key, two open hearts for our love, and a starfish and a shell for the ocean. I'm going to glitter paint the starfish and tie seven charms onto each with a silver string. It will also be the seating card."

"I love it." My mom pursed her lips in thought. "You can use my white wooden tray to put them in. We can fill it with sand."

"I'm also going to make the wedding invitations. I found blanks online for twenty dollars and we can print them here. With a little ribbon and a starfish charm, they'll be beautiful." We walked to the back deck. "After the ceremony, the cocktail hour will be here. I've spoken to Jean-Luc and we've decided to keep the drink choices down, which will also keep the budget down. So we're going to make sangria and offer pastis, whiskey, and white and red wine—the same wine we'll serve at dinner."

"What about vodka? Or tequila shots?"

"Mom, it's a wedding. We don't want people to get bombed and then have to drive down the canyon road." I grimaced. "And vodka leads to divorce."

Wherever there was a yin, there was a yang, and nature found its balance. If bad things happened for a reason, so did the good things. I was a true believer in karma now. Finally, my birth certificate arrived. I didn't know who was responsible for getting it to me so quickly— Governor Schwarzenegger or Senator Pavley's office—but in any case, I sent them both thank-you notes via email. I also received word from my attorney that my discharge had gone through, the trustee having accepted the revised file. I was debt-free and would be receiving a notice in the mail within the next month or two.

In addition to this, the biopsy for cervical cancer came back normal, as well as my most recent Pap, and according to the ultra-sound and mammogram, the lumps in my breast were fibroadeno-mas, just like in high school—nothing serious. With the health and money scares put behind me, I could finally move forward without fear. Chest out, marching proudly, I worked quickly to have the nec-essary Apostille applied onto my birth certificate, praying it didn't get lost in the mail.

I called Jean-Luc when I got home.

"Honey, I'm a free woman. I'm debt-free. I'm cancer-free. I have my birth certificate. And I'm all yours. Make me your wife!"

A few minutes later, Jean-Luc sent me my itinerary, having used frequent-flyer miles to buy my ticket once again. I'd arrive in

Toulouse two days before his birthday. Along with something sexy that begins with Victoria's and ends with Secret, I had an idea for a perfect gift for him. Something very special that would last an eternity.

I had less than a fortune to spend, but I purchased both of our wedding bands—the total coming to a little over three hundred and fifty dollars. His was a plain white gold band I'd ordered on Amazon. Mine was also white gold, a delicate X shape encrusted with pavé diamonds, which I'd found on eBay.

After that, I had four hundred and seventy-five dollars left to my name.

Regardless of my finances, there was so much to celebrate. I looked at my watch. "Mom, we've got to pick Tracey up at the airport!"

Best friend by my side, my world was complete. The second we got back to my parents' house, Tracey and I pored through the old photo album from our 1989 European adventure. Then we read Jean-Luc's and Patrick's letters and her old journal, giggling at all the memories like two giddy schoolgirls.

"I can't believe you're marrying Jean-Luc," she said.

"I can't believe I'm moving to France."

"I can't believe I have another awesome place to visit."

"It is awesome, isn't it?" I smiled and flipped a page in the photo album over to Patrick's picture. "I wonder what happened to him. Do you?"

"Sometimes," she said. "But Michael and I are really happy."

Michael had been Tracey's partner for the past eight years. We'd met him in high school, where he'd always had the hots for Tracey. We'd called him her red phone boy. When Tracey's car would break down, she'd call Michael. If she went through a bad breakup, she'd call Michael. His persistence and patience finally paid off and he got the girl of his dreams.

"You may not be curious, but I am. Jean-Luc and Patrick lost touch right after they met us." I opened the cover on my computer. "What was his last name? Maybe he's on Facebook." She told me, I searched, and there he was. Still movie-star good-looking, he hadn't changed a bit. Tracey and I both raised our brows. His Facebook page wasn't privacy protected, so we were able to view some photos. He looked happily married to a lovely French woman; they had two beautiful kids.

"I'm sending him a note. Do you mind?" I asked. "I want to let him know I finally wrote to Jean-Luc."

"Why would I mind? Write him. I'm kind of curious if he'll respond."

With Tracey looking over my shoulder, I sent a Facebook friend request to Patrick, along with the news Jean-Luc and I were to be married. Patrick responded two seconds later, in French. I pulled up Google Translate in a browser window and pasted the note in:

Congratulations, it's really amazing, like when lightning strikes; it leaves traces, even years later. If you and Jean-Luc are ever in Paris, please, look me up. I'd love to see both of you. And please, give my hello to Tracey.

"Wow, that was quick," said Tracey. "Lightning fast."

"Amazing, the power of the Internet, huh? Do you want me to let him know you're here? With me now?"

"Nah," she said. "I'm already with my guy from the past. But if you ever do see him again, tell him I say hi back."

The phone rang, an international call. "Speaking of hellos, answer it. It's Jean-Luc. I'm sure he'd love to speak with you."

She didn't hand me the phone back for well over an hour. I was only able to speak with Jean-Luc for five minutes, just enough time to alert him that Tracey, my mom, and I would be taking off for the desert in a few minutes to stay with Debra for two days.

"Is it a party for the bride-to-be?" he asked.

"No, more like we're saying good-bye to my old life and hello to my new life with you in France."

"Well, then I won't call you."

"You can."

"No, Sam, spend some time with your friends. Drink champagne, but not too much. I'll be waiting for you upon your return."

. And return I did. Two weeks later, I was back in France.

The moment I arrived in Toulouse, I called the U.S. consulate general in Marseilles to make an appointment to pick up the *certificat de coutume* and *certificat de non-remariage*, speaking with a man whose voice was reminiscent of James Earl Jones, deep and unmistakable. I explained my situation, how I'd hired an attorney to draw up both forms but that the *mairie* wouldn't accept them, that I was supposed to pick them up at the consulate. He chuckled—not teasingly or condescendingly, but warmly. "Ahhh, the French paper trail! It's a fun and never-ending path to follow, isn't it? When do you want to come in?"

"Tomorrow at one?"

"That will be fine." He took down my information. "We'll see you tomorrow."

I was expecting a roadblock. But no, on a four-hour drive, we didn't even hit traffic along the way.

Jean-Luc waited for me at a coffee shop while I met the man behind the voice, the consul himself—a burly man, tall and dark, with kind eyes and a boisterous laugh. I filled out the required paperwork and paid. The consul handed me the two certificates. "If they give you any problems," he said, "you call me."

I was about to faint. For once! Someone on my side! I may have called him my personal savior. I thanked the consul profusely.

The following day, with all our documents in hand, all certified and translated, complete with an Apostille, Jean-Luc and I made our way to the *mairie's* office. The woman was beginning to argue about one of my documents, saying something about not meeting Toulouse's requirements, but Jean-Luc cut her off. In French he said, "We have everything required on the list as far as Toulouse is concerned. I've looked. We've also spoken with the American consulate in Marseilles. I really hope you don't force me to get the *mairie* involved."

And that did it.

She opened up her calendar, looking over the dates.

"*Le sept mai, ça marche?*"

The smile stretched across my face.

Oh yeah, the day worked. The seventh of May was the exact day I had written the first "love blog" post, a year ago, when I was still unsure about my future.

How serendipitous.

While we waited with anticipation for the big day, Jean-Luc signed me up for one month of intensive French classes at the Institut Catholique de Toulouse—every morning, five days a week for four hours a day. It was time for me to integrate into the French culture a bit better and make fewer faux pas, as well as find a better way to communicate with the kids, who laughed at my remedial language skills and only taught me words like *dégueulasse* (disgusting), *nul* (loser), and *méga moche* (not just ugly but super ugly). Surprisingly, I tested into "*Elémentaire II*," two notches above beginner, but not quite intermediate. Not so surprisingly, I was the oldest person by twenty years and the only American in the classroom of ten other students—a beautiful girl from Ethiopia, a suave guy from Argentina, and a funny Vietnamese fellow named Paul who flirted with the Japanese girls in class—who comprised the rest of my fellow linguists.

"Hey," Paul said, sitting down at the desk next to me. He looked at my ring, waggled his brows. "*Tant pis.*"

Too bad? Not at all. Things were looking up. I was able to relearn all those dreaded conjugations and build up my vocabulary, which made it so much easier to speak with Max and Elvire. Nobody challenged Jean-Luc's and my union, and the *publication des bans* was taken out of the window of city hall. One week more and we would be legally bound as French husband and American wife. All we had to do was show up on May 7. And all of a sudden, the special day had arrived.

It was twenty minutes to four and I was ready for the civil

ceremony, save for putting on my dress. I ran to the closet and took it off the hanger. It was a simple cream, tiered, strapless cocktail-length dress with a belt with a single rosette on it. The bridal shop I'd purchased the "real" dress from had thrown in this dress for fifty dollars. Who was I to say no? Unfortunately, I hadn't tried it on in months and I was having problems with the zipper, meaning it wouldn't pull up and was stuck right at my ribcage.

Screw the myth about the groom not being able to see the bride before the ceremony. He'd be driving us to the town hall anyway. "Jean-Luc!" I screamed. "I need your help!"

He ran into the bedroom. "Ouf, honey, maybe you should stay away from the pastries. I think you may have gained—"

"That isn't funny." I turned around. "Help!"

I pulled the sides of the dress in while he yanked the zipper. "Honey, maybe you should wear something else. We have to leave in two minutes—"

"I don't have anything else to wear." I turned to face him, my voice shaky. "This will work. It has to."

"Take the dress off. We'll try pulling it over your head."

So we did just that. And he was pulling and tugging and tugging and pulling. I'd put fresh roses from the garden into my hair, now up in a very messy French twist. Petals dropped to the floor. "Oh no! My hair!"

"Honey, please figure something out. This isn't working." He laughed. "Your dress, *évidemment*, doesn't fit and we have to leave now. You might have to get married naked."

I sat down on the bed. French women may not get fat, but put an American woman in France with all the lovely breads and cheeses and you have Miss Piggy in the making. Jean-Luc wiped the tear forming in the corner of my eye.

"Are you sure you want to marry me?" I puffed out my bottom lip. "Because now would be the perfect time to change your mind."

"I thought you came with a no-return policy." Jean-Luc stroked my chin. "Come on, Sam, stop pouting, we have to go."

"At least I've gained pounds of happiness," I muttered, a solution to the problem coming to mind. The dress was somewhat on, and Jean-Luc was able to hitch the top eyelet. I bolted back to my closet and grabbed a little black jacket with a black rosette from Forever 21 to hide the fact the zipper was open midback. Not what I'd had in mind, but the dress wouldn't fall off, and it would have to do. Then I ran to the bathroom, smoothed out my hair, puffed up the crushed flowers, and reapplied my lipstick.

"Honey, we have to go," cried Jean-Luc. "We have two minutes to get to the ceremony."

I threw the rings in my purse, and Jean-Luc and I raced to the car. The kids were at school. We'd decided to only torture them with one wedding—the special one in July.

Jean-Luc floored it the three blocks to the *mairie*. My head lurched backward from the speed, crushing the flowers in my hair again. He dropped me off in front of the hall where Christian and Ghislaine, our witnesses, were waiting and screeched into a parking spot. Ghislaine greeted me with a wide smile and handed over a beautiful bouquet— white roses, lilies, and freesia, with elegant greens.

This, I was not expecting.

"*Merci*," I said. Her kind gesture turned what was supposed to be an administrative day into something really special. We headed inside the marriage hall where Jean-Luc joined us a few minutes later.

Today, the deputy mayor of our town was performing the ceremony. He wore a gray suit with a blue, white, and red sash over it. We took our places in front of a large wooden table. Ghislaine sat next to me while Christian snapped picture after picture as the French civil code was read. Five minutes later, Jean-Luc and I signed the marriage booklet, which Ghislaine and Christian signed as well.

Was I married?

"*Les bagues?*" asked the deputy mayor.

The rings. These were about the only two words I understood throughout the whole ceremony. I pulled the box out of my purse, opened it, and slid the white gold ring onto Jean-Luc's finger. I took off my engagement ring and set it on the table. Jean-Luc gingerly took me by the hand and a wedding band soon adorned my left ring finger. After sliding my engagement ring back in place, I raised my hands in victory, pumping them up twice. Everyone laughed.

Ahh, Americans! We were such an amusing species.

Et voilà! The deputy mayor handed Jean-Luc the *Livret de Famille*, a thin red booklet, and then presented another bouquet of flowers—a congratulatory gift from the town. "*Félicitations, Madame et Monsieur Vérant!*"

"*Félicitations!*" echoed Christian and Ghislaine.

After months of stress, now, now it was over? I looked at Jean-Luc, relief flooding my whole system. "What did I just sign?"

"I now own you. You have to do whatever I say." Jean-Luc pulled me close to him. "So kiss me, Madame Vérant."

Letter Six
Paris, August 16, 1989

My sweetest Sam,

Tonight I wanted very much to write you some words, the sweetest I hope in order to communicate my feelings. I am listening to Bach, a beautiful piece of classical music. It takes you to tears, shows that your hidden feelings can be awakened in your conscience by the beauty of sound. You want to forget everything for a while, the only thing remaining you and your thoughts. Can my thoughts reach you as arrows to open your heart to mine?

Every word I write to you is as fresh as the air I breathe in. Water and air are the basis of life. And so is fire. You still burn deep in my skin when I think of you. Sometimes I wonder if the stars are sparkling or if it is the light of my eyes stimulated by your memory, projected to them. So when you will look toward the sky, and when you see the stars, maybe at the same time I will be looking at them too.

Lovely,
Jean-Luc

The Third Time's the Charm

Since I couldn't stay in France longer than three months in a six-month period thanks to travel restrictions, I was forced to return home at the end of May. I'd spent a lot of time being a boomerang, bouncing back and forth from France to California. This time, when I returned to France, it would be for keeps—at least that was the plan. I now had my long-term visa as the spouse of a French citizen, a gift from the French consulate in Los Angeles. It had been over a month, and I was missing my husband and the kids something fierce. To thwart impending insanity, I set up a blog, *The Frog and a Princess: Life, Love and Living in France,* as a distraction, having decided blogging was a good way to meet other expats and share bits and pieces of my new life with my friends. I posted a link on Facebook to my first post: "Looking for Prince Charming?" He wasn't a rare, elusive creature lurking in a pond; he was real. I found him.

Finally, on a sunny day toward the end of June, Jean-Luc and the kids arrived in California. It was a good thing Jean-Luc had over forty days of vacation, because he was using most of them. My parents became instant grandparents, which thrilled them to bits. We went boating and beaching and biking. We ate American-style—classics like barbecued ribs and grilled burgers and hot dogs. Once again time blurred, and the biggest day on this crazy love adventure had arrived. My mom and I lounged by the pool, watching the kids play in it.

"What are they going to call me?" she asked. "How about Me-Me? I like that."

"*Meme* is what they call their grandmother."

"What about Kiki?" she asked.

"Um, that's slang for a penis."

My mother's eyes widened.

Max jumped into the pool cannonball style and splashed Elvire. "*Viens dans la piscine avec nous, Sam! Viens!*"

I got off my lounger, said, "Be happy they call you Anne," and dove into the water. When I emerged, I smiled and swam after Max and Elvire, splashing them. "After all, I'm happy with being Sam. I am!"

Soon, we only had two hours before our guests for the "all-American and French barbecue" danced into the garden. Jean-Luc had rolled five of the rental tables out from the garage, which Elvire and I decorated with blue and white checked tablecloths, blue clay pots from the dollar store—each with one little French and American flag—and bright, happy sunflowers. We were expecting forty people that afternoon, mostly out-of-town guests and family, and seventy for the wedding celebration.

For the most part, everything for the "big night" was set. The previous week, Elvire and I had bonded over making all the starfish gifts and decorations, while Maxence, who wanted nothing to do with girly things, swam in the pool and played with the dogs, Jean-Luc hung all the Christmas lights, and I wired the remaining starfish into the arbor and into bushes.

A true garden by the sea.

A friend of my mother's, Diane Lotny, was a professional musician. As a wedding gift, she would perform with her band after flamenco guitarist Marco, whom I'd booked for the ceremony, cocktail hour, and dinner, finished. No longer having to rely on my iPod and outside speakers for dancing, I was thrilled with the gift. We were

going to rock the canyon. Additionally, M. C., another friend of my
mother's and also a professional ballroom dancer, had gifted Jean-
Luc and I with private dance lessons. Little did I know that my man
could bust a move like there was no tomorrow.

My grandmother and her sister, my aunt Bobby, had pre-tied
organza wraps and starfish decorations, so all we had to do was slip
them onto the chairs in the morning. My godmother, Diane, who
was a stylist, offered to handle all the floral arrangements including decorating the arbor, which Jean-Luc and I would be married
under—again.

Tracey and Michael came over early, offering their assistance.
They were on a budget and I wanted my best friend staying close by,
so I'd set them up with new friends Rob and Edina, who lived at the
bottom of the street. Besides enjoying myself, nothing else needed to
be done. The caterers would handle the rest. The photographer was
confirmed. Everything was going as planned, including my dress
which, thankfully, still fit. Okay, it was tight, but it still zipped up.

Jean-Luc and I hired Rayna, my mom's cleaning woman, and her
daughter, Yvette, to work the rehearsal dinner. At the ceremony, they
would be guests, members of our family. As a surprise, Yvette, who
happened to work in catering as well as going to school, prepared a
delicious salad and small pizzas to snack on. The caterers dropped
off the dishes—an American French barbecue on a budget of eight
dollars a person. While Yvette set up the buffet and Rayna made
fresh lemonade, I tied forks, knives, and spoons into red and blue
napkins with a white ribbon and put them in a basket. This wedding
was truly a community effort.

One by one, the other guests arrived. Jean-Luc's French
contingency—his sisters and Muriel's husband, Alain, and, save for
Anaïs, their children; Gilles, Nathalie, Claude, and Danielle; and
Christian, Ghislaine, and their daughter, Anne.

My graceful grandmother, Nanny, and her sister, Aunt Bobby.

Rob and Edina, my neighbors.

My aunts, my uncles.

Lori, my best friend from college, and her husband, Jonathan.

Barbara, my favorite dog-walking client, and Stacy, the owner of the company.

My friends, some old, some new. My family.

Before I knew it, the party was in full swing. French music played in the background. People danced and ate and the sound of laughter echoed across the canyon. The buffet table displayed a colorful explosion of salads and drinks. The molasses baked beans, corn on the cob, and barbecued chicken were served in warming trays, while Yvette cooked up hot dogs and hamburgers to order, all the fixings placed to the side. Max didn't know where to turn first; it was his idea of heaven.

I took a plate and sat down with Lori and Tracey. Stephen, a friend of my mother's who had offered to take pictures of the event, stood poolside, his professional camera in hand. Gilles ran around the yard handing everybody a pink printout. "Are you ready?" he asked before darting into the house.

They were up to something. I bit my bottom lip and looked to Jean-Luc, who just shook his head in resignation. He knew a little pain was coming our way. A dish best served with humor. I hoped.

"Samantha and Jean-Luc," said Stephen, waving his hands. "These people claim they have a song dedicated to you guys in honor of something that's happening tomorrow at seven o'clock. I don't know what that's about." Stephen raised his shoulders. "Is everybody ready?"

"*Oui,*" came the resounding cheer.

Jean-Luc groaned.

"Cue the music," said Stephen.

After an *un, deux, trois*, Jean-Luc's family and friends, including Max and Elvire, launched into a song hazing Jean-Luc. Sung to the tune of a folk song from their hometown of La Ciotat, a little off-key and in French, they teased him about how he'd fantasized about one of his teachers, how he spoke a few languages, namely Russian and English, only because of girls, and how he grew up by the sea. The last verses, however, were quite sweet and included the children, Jean-Luc, and me and how we would all live happily ever after together.

We applauded and we screamed and we cheered.

Out of the corner of my eye, I saw my little hummingbird perched on his branch. When I turned my head to face him, he twittered and flew away. I guessed his work with me had been completed.

There wasn't much to do on the big day. Shortly after the flowers arrived, I showed my godmother how I'd envisioned the arrangements to look and where the extra flowers were needed around the property. I gave her a free hand, knowing that everything would look fantastic. The scent of flowers filled my mom's yoga room, which was where all the wedding supplies were being stored. Of course, I had the florist arrange the personal items. I could only imagine the creative mess I would have made of a bouquet.

Elvire would carry a miniature version of my bouquet consisting of ivory roses, freesia, and green cymbidium orchids. My mother, Jessica, Tracey, my Nanny, and Jean-Luc's sisters would all wear cymbidium orchid and rose wrist corsages. For the men—my dad, Jean-Luc, and Maxence—I'd arranged orchid boutonnieres. I set aside fifteen stems of dendrobium orchids for the caterers, placing them on the kitchen counter with a note: "Please use these as you see fit—on the cake, the tables, and anywhere else! Thank you, the Bride!"

Per my instructions, Jean-Luc had already rolled out the remaining tables from the garage. While Michael and Jean-Luc moved all of the rental chairs to the garden, Tracey, Jessica, and I slipped the organza wraps with starfish ties onto the chairs. After setting up hurricane lamps with battery-operated candles on the back ledge, which took all of two minutes, the only thing left to do was make the sangria.

All the busy work was completed by ten in the morning. Jean-Luc kissed me on the forehead before he took off with my dad to pick up the cake. As they walked away, Jean-Luc smiled at my dad. "Before, she was a boomerang, but I've caught her."

"I'm holding you to that," said my dad with a laugh.

With nothing to do but relax, I sat poolside with Tracey and the kids. Since the linens hadn't been set out yet, I let Maxence and Elvire go mental in the pool. I'd joked with Tracey that she and Michael should've tied the knot right along with us. But once she'd mentioned putting the Irish flag into the all-American barbecue pots, right next to the French one, I reconsidered the wisdom of that idea. Not to mention how the extra guests would freak my mother out. I'd had a hard enough time convincing her to let me host *both* the barbecue and the wedding at the house.

Michael came up behind Tracey and put his arms around her. Tracey smiled. "Do you need anything else? Otherwise we're going to go explore Santa Monica a bit while we can."

"Nope. It's all good. Thanks for your help."

"It looks really beautiful, Sam." She gave me a hug.

"Thanks." I squeezed her tight. "I'm so glad you guys are here."

"I wouldn't have missed this for the world." She laughed. "What a story. I'm thrilled to be a part of it."

So was I.

They left, and I decided to walk the dogs to diffuse my nervous energy. I was in the garage putting away the dogs' leashes when my dad and Jean-Luc drove up in my mother's SUV. Jean-Luc sat in the backseat, licking his fingers. And…

Oh my god! The cake!

I ran up to the window and peered in to find Jean-Luc's hand covered in white frosting, a smidgen on his nose. He regarded me wide-eyed, probably expecting me to go ballistic. "We went around the corner and it slid. I tried to stop it, but—"

"Sorry, Sam," said my dad. "It'll still taste good, right?"

I burst out into hysterical, uncontrolled laughter.

By the worried expression on their faces and the way neither of them were able to meet my gaze, I could tell they both felt terrible. I surveyed the damage. It wasn't that bad. Just some smudged frosting and a couple of indentations from Jean-Luc's hands. My laughter came harder. Stuff like this? 'Twas only a cake wound. Life was filled with much bigger problems. "The caterers just got here. They'll be able to fix it."

In a matter of minutes, one of the chefs worked his magic. I thanked my lucky stars I had ordered the extra dendrobium orchid stems. The flowers were placed on each of the three tiers, surrounding the bottom. A few cymbidiums covered up the major damage. When the chef was finished playing doctor, there was no sign of injury.

"Thank you," I said. "You're a real cake saver."

"No worries. We're used to this kind of thing happening all the time." The chef placed the cake topper—a porcelain princess holding a small green frog in her hand. It was perfect. He pointed to me and then to Jean-Luc. "Ahhh, I get it. You're the American princess and he's the French frog."

At four o'clock, it was time for us girls to get ready. Jessica, my mom, Elvire, and I scurried to my parents' room, bringing along a bottle of champagne and taking it over as the bridal suite. Elvire took a sip from my glass. By the way she smiled, I knew she loved being included, feeling like one of the grown-ups, one of the girls.

My ivory-colored dress hung off the armoire. Designed by Maggie Sottero, it was less of a bridal gown and more of an evening dress, and the highlight was the back. Ruched gossamer chiffon, the bodice was fitted with crystal-encrusted halter straps which joined together at the nape of the neck into one sensational bar back treatment; it was sexy and glamorous and, even better, since it was a sample, it was cheap. My hair was styled into a simple half up-do—a bit reminiscent of the sixties and Brigitte Bardot—and held in place with a beautiful starfish and pearl comb.

Elvire's dress was a brand-new, navy blue, empire-waisted, silk chiffon BCBG dress I'd found on eBay that had silver paillettes around the bust line—and she looked stunning in it. My mother's strapless silk chiffon in teal with a small rhinestone detail at the waist fit her perfectly. And Jessica's dress was a sexy blue jersey with crystal-beaded details reminiscent of mine. An ocean of blues for a wedding in a garden by the sea.

Pam, a friend whose father studied with Ansel Adams, knocked on the door and offered to do some sexy boudoir shots of me while the girls got ready. I poured her a glass of champagne. Soon, I was half-naked, lounged in a white armchair, my arm draped over my chest. Elvire raised an eyebrow but otherwise didn't say a word.

"Here's to sexily ever after," said Pam, lifting a glass.

Little did she know.

Our nondenominational ceremony was less about religion and more about celebrating love and was supposed to start at seven sharp, but we were running a few minutes behind. Five minutes before the hour, I sent Jessica to the back porch to get everybody seated in the garden and to grab Maxence and my dad. It was a race against the clock. Or maybe I'd put too much thought into this? I ran over the coincidences in my head.

Seven was my lucky number.

Jean-Luc and I were seven years apart in age.

He'd written me seven beautiful letters.

I'd written my seven-post blog.

Our civil ceremony was held on May 7, exactly one year after the first "love blog" posting. We met on July 24, 1989, near the end of the seventh month of the year, exactly twenty-one years earlier. Did I dare tell a skeptical rocket scientist that I suspected fate had played a hand in getting us together?

I eyed the clock in the bedroom. It would have to wait.

Maxence ran up in his blue slip-on Converse sneakers, looking adorable and very California-casual in his long blue shorts and untucked white collared shirt. The same went for my dad, who was wearing sage linen pants and an ivory shirt, his face adorned with day-old scruff.

We exited the house out of the front door to the gate that would lead us to the garden.

After checking out the arbor, which carried a sense of enchantment with the orchid and starfish decorations, I caught the guitarist's eye and nodded. After a quick transition, Marco launched into a beautiful strummed rendition of Bach's *Air on a G String*. My mother and my sister made their entrance, followed by Max and Elvire. The officiant, Greg, stood under the arbor, Jean-Luc to his left.

I glanced at my dad's watch. It was *seven* past *seven*, and I could live with that.

My dad escorted me to Jean-Luc and then took his place next to my mother and my sister. Jean-Luc took both of my hands. We gazed into each other's eyes and he mouthed, "You look beautiful, the prettiest rose in this garden." Jean-Luc was more handsome than ever, wearing a cream-colored shirt with black pants and black shoes.

Greg commenced with the service. "Friends and family of Samantha and Jean-Luc, welcome and thank you for being here on this special day…"

In a daze, I faced Jean-Luc, holding his hands, smiling like a fool. Before I knew it, Greg was saying, "*Vous pouvez embrasser la mariée.*"

Jean-Luc placed a hand on my back and dipped me, planting a huge kiss on my lips.

The crowd cheered.

The rest of the evening passed beautifully. Everybody was impressed with both the flamenco guitarist, who switched from Sting to Gipsy Kings flawlessly, and the appetizers served during the cocktail hour. The caterers offered chili-herbed shrimp with a Thai dipping sauce, filet mignon on canapés, goat cheese and fresh fig turnovers, tuna tartare on a phyllo pastry, and Belgian asparagus spears with a blueberry balsamic glaze. People sipped on pastis or sangria or made-to-order mojitos, enjoying each other's company. Even the jasmine-scented air smelled of magic.

For the main course, we moved to the poolside tables. I sat Jessica at our table, along with Isabelle, Muriel, and Alain. The children were happy sitting with their cousins. The floating candle and cymbidium orchid displayed in the center was aglow, small tea lights surrounding it. Each napkin had one dendrobium orchid resting on it.

Along with a delicious Pinot Noir, we enjoyed an organic field green salad with grilled pears and caramelized walnuts, followed by an organic boneless chicken breast with fresh mango salsa, accompanied by fingerling potatoes, haricots verts, and ginger-glazed carrots. Before I could blink, Diane Lotny and the band took the stage. "Ladies and gentlemen, please welcome Jean-Luc and Samantha Vérant to the floor."

The music kicked in.

Jean-Luc took me by the hand, leading me to the dance floor for our song: Van Morrison's "Moondance." We'd chosen this particular piece because the lyrics resonated with us, and also because I couldn't think of a better song to dance to under the stars with my rocket scientist. Thousands of stars dotted the sky, one sparkling constellation after the other. And then, just as if I'd ordered it for the occasion, a full moon rose big and bright right over our heads.

Jean-Luc spun me around and pulled me back toward him. I whispered, "I finally found the space station, the brightest point in the sky." I nuzzled up to his ear. "It's always been right here with you. It's in my heart and it has been there ever since we first met twenty years ago."

With one hand planted firmly on my back, holding me to earth, Jean-Luc dipped me under the stars.

A Rebooted Heart

Life took a magical turn and suddenly everything just flowed. A reprieve from the eighty-degree weather typical of summer in southwestern France, there was a nice breeze. I opened the *volets* off the kitchen wider and locked the heavy wooden doors into position with an iron latch, carefully pushing the branches of my favorite rose bush to the side. Bursting with at least a hundred scarlet clusters, its vines climbed up the rustic beams on the back of our townhouse and nestled onto the small terra-cotta-tiled roof protecting our kitchen from the sun. The heady scent of lavender and roses filled the air. Oddly, all the flowers had bloomed a second time. Like me.

The kids were at their grandmother's for the remainder of the summer, giving us newlyweds some time alone. When they returned, I wanted to have the house in order—warm and inviting, to offset the impending chill I expected to be present when they returned home, thanks to their grandmother's dislike of Jean-Luc.

I was a woman with a plan.

Jean-Luc's gaze shot over to the small bookcase in the hall. Handy with a drill, I'd hung three carved plaster plaques, the ornamental and architectural work of an artist named Sid Dickens, over it. Along with pictures of the family I'd placed on top of the bookcase, I found a beautiful wooden ship in the garage. It was about three feet long and one foot wide and impressively detailed, from the planked wooden floor to the sails. Jean-Luc regarded it with pride. "My father built that, every piece carved with his own two hands."

I ran my fingers across the delicate helm, then the mast. "It wasn't a kit?"

"*Non.*"

"Wow, that's incredible."

His eyes softened. "No, you're incredible. I love what you're doing here. Really, it all looks great. You've done so much in so little time."

Skype flashed on my computer.

I turned to Jean-Luc. "I can call her back later."

"Answer it," he said. "It's your mom."

"I love you," I said.

"I know."

I clicked the video screen open. "Hi, Mom!"

"I'm so excited to see all the work you've done to your house. Show me."

"Hello, Anne," said Jean-Luc. Although he would spend hours on the phone with my mom, which was something I loved about him, Jean-Luc wasn't a fan of video. He pecked me on the cheek and waved to the screen before sneaking down the stairs, leaving me to take my mom on a house tour. She oohed and aahed.

A few days later, we picked up the kids at the airport. They were a bit quieter and more reserved, hesitant. But when they opened the door to the kitchen, now painted orange with two Italian paintings adorning once-bare walls and the big silver bowl filled with fruit on the breakfast bar, their smiles widened. When they walked into the living room, their eyes darted back and forth. A rug now decorated the floor. Add the green accent colors of throw pillows, blankets, candles, and plants—all thanks to the wonders of IKEA and the cash we received as wedding presents—and I could tell they were thrilled.

But it was when we went upstairs that the kids saw the biggest change. The IKEA bookcases were put together, the computer and printer sat on the new desk, shaggy burgundy carpet adorned the floor, and the once-naked walls were painted and decorated with pictures of the family. I retrieved an empty picture frame from the bookshelf. It was silver-painted wood with carved flowers. *"C'est pour la photo de ta mère."*

"Merci," Elvire said. *"Merci."*

No matter what their grandmother had told them, no matter what they had gone through with Natasha, they both needed to know I wasn't going anywhere. This was my home now and there was no revolving door. I was there to stay. I knew I'd never replace their mother, but I was now a part of their lives.

"D'accord," said Jean-Luc. *"Range tes sacs. On partira demain."*

We were leaving tomorrow?

"Ah, oui," said Max. *"On ira en Espagne."*

I'd been so busy I'd almost forgotten we had the annual trip with Jean-Luc's scuba club that weekend. It was time to experience Jean-Luc's underwater passion, something neither the kids nor I had ever done. The following afternoon, we loaded up the car and drove a little over three hours to L'Estartit, a seaside village located in the Costa Brava region of northern Spain. Elvire, Max, and I would be joining the group for one morning dive—a *baptême de plongée*. We walked to the dive center, passing by restaurants and numerous shops typical of any European beachside community—the kind selling sunscreens, rafts, sarongs, and tchotchkes, the kind of store Elvire and Max could spend hours in. They stopped in front of one of the boutiques.

"À plus tard," said Jean-Luc.

Later would mean now. The kids bounded into the shop. Jean-Luc gave them three minutes until he pulled them out.

While my dive-master husband was occupied with his co-workers, the kids and I were placed in the hands of our instructor—a fiery, redheaded Catalan lady who spoke both Spanish and French. But she didn't speak English and this made me extremely nervous. While I understood the basic concepts of scuba diving, I hoped I didn't miss anything important. Because I could die. Max was the first to raise his hand when she asked who wanted to go first. Elvire was second. I was last.

"*C'était bon?*" I asked Max when he returned from the sea to the boat.

He shot me a thumbs-up.

"*Tu as eu peur?*" God knew I was scared.

He shrugged. "*Non, pas vraiment.*"

Fifteen minutes later, Elvire climbed up the ladder, her blue eyes glimmering in the Spanish sun. With a grunt and a nod, a salty man with a stubbly beard called me over. He reminded me of a pirate— all that was missing was an eye patch. First, he put a weighted belt around my waist then he pointed to a pair of fins, which I put on. He handed me a mask and threw the stabilizing vest and tank into the water. "*Sautez!*" he said.

One flipper at a time, I made my way to the ladder and jumped in the water, treading for a few minutes, waiting for our instructor, who was easy to spot since her wet suit was equipped with red horns on the hood and a pitchfork tail on her rear. She swam over to me, helped me strap on my vest, and in French, told me to the put the regulator in my mouth and to breathe.

Hand in hand with the devil, I began the slow descent into the Mediterranean Sea. The first three minutes were absolute hell. My fear wasn't of the marine life swimming around me; it was of suffocation. I'd always thought the first time I'd try diving would be in a swimming pool. But here I was in open water. The instructor adjusted my vest, making it easier for me to get my bearings. Little by little, my nerves calmed and my breathing became more natural, stable. The sea life was plentiful—hundreds of tiny, fluorescent purple fish, large black-and-white striped fish, little yellow ones, blue ones, and even a couple of starfish. Gripping her hand, I relaxed a bit and enjoyed—or tried to enjoy—the world around me.

Five minutes later, we emerged. I was still alive, felt more than alive. I conquered another one of my fears. Jean-Luc smiled at me from the deck. With love on my side, I realized, I could do anything.

September eased in and the kids returned to school, Jean-Luc returned to work, and I did my best to settle into this new life as a stay-at-home immigrant stepmom—for now. During the day, I tackled the weeds in the garden and pruned the rose bushes while making small talk with my neighbors through the wire fence separating our properties. A couple in their midseventies, Claude and Paulette, bestowed me with softball-sized *coeur du boeuf* tomatoes from their garden and homemade *foie gras*. Although my French had improved, it was still sometimes difficult to communicate with them—but I was trying.

One day, I idly checked my Facebook page. What I found stunned me into a stuttering stupor. My biological father had not only tracked me down, he had sent me a friend request and a message about how lucky I was to live in France and, moreover, how I had a sixteen-year-old half-brother who I should meet someday.

It had been over twenty years since I'd last heard from him. And this? This was what he sent? His nonchalant, laissez-faire attitude appalled me. I couldn't stop the tears from falling when I told Jean-Luc. I choked back my anger. "I need to end this with him now. I don't want him in my life anymore, showing up like this unannounced."

"Sam, I've told you this once before, you have to suck out all of the poison in your life. If you don't, it will kill you." He squeezed my shoulders. "So do it."

It took me three days to find the right words:

Dear Chuck:

Sorry, Charlie, you are a complete stranger and my hand in friendship is not up for grabs. No, I don't hate you or harbor you any ill will, but nobody needs to dredge up painful memories from the past when they've already moved on. As for your son, if he or I ever want to reach out to one another, we will. Please respect my wishes and continue on with your life the way it's been—without my mother or me in it.

Wishing you all the best,

Samantha Platt Vérant

Able to say good-bye on my terms, I finally had the closure I needed. Poof. All my pent-up anger was gone. Even my heart felt lighter. I called Tracey to fill her in on my latest victory.

"Aren't you curious about your brother?" she asked.

"I am. Do you think we'll look alike?"

"There's only one way to find out. Ask for a picture."

"I can't, Tracey. In a way, I'm relieved I finally got to say my piece after all these years. I'm happy Chuck is out of my life."

"You sure?"

"About Chuck, yes."

"And about your would-be brother?"

"Only time will tell."

Much as I'd rewritten my past with Jean-Luc, I'd also been able to close the book on a haunting history that held me from completely moving on. But had I really let go? Again, there was only one way to find out. I pulled Jean-Luc's seventh letter out from the blue plastic folder and reread it.

Letter Seven
Paris, November 23, 1989

Samantha,

I've never received any news from you, not even a single letter with a "How are you, guy?" I am sure now that my letters surprised you in a bad way. You probably wondered if I was a complete fool and the only way to stop this nonsense is not to answer me. I think you are wrong to behave this way. Of course, we only knew each other for a short time, but we are human beings and we don't work as machines with a previous program. I don't regret anything, neither spoken nor written.

I really hope you will answer this letter. I would like very much to get some news of you. Just because there are five thousand kilometers between us it doesn't mean we have to rub out friendship. I'd like to know the reasons behind your silence.

Perhaps you are right. No matter. That's life. I won't write you again if you don't desire it. So I wish all is all right for you in Syracuse.

Friendly,
Jean-Luc

I squeezed my eyes shut tightly, thankful I finally garnered up the courage to write Jean-Luc back. I'd found my everything. I tucked the letter back into the protective pocket that separated Jean-Luc's seven letters from the stack of other letters at least two inches thick.

Who were all these other letters from? And why on earth was I keeping them? No longer did I need to hold on to my past, looking for emotional validation or ego boosts. Not when I had everything I'd ever wanted in the present. Inspiration hit.

Lighter in hand, I booked it to the backyard, ready to purge. Breathless with excitement, I placed a stack of letters on the barbecue grill and lit one corner. Pages crinkled, curling up and turning gray then black, finally settling into a pile of smoldering ash. Plumes of smoke billowed up to my nose. Engulfed in orange flames, souvenirs from past relationships crackled and hissed, and names long forgotten vanished. Vapors of charcoal and dust filled my lungs. I choked back a cough and threw more letters into the pile—saying *au revoir* to a secret admirer and a final *adieu* to high school and college sweethearts. My eyes watered and burned, but I didn't stop the cleanse. I held my breath and threw another old letter onto the flames in celebration. It was the "Play with it again, Sam" card from Chuck.

A strange sense of pleasure flooded my body. I watched Chuck's card burn until it settled into a pile of ash. Then I threw another letter onto the blaze, tempted to dance around the fire in some kind of bizarre tribal ritual while chanting, "Free at last."

Jean-Luc came home from work to find me in the garden, surrounded by a cloud of smoke, prodding the fiery blaze with a rebar pipe. His eyes darted to the massive pine tree above the grill. "Sam, what in the world are you cooking?"

"I'm burning all my old letters." I turned to face him, poker in hand. "Except for yours, of course. And a couple from Tracey."

His laughter started off slow then it boomed. "But we could have read them together. And we could have laughed."

He already had all the dots making up my life; he didn't need to connect them. My brows furrowed. "But I thought it was a romantic, a symbolic gesture…"

"It is."

Jean-Luc popped his lips, put his hands on my waist, and pulled me in for a kiss. *Soupe de langues!* The honeymoon period was far from over. I withdrew from his embrace before we overheated. "Do you think it will last? This passion?"

Jean-Luc stifled another laugh. "Sam, like I told you in one of my letters, a life without passion is like a sky without a moon or the stars, like a sea without little fishes."

"But you don't write me love letters anymore," I teased.

"I don't have to. You're here with me, right now, right where you're supposed to be."

Yes, there I was, in the here, in the now, living in the South of France, married to a man I'd met over two decades before. As my parents had told me shortly after my adoption, love didn't come from DNA; it came from opening up your heart, just like my real dad, Tony, had done for me. Just like I could do wholeheartedly now. The rest, as they say, was history.

Twenty years ago, I was terrified of love, of letting myself be loved, and I left Jean-Luc standing alone on a platform at Gare de Lyon. But the train had finally stopped at my station. When I let go of anger, guilt, and fear, I finally let love in. For once, my entire life jumped onto the right track, and it was cruising along, moving full speed ahead.

L'amour! Encore l'amour! Toujours l'amour!

Acknowledgments

Sometimes it takes a village to transform a book from a dream into actual publication. I'd like to start by thanking Anna Klenke, my fabulous editor, who picked my story out of the Sourcebooks slush pile and believed in it enough to take it from a mere dream to a finished project. *Merci mille fois!* Likewise, I'd like to thank the Sourcebooks team. Thank you all so much for believing in my story and in me.

To my parents, Anne and Tony Platt, where do I start? Thank you for your unwavering love and for not letting me sink when life dragged me down. And Dad? Thank you for turning the page at the sexier parts. The same goes to Dottie Thomas, my grandmother. Also, I raise my glass to my two best friends in the entire world, Tracey Biesterfeldt and my sister, Jessica. This story is your story too.

A special shout goes out to all the wonderful writers who have been with me on this journey from almost day one. Thanks to my alpha readers Susan Oloier and Christine Sarmel, whose candor and honest critiques helped my book to grow. Thanks to my army of beta readers: Sara Raasch, Jill Hathaway, the Roecker sisters, Kelly Polark, Jaye Robin Brown, Stephanie Hayes, Rachel Eddey, Pam Ferderbar, Judy Mintz, Colene Beck, Mary Metzger, Robin Tolbert, Stina Lindenblatt, Wendy Forsythe Van Dyk, Stephen Fisch,

Diane Lotny, M. C. Callaghan, Debra Wolf, Kim O'Brien, Pam Serp, Stacy Mahoney, Karla Wheeler, Liz Johnson, Meg Vernon, Michelle Cassera, Christina Schmitt, Kristin Gaudio, Judy Ravitz, Karin Barnes, and Edina and Rob Markus. And, finally, thank you to the expert advice of industry pros Stephanie DeVita, Jay Schaefer, Candace Walsh, Victoria Twead, and my aunt, Randi Platt. Whether you delivered a full critique, took my author photos, taught me to mambo, read a few chapters here and there, or just cheered me on, I need for you all to know it meant (and still means) the world to me.

Moving to a new country can be a daunting experience. So a huge and heartfelt thanks goes to the Toulouse *"les chicks"*—Monique Nayard, Oksana Ritchie, Trupty Vora, Lindsey Hebblethwaite, Zoe Levi, and Melissa Hall, who not only read for me but also became instamatic friends.

I'd be remiss if I didn't mention all the lovely souls I've met thanks to social media—on AbsoluteWrite.com, on Verla Kay's blueboards, on Twitter, and on Blogger, especially my French contingency of expats—Sara Dillard Sylvander, Sarah Hague, Kasia Dietz, Lindsey Tramuta, Kristin Espinasse, and Aidan Larson, whose blogs provided much needed friendship and advice.

Thanks to Jean-Luc's parents, Marcelle and André, to his sisters Isabelle and Muriel, and to their spouses and children. To my adoptive French parents, Christian and Ghislaine, and their daughter, Anne; and to all of Jean-Luc's friends. Thank you all for not placing bets on how long my marriage to Jean-Luc would last.

To Max and Elvire, I am the luckiest woman in the world to have both of you in my life. As for Jean-Luc, I know you wanted for me to tell our story as a fictional account, killing you off in the end! But the truth is *always* better than fiction. You have my heart in your hand. *Je t'aime très fort. Je t'aime.*

Finally, I'd like to thank you, dear reader, for joining me on this love adventure. Now put this book down and live and love your life to its fullest—without fear, without anger, and without regret. *L'amour! Encore l'amour! Toujours l'amour!*

About the Author

Samantha Vérant is a travel addict, a self-professed oenophile, and a determined, if occasionally unconventional, French chef. She lives in southwestern France, where she's able to explore all of her passions, and where she's married to a sexy French rocket scientist she met in 1989 but ignored for twenty years.

Photo credit: Stephen Fisch